SAME·DAY RESUME

Write an Effective Resume in an Hour

Third Edition

LOUISE M. KURSMARK

jist Works
America's Career Publisher®

PART OF JIST'S HELP IN A HURRY™ SERIES

SAME-DAY RESUME, THIRD EDITION

© 2012 by JIST Publishing

Published by JIST Works, an imprint of JIST Publishing
875 Montreal Way
St. Paul, MN 55102
E-mail: info@jist.com

Visit our Web site at **www.jist.com** for information on JIST, free job search tips, tables of contents, sample pages, catalogs, and ordering instructions for our many products!

Trade Product Manager: Heather Stith
Development Editor: Grant E. Mabie
Production Editor: Jeanne Clark
Cover Designer: Alan Evans
Cover and Interior Layout: Jack Ross
Proofreader: Laura Bowman
Indexer: Cheryl Ann Lenser

Printed in the United States of America
18   17   16   15   14   13   12   9   8   7   6   5   4   3   2   1

Library of Congress Cataloging-in-Publication Data is on file with the Library of Congress.

ISBN 978-1-59357-906-7

About This Book

Writing a resume doesn't have to be difficult. You can do a simple one in about an hour, and a few more hours will give you a very nice resume. That's what Chapters 1, 2, and 3 are about: getting an acceptable resume finished quickly. My point is to help you get your resume done today, so that you can get started on your job search this afternoon. After all, your desire is not to do a perfect resume—it is to get a perfect job.

But this book consists of a lot more than resume advice. After you've done your resume, you can learn about cover letters, thank-you notes, and the innovative JIST Card—a mini-resume for getting the word out quickly about your skills and qualifications—in Chapter 4.

Chapter 5 shows you how to put your resume to use both online and off. Chapter 6 shows you how to go back, when you have time, and refine the resume you created in earlier chapters.

And finally, Chapter 7 is a stupendous collection of nearly 50 real resumes written and designed by Academy Certified Resume Writers. You can use these samples to get ideas for the wording, layout, and design of your own resume.

In short, this little book gives you all the information you need to get your resume into employers' hands today—so that you can start getting interviews that will lead to job offers. Good luck!

Contents

About This Book... iii

A Brief Introduction to Using This Book 1

Of Course, You Can't Just Read About It. 2

Why This Is a Short Book 2

Chapter 1: Quick Tips for Creating and Using a
Resume.. 3

What Is a Resume?...3

Some People Say You Don't Need a Resume 3

Resumes Aren't Good Job Search Tools...................................*4*

Some Jobs Don't Require Resumes..*4*

*Some Job Search Methods Don't Require Resumes—At Least
Initially* *4*

Some Resume Experts Call a Resume by Another Name............*4*

Some Good Reasons Why You Should Have a Resume 5

Employers Often Ask for Resumes *5*

Resumes Help Structure Your Communications *5*

*If Used Properly, a Resume Can Be an Effective Job
Search Tool* *5*

Resume Basics..5

Length..*6*

Eliminate Errors *6*

Appearance *7*

Word Processing *7*

Photocopying and Printing *7*

Use Good Paper *7*

Use Action Words and Stress Your Accomplishments................*8*

Break Some Rules...*8*

The Most Important Rule of All: Do a Basic Resume Today.......*9*

Types of Resumes...9

Chronological and Hybrid Resumes..............................9

Skills, or Functional, Resumes.................................10

Creative Resumes..10

The Curriculum Vitae and Other Special Formats...................11

"Send Your Resume to Lots of Strangers and, If It Is Good Enough, You Will Get Job Offers" and Other Fairy Tales........11

Chapter 2: Write a Simple Chronological Resume in About an Hour 14

Chronological Resume Basics...................................14

Two Chronological Resume Samples 14

Writing the Major Sections of a Chronological Resume...........15

Name...15

Mailing Address...18

Phone Numbers and Email Address 18

Job Objective 19

Education and Training...22

Work and Volunteer History 23

Professional Organizations....................................25

Recognition and Awards.......................................25

Personal Information...25

References 25

The Final Draft..26

Chapter 3: Write a Skills Resume in Just a Few Hours....34

The Skills Resume 34

A Sample Skills Resume...35

Writing Your Skills Resume 37

Job Objective 37

The Skills Section..38

Tips for Editing Your Draft Resume into Final Form 41

More Sample Skills Resumes....................................42

Darrel Craig's Resume 42

Thomas Marrin's Resume......................................44

Peter Neely's Resume *45*

Andrea Atwood's Resume *47*

Chapter 4: The 15-Minute Cover Letter and Other Job Search Correspondence 49

Cover Letters 49

Seven Quick Tips for Writing a Superior Cover Letter *50*

Writing Cover Letters to People You Know *51*

Writing Cover Letters to People You Don't Know *57*

The Hardworking JIST Card® 60

Think of a JIST Card as a Very Small Resume *60*

JIST Cards Get Results *60*

How You Can Use Them *61*

JIST Card Paper and Format Tips *61*

Sample JIST Cards *61*

Thank-You Notes 64

Three Times When You Should Definitely Send Thank-You Notes—and Why *64*

Six Quick Tips for Writing Thank-You Notes *67*

Chapter 5: Use Your Resume Online and Off 69

Adapting Your Resume for Electronic Use 70

Sample Text-Only Resume, with All Graphics and Formatting Removed *71*

Converting Your Resume to Electronic Format *74*

The Importance of Keywords 75

Quick Tips for Selecting Keywords to Include in Your Resume *75*

Sample Keyword Resumes *76*

Managing Your Online Identity 76

Google Yourself *76*

LinkedIn and Other Professional Profiles *77*

Blogs and Tweets *78*

Online Career Portfolios and Personal Websites *79*

Resume Banks, Job Boards, and Online Information 79

Chapter 6: Write a Better Resume Now 81

If You Aren't Good at This, Get Some Help 81

Professional Resume Writers 81

Career or Job Search Counselors and Transition Services 84

Improve Your Resume 85

Write or Expand Your Summary Section 85

Quantify Your Accomplishments 85

Expand Your Education and Training Section 85

Add New Sections to Highlight Your Strengths 85

Portfolios and Enclosures 86

Gather Information and Emphasize Accomplishments, Skills, and Results 86

More Quick Resume-Writing Tips 99

As Much as Possible, Write Your Resume Yourself 99

Don't Lie or Exaggerate 99

Never Include a Negative 100

This Is No Place to Be Humble 100

Use Short Sentences and Simple Words 100

If It Doesn't Support Your Job Objective, Cut It Out 101

Include Numbers 101

Emphasize Skills 101

Highlight Accomplishments and Results 101

The Importance of Doing Drafts 101

Edit, Edit, Edit 102

Get Someone Else to Review Your Resume for Errors 102

More Tips to Improve Your Resume's Design and Appearance 102

Increase Readability with Some Simple Design Principles 102

Avoid "Packing" Your Resume with Small Print 103

Use Two Pages at the Most 103

Use Type Fonts Sparingly 103

Consider Graphics 103

Edit Again for Appearance *104*

Select Top-Quality Paper and Matching Envelopes *104*

Final Comments 104

Chapter 7: A Stupendous Collection of Professionally Written and Designed Resumes 105

How to Use the Sample Resumes in This Section 105

Resumes for All Types of Jobs 106

Health Care *107*

Science, Engineering, and Technology *112*

Education *119*

Clerical, Administration, and Human Resources *123*

Sales and Marketing *130*

Logistics and Operations *144*

Accounting and Finance *147*

Media *153*

Hospitality and Services *156*

Executives *159*

New Grads *163*

Career Changers *170*

Military-to-Civilian Transitions *174*

Appendix: How to Contact the Professional Resume Writers Who Contributed to This Book 178

Index 180

A Brief Introduction to Using This Book

Most people spend too much time worrying about their resumes. Instead, this book shows you how to write an acceptable resume in just an hour or so, and then a better one later, if you need one.

Because you obviously want to put together a resume, I assume that you are also looking for a job or are thinking about doing so. That being the case, here are my suggestions on the best way to use this book:

1. **Read the Table of Contents.** This introduces you to the content of the book and its chapters.

2. **Complete a basic resume, as described in Chapters 1, 2, and 3.** These short chapters *show* you how to put together a resume that will be fine for most situations—and help you do this in just a few hours. You might also want to review the sample resumes in Chapter 7 to help you write your own resume.

3. **Create and circulate your JIST Card, as described in Chapter 4.** A JIST Card® is a mini-resume that will get your foot in the door in places where a resume might not.

4. **Begin looking for a job.** Once you have a basic resume and JIST Card, see the sidebar on page 12 for a quick review of self-directed job-search techniques. These techniques can reduce the time it takes to find a job. You should also read Chapter 5, "Use Your Resume Online and Off," so you understand the realities of online job searches and the importance of in-person networking. Then go out looking for your next job.

5. **If you really need to, and as time permits, write a better resume.** Although it will take more time, you might want to revise your resume and create one that is, well, better. Chapters 6 and 7 provide lots of good information and sample resumes to help you in this task. But keep in mind that your priority is to get a good job and *not* to stay home working on your resume.

Of Course, You Can't Just Read About It...

To get results, you will have to actively apply what you learn in this book. One of the biggest reasons some people stay unemployed longer than others do is that they sit at home waiting for someone to knock on their door, call them up, or make them an offer via email. That passive approach too often results in their waiting and waiting, while others are out there getting the offers.

I know you will resist completing the worksheets. But trust me—they are worth your time. Doing them will give you a better sense of what you've accomplished, what you are good at, what you want to do, and how to go about doing it.

The interesting thing is that, when you finish this book and its activities, you will have spent more time planning your career than most people do. And you will know more than the average job seeker about writing a resume and finding a job.

Why This Is a Short Book

I've taught resume writing and job-seeking skills for many years, and I've written longer and more detailed books than this one. Yet I have often been asked to tell someone, in a few minutes or hours, the most important things they should do in their career planning or job search. Instructors and counselors also ask the same question because they have only a short time to spend with the folks they're trying to help.

I've thought about what is most important to know, if time is short. This book is short enough that you can scan it in a morning and write a basic resume that afternoon. Doing all the activities and making the improvements suggested in Chapter 6 take more time but prepare you far better— again, should you need it.

I've written this book to help you over the resume hurdle. It will help you get a resume done quickly and go about the more important task of getting a job. I hope it helps.

Chapter 1

Quick Tips for Creating and Using a Resume

This book's objective is to help you get a good job in less time. Creating a superior resume alone will not get you a job. No matter how good your resume is, you will still have to get interviews and do well in them before you get a job offer.

So a legitimate question might be "Why have a resume at all?" This chapter answers that question by presenting both sides of the argument, as well as my own conclusions. I also give you an overview of some guidelines for writing your resume and tips on how to use it.

What Is a Resume?

As a first step in creating a resume, examine what a resume is and consider what it can and cannot do.

The word "resume" describes a one- or two-page summary of your life and employment history. Although resumes traditionally have been submitted on paper, they are now most often sent in electronic form—either as files attached to email or as an upload to an employment site. Whatever a resume's form, the idea is to select specific parts of your past that demonstrate that you can do a particular job well.

A resume presents you to prospective employers who—based on their response to the resume—may or may not grant you an interview. Along with the application form, the resume is the tool employers use most often to screen job seekers.

Some People Say You Don't Need a Resume

For a variety of reasons, many career professionals suggest that resumes aren't needed at all. Some of these reasons make a lot of sense and are detailed in the following sections.

Resumes Aren't Good Job Search Tools

It's true; resumes don't do a good job of getting you an interview. Trying to get an interview by submitting lots of unsolicited resumes is usually a waste of effort. When used in the traditional way, your resume is more likely to get you screened out than screened in. There are better ways to get in to see people, such as networking with people you know and just picking up the phone to talk to those you don't.

Five Easy Ways to Develop a Network of Contacts
1. Make lists of people you know.
2. Contact them in a systematic way.
3. Present yourself well.
4. Ask contacts for leads.
5. Contact these referrals and ask them for leads.

Some Jobs Don't Require Resumes

Employers of office, managerial, professional, and technical workers often want the details that a resume provides. But for many jobs, particularly entry-level, trade, or unskilled positions, resumes might not be required.

Some Job Search Methods Don't Require Resumes—At Least Initially

Some people get jobs without using a resume at all. In most cases, these people get interviews because the employer knows them or they are referred by someone. In these situations, a resume might be requested at a later point in the process and is used primarily to document the candidate's experience and qualifications and not as a primary way to screen or select the candidate.

Some Resume Experts Call a Resume by Another Name

Many other names are used in place of the word "resume," including "professional job power report," "curriculum vitae," "employment proposal," and other terms. One resume book author, for example, advises you not to use a resume. Instead, he advises you to use his "qualifications brief." In all their forms, though, they are really various types of resumes.

Some Good Reasons Why You Should Have a Resume

In my opinion, there are several good reasons to have a resume.

Employers Often Ask for Resumes

If an employer asks for a resume (and many do), why make excuses? This alone is reason enough to have one.

Resumes Help Structure Your Communications

A good resume requires you to clarify your job objective; select related skills, education, work, or other experiences; and list accomplishments—and present all this in a concise format. Doing these things is an essential step in your job search, even if you don't use the resume.

If Used Properly, a Resume Can Be an Effective Job Search Tool

A well-done resume presents details of your experiences efficiently so that an employer can refer to them as needed. Also, because interviewers often use the resume as a starting point for questions, you can help guide your interviews in the direction you want simply by virtue of what you choose to put on your resume.

Resume Basics

In the following sections you'll find some basic guidelines for developing your resume. These aren't rules, but you should carefully consider the suggestions because they are based on many years of experience, and they make good common sense.

Many of these guidelines assume a traditional, printed-on-paper format rather than a resume that is submitted electronically (more on that in Chapter 5). But you will likely need a paper resume *and* an electronic resume, and this advice will help in either case.

> **TIP:** If you show your resume to any three people, you will probably get three different suggestions on how to improve it. So one problem with resumes is that everyone is an expert, but few of these experts agree. This means that you will have to become your own expert and make some decisions on how to do your resume. I'm here to help.

Length

Opinions differ on length, but one to two pages is usually enough. If you are a recent high school or college graduate (within the last two years), regardless of what field you are going into, try to keep your resume to one page. If you are seeking a managerial, professional, or technical position—where most people have lots of prior experience—two pages is the norm. In most cases, a busy person will not read a resume that is any longer than two or three pages. Shorter resumes are often harder to write; but, when you do them properly, they can pay off.

However, don't try to cram so much information onto one page that it becomes difficult to read. And don't omit important information just because you think you "should" have a one-pager. Again, use common sense—include the information you think is relevant and important, and format the resume so it can be easily skimmed and read.

Honesty Is the Best Policy

Some people lie on their resumes and claim credentials, education, or experience that they don't have, hoping that no one will find out. Many organizations now verify this information, sometimes long after a person is hired, and people lose their jobs over such lies.

Never lie on your resume. But that does not mean that you have to present negative information! Make sure that everything you put in your resume supports your job objective in some direct way. If you really can do the job you are seeking, someone will probably hire you. Be confident about what you *do* have, and don't obsess over what you don't.

Eliminate Errors

I am amazed how often an otherwise good resume has typographical, grammar, or punctuation errors. Employers who notice will not think kindly of you. So don't have any!

Even if you are good at proofreading, find someone else who is good at proofreading also and ask this person to review your resume—carefully. If possible, wait at least one day after you've written it (or longer, if you can) before reading your draft. A day's delay will allow you to notice what your resume says, rather than what you think it says.

Then, after you've read your resume, read it again to make sure you catch the errors. Then go over it again.

Appearance

Obviously, your resume's overall appearance will affect an employer's opinion of you. In a matter of seconds, the employer will form a positive or negative opinion. Is your resume well laid out? Is it crisp and professional looking? Does it include good use of white space? Does it have any errors?

> **TIP:** *Even if you spell-check your resume on your computer, you still won't catch all the errors. For example, spell check won't tell you that you should use "their" instead of "they're" in cases that call for a possessive pronoun. So there is no substitute for proofing your resume carefully.*

Word Processing

Your printed resumes should be created with word-processing software (preferably Microsoft Word) and produced on a high-quality inkjet or laser printer. If you don't have the capability to produce it yourself, get some help! Perhaps you have a friend who has an up-to-date computer and good-quality printer. Or visit your local library—you might be amazed at the services it provides for free.

Most quick-print shops, including national chains such as FedEx Kinko's and Sir Speedy, will do the word processing and printing for a modest fee. Ask to see samples of their work and fees—and be willing to go to a few places to get the quality you want.

Photocopying and Printing

If you have your own computer and high-quality printer, individually printed resumes can present a better appearance than photocopies and, of course, will allow you to target your resume to a particular job or employer.

You can also take your resume to most small print shops and have them print a few hundred copies for a reasonable price. Just make certain that the quality is very good. However you produce your resume, make sure you have plenty on hand to use as needed. Even if you are submitting most resumes electronically, you will need multiple copies for interviews, job fairs, networking meetings, and other in-person events.

Use Good Paper

Never go with cheap paper like that typically used for photocopies. Papers come in different qualities, and you can see the difference. Papers that include cotton fibers have a richer texture and feel that is appropriate for a professional-looking resume. Most stationery and office-supply stores carry better papers, as do quick-print shops.

Although most resumes are on white paper, I prefer an off-white bone or ivory color. You can also use other light pastel colors such as light tan or gray, but I do not recommend red, pink, or green tints. Your resume is a professional document and in most cases should have a conservative and professional look and feel.

> **TIP:** *Always send a potential employer a thank-you note after an interview or other face-to-face meeting. Employers are impressed by and will remember candidates who follow up in this way. Thank-you notes can be handwritten or typed.*

Once you've selected your paper, get matching envelopes. You might also find matching "Monarch" size paper and envelopes. This smaller-sized paper, when folded once, makes for an inexpensive and perfectly acceptable thank-you note.

Use Action Words and Stress Your Accomplishments

Most resumes are boring. So don't simply list what your duties were—emphasize what you got done! Make sure you mention specific skills you have to do the job, as well as any accomplishments and credentials. Even a simple resume can include some of these elements.

Don't Be Humble

Like an interview, your resume is no place to be humble. If you don't communicate what you can do, who will?

> **TIP:** *The list entitled "Use Action Words and Phrases" in Chapter 2 will give you ideas of action words to use, as will the sample resumes throughout the book.*

Make Every Word Count

Write a long rough draft and then edit, edit, edit. If a word or phrase does not support your job objective, consider dropping it.

Break Some Rules

This will be *your* resume, so you can do whatever makes sense to you. Most resume rules can be broken if you have a good reason.

The Most Important Rule of All: Do a Basic Resume Today

> **TIP:** *In an active job search, you network and call potential employers for interviews. You don't wait for employers to respond to your resume.*

In the rest of this and the next two chapters, you will learn about the types of resumes and see a few basic examples. You'll see more examples in Chapter 7. Although many additional details will follow, remember that it is often far more useful to you to have an acceptable resume as soon as possible—and use it in an active job search—than to delay your job search while working on a better resume. A better resume can come later, after you have created a presentable one that you can use right away.

Types of Resumes

Three common resume types are the chronological resume, the skills (or functional) resume, and the creative resume. I also mention the curriculum vitae (CV), which is used for some specialized professional careers.

Chronological and Hybrid Resumes

The word "chronology" refers to a sequence of events in time. The primary feature of this type of resume is the section of jobs you've held, listed in reverse order from the most recent to least recent.

Over time, the chronological resume has evolved to include—in addition to the chronological listing—some "up-front" information that can help position you for the job you're looking for now rather than letting the employer make an assumption based on your past job titles. Often referred to as a "hybrid" resume, it is the most common type in use today—and the type most preferred by employers.

It's easy to understand why the hybrid resume is so popular. Employers want to know where you've worked, when you worked there, and what you did on the job. The chronology gives them that information. You, on the other hand, want them to know more! You want them to know who you are and your strongest skills and experiences as they relate to your current goals. The introductory section of the hybrid resume lets you share this important information.

Chapter 2 walks you through the process of creating a simple chronological/hybrid resume. In addition, most of the resume samples in this book are hybrids, featuring some introductory information followed by a chronological work history describing activities and accomplishments.

However, the chronological/hybrid format might not work well for people who do not have a relevant work history (or any work history—such as new graduates), those whose backgrounds are unconventional, people who want to make a drastic career change, or anyone who has a less-than-ideal work history such as job gaps.

Understand that employers prefer the chronological format, but don't feel bound by it if it doesn't present you and your skills in the best possible way.

Skills, or Functional, Resumes

Rather than list your experience under each job, this resume style clusters your experiences under major skill areas. For example, if you are strong in "communication skills," you could list a variety of work and other experiences under that heading.

This format makes little sense, of course, unless your job objective *requires* these skills. For this reason and others, a skills resume is often more difficult to write than a simple chronological resume. But if you have limited paid work experience, are changing careers, or have not worked for a while, a skills resume might be a better way to present your strengths.

A skills resume is often used in situations where the writer wants to avoid displaying obvious weaknesses that would be highlighted on a chronological resume. For example, someone who has been a teacher but who now wants a career in sales might choose a skills resume. A skills resume can help hide a variety of other weaknesses as well, such as limited work experience, gaps in job history, lack of educational credentials, and other flaws. This is one reason why some employers don't like skills resumes—they make it harder for employers to quickly screen out applicants.

If you decide this is the best option for you, Chapter 3 shows you how to write your own skills resume.

Creative Resumes

Remember, don't be bound by the rules in writing your resume!

Some job seekers have come up with creative formats that defy any category but that are clever and have worked for them. These resumes use innovative formats and styles. Some use dramatic graphics, colors, and shapes. I've seen handwritten resumes (usually *not* a good idea); unusual paper colors, sizes, and shapes; resumes with tasteful drawings and borders; and lots of other ideas. Some of these resumes were well done and well received; others were not. Graphic artists, for example, might use their resumes as examples of their work and include various graphic elements. An advertising or marketing person might use a writing style that approximates copywriting and a resume design that looks like a polished magazine ad.

Bottom line: Use a creative resume if it best represents you *and* if it is the best possible way to showcase your skills. Just be aware that you'll get a stronger reaction (positive *and* negative) to a creative resume than to a more traditional format. Because this book is designed to provide "help in a hurry," I haven't included examples or instructions for producing creative resumes but rather have focused on the two most useful formats: chronological/hybrid and skills/functional.

The Curriculum Vitae and Other Special Formats

Attorneys, college professors, physicians, scientists, and people in various other occupations have their own rules or guidelines for preparing a "professional vitae" or some other special format. If you are looking for a job in one of these specialized areas, you should learn how to prepare a resume to those specifications. These specialized and occupation-specific resumes are not within the scope of this book; therefore, examples are not included. But many books provide information on these special formats.

"Send Your Resume to Lots of Strangers and, If It Is Good Enough, You Will Get Job Offers" and Other Fairy Tales

As I will say throughout this book, your objective is to get a good job, not to do a great resume. I have written this book to teach you the basics of putting together a useful

> **TIP:** Contrary to the advice of many career "experts," writing a "dynamite" or "perfect" (or whatever) resume will rarely get you the job you want. That will happen only following an interview, with just a few odd exceptions. So the task in the job search is to get interviews and to do well in them. Sending out lots of resumes to people you don't know is, essentially, a big waste of your time, energy, and other resources that you could be spending on much more productive activities.

and effective resume, but any resume will only be as good as how you use it. And the big problem with resumes is that most people don't understand that a resume alone will not get them a job.

That is why I suggest doing a simple resume early in your job search—one you can create in a few hours. This "same-day" approach allows you to get on with actively getting interviews instead of sitting at home working on a better resume or blindly sending out resumes to every company and every posting you can find. Later, as you have time, you can do an improved resume.

Seven Steps to Getting a Job Fast

Here are the key elements of getting a good job in less time:

1. **Know your skills.** One employer survey found that about 80 percent of those who made it to the interview did not do a good job presenting the skills they had to do the job. If you don't know what you are good at and how this relates to a particular job, you can't write a good resume, can't do a good interview, and are unlikely to get a good job.

2. **Have a clear job objective.** If you don't know where you want to go, it will be most difficult to get there. You can write a resume without having a job objective, but it won't be a good one.

3. **Know where and how to look.** Because three out of four jobs are not advertised, you will have to use nontraditional job search techniques to find them.

4. **Spend at least 25 hours a week looking.** Most job seekers spend far less than this and, as a result, are unemployed longer than they need to be. So, if you want to get a better job in less time, plan on spending more time on your job search.

5. **Get two interviews a day.** It sounds impossible, but this *can* be done once you redefine what counts as an interview (see the sidebar on the next page). Compare getting two interviews a day to the average job seeker's activity level of four or five interviews a month, and you can see how it can make a big difference.

6. **Do well in interviews.** You are unlikely to get a job offer unless you do well in this critical situation. I've reviewed the research on what it takes to do well in an interview and found, happily, that you can improve your interview performance relatively easily. Knowing what skills you have and being able to support them with examples is a good start. Chapter 3 helps you identify your key skills and prepare for interviews—as well as write a superior resume.

7. **Follow up on all contacts.** Following up can make a big difference in the results you get in your search for a new job.

No one should ever say that looking for a job is easy. But I have learned that you can take steps to make the process a bit easier and shorter than it typically is. Getting your resume together is something that hangs up many people for entirely too long. The next two chapters should help you solve that problem.

The New Definition of an Interview

An interview is any face-to-face contact with someone who has the authority to hire or supervise a person with your skills—even if no opening exists at the time you talk to them.

Chapter 2

Write a Simple Chronological Resume in About an Hour

You *can* write a basic resume in about an hour. It will not be a fancy one, and you might want to write a better one later, but I suggest you do the simple one first. Even if you decide to create a more sophisticated resume later (see Chapter 6), doing one now will allow you to use it in your job search within 24 hours.

Chronological Resume Basics

A chronological resume is easy to do. It works best for people who have had several years of experience in the same type of job they are seeking now. This is because a chronological resume clearly displays your recent work experience. If you want to change careers, have been out of the workforce recently, or do not have much paid work experience related to the job you want, a chronological resume might not be the best format for you. In these instances, you might want to use a skills resume, which is presented in Chapter 3.

Remember, you can edit and improve your resume at any time! Start with a basic resume, and put it to work immediately. When you have time, you can develop a more sophisticated resume.

> **TIP:** *The important point is to get together an acceptable resume quickly so that you won't be sitting at home worrying about your resume instead of being out job hunting.*

Two Chronological Resume Samples

Two sample chronological resumes for the same person follow. The first (Figure 2-1) is a simple one, but it works well enough in this situation because Judith is looking for a job in her present career field, has a good job history, and has related education and training.

Note that she wants to move up in responsibility, and her resume emphasizes the skills and education that will assist her.

One nice feature is that Judith put her recent business schooling in both the Education and Experience sections. Doing this filled a job gap and allows her to present recent training as equivalent to work experience. This resume includes the extra Personal section, where she presents some special strengths that often are not included in a resume.

> **TIP:** *If you will be submitting your resume to resume databases, a resume format like this one can be used without modification. More elaborately formatted resumes must be stripped of their more decorative elements to become electronic resumes. Chapter 5 has much more detail on writing and formatting your resume for electronic submission.*

The second example (Figure 2-2) is an improved version of this same resume. The improved resume adds a number of features, including a Summary instead of a job objective, a Knowledge and Skills section, and more accomplishments and skills. Notice, too, the impact of the numbers she adds to this resume in statements such as "top 30% of class" and "decreased department labor costs by more than $45,000 a year."

You should be able to do this sort of resume with an hour or two of additional work over the preceding one. As I think you will realize, most employers like the additional positive information it provides.

Writing the Major Sections of a Chronological Resume

Now that you have seen what both basic and improved chronological resumes look like, it's time to do your own chronological resume. Use the Instant Resume Worksheet beginning on page 27 to complete each part of your basic chronological resume.

Name

Remember, your resume is a business document, so be sure to use the name you will use in business settings. It's fine to use a nickname or variation of your name as long as it sounds professional and won't cause any confusion. Traditionally, most people have used their full, formal name on their resumes.

Figure 2-1: A Simple Chronological Resume

Judith J. Jones

115 South Hawthorne Avenue
Chicago, IL 66204
312-653-9217
judithjones@gmail.com

JOB OBJECTIVE

Desire a position in the office management, accounting, or administrative assistant area. Prefer a role that requires responsibility and includes a variety of tasks.

EDUCATION AND TRAINING

Acme Business College, Lincoln, IL
Graduate of a one-year business program, 2008

John Adams High School, South Bend, IN
Diploma, business education, 2003

U.S. Army
Financial procedures, accounting functions.

Other: Continuing-education classes and workshops in business communication, computer spreadsheet and database programs, scheduling systems, and customer relations.

EXPERIENCE

2008–present—Claims Processor, Blue Spear Insurance Co., Wilmette, IL. Handle customer medical claims, develop management reports based on spreadsheets I created, and exceed productivity goals.

2007–2008—Returned to school to upgrade my business and computer skills. Took courses in advanced accounting, spreadsheet and database programs, office management, human relations, and new office techniques.

2004–2007—E4, U.S. Army. Assigned to various stations as a specialist in finance operations. Promoted prior to honorable discharge.

2003–2004—Sandy's Boutique, Wilmette, IL. Responsible for counter sales, display design, cash register, and other tasks.

PERSONAL ATTRIBUTES

I am reliable, hardworking, and good with people.

Figure 2-2: An Improved Chronological Resume

Judith J. Jones

115 South Hawthorne Avenue • Chicago, IL 66204
312-653-9217 • judithjones@gmail.com

SUMMARY

Administrative professional with eight years of experience managing a high volume of complex insurance, accounting, and customer transactions. Problem solver who developed new processes and systems that increased efficiency and reduced costs. Effective supervisor and team member.

Knowledge and Skills

Administration: Insurance Claims Management • Office Management • Internal Systems & Processes • Purchasing • Vendor Management

Accounting: Accounting Theory & Systems • General Ledger Posting • Accounts Receivable • Accounts Payable • Invoice Management • Cash Balances • Bank Deposits

Technology: Microsoft Office (Word, Excel, Access, Outlook) • Accounting Software

Personal: Dedicated work ethic and excellent attendance record • Strong interpersonal, written, and oral communication and math skills.

EXPERIENCE

2008–present—Claims Processor, Blue Spear Insurance Company, Wilmette, IL
Handle 50 complex medical insurance claims per day, almost 20% above department average. Created a spreadsheet report process that decreased department labor costs by more than $45,000 a year (eliminating one full-time position). Received two merit raises for performance.

2007–2008—Returned to business school to gain advanced skills in accounting, office management, sales, and human resources.

2004–2007—Finance Specialist (E4), U.S. Army
Responsible for the systematic processing of more than 200 invoices per day from commercial vendors. Trained and supervised eight employees. Devised internal system that generated 15% increase in invoices processed with a decrease in personnel. Managed department with annual budget of more than $350,000. Honorable discharge.

2003–2004—Sales Associate promoted to Assistant Manager, Sandy's Boutique, Wilmette, IL
Made direct sales and supervised four employees. Managed daily cash balances and deposits, made purchasing and inventory decisions, and handled all management functions during owner's absence. Sales increased 26% and profits doubled during my tenure.

EDUCATION AND TRAINING

2008—Acme Business College, Lincoln, IL
Completed one-year program in Professional Office Management, earning grades in top 30% of my class. Courses included word processing, accounting theory and systems, advanced spreadsheet and database programs, time management, and basic supervision.

2003—John Adams High School, South Bend, IN
Graduated with emphasis on business courses. Earned excellent grades in all business topics and won top award for word-processing speed and accuracy.

Other: Continuing-education programs at my own expense, including business communications, customer relations, computer applications, sales techniques, and others.

Mailing Address

Don't abbreviate words such as "Street" or "Avenue." Do include your ZIP code. If you might move during your job search, ask a relative, friend, or neighbor whether you can temporarily use his or her address for your mail. As a last resort, arrange for a post office box. Forwarded mail will be delayed and can cause you to lose an opportunity; get an address at the new location so you appear to be settled there.

For security purposes, it's fine to omit your address when uploading your resume to a resume bank or job site. You can omit it entirely or you can include a general geographic qualifier—"Chicago Area"—if you want to send the message that you are a local candidate.

> **TIP:** Look at the many sample resumes in Chapter 7 to see how others have handled details such as address and contact information. Those resumes present lots of good ideas.

Phone Numbers and Email Address

An employer is more likely to phone or send an email than to contact you by mail. So it is essential to provide this contact information on your resume.

Let's start with the telephone. Always include your area code. Use a phone number that will be answered throughout your job search—for many people, that's a mobile phone. As long as your primary number is reliable and has a voicemail option, there's no need to include a secondary number such as your home phone.

I suggest that you call your number and listen to your voicemail message—what it says and how it is said. Is it professional? Does it clearly identify you? If your message has some cute, boring, or less-than-professional message, change it to one you would like your next employer to hear.

> **TIP:** Keep in mind that an employer could call at any time. Make sure that anyone who will pick up the phone knows to answer professionally and take an accurate message, including a phone number. Practice with these people if you need to. Nothing is as maddening as a garbled message with the wrong number.

Always include your email address. Email is the primary communication during most job searches.

Ideally, your email address should be simply your name "at" your email provider. You might need to add some numbers or additional information if your name is a common one. If you have an email address that you like but that doesn't convey a professional image (such as "catlover@aol.com" or "fratboy@gmail.com"), you can keep that email for private use and get a separate email address just for your job search.

Now, take a moment to complete the Identification section in the Instant Resume Worksheet on page 27.

Job Objective

Should you include a job objective on your resume? As you'll see from most of the sample resumes in this book, job objectives have largely been replaced by summary sections—for many very good reasons. The summary allows you to present a cohesive introduction to the rest of the resume and highlight your most important qualifications. Rather than telling an employer what you want, it states what you have to offer.

However, when you are writing a basic resume in an hour or so, it's wise to start with a job objective. Doing so will allow you to select resume content that will directly support the job you want. Later, when you are refining your resume, you can transition to a summary.

Carefully write your job objective so that it does not exclude you from a variety of related jobs you would consider. For example, if you use a job title such as "administrative assistant," you might exclude yourself from other jobs that call for similar skills. Look at how Judith Jones presented her job objective in her basic resume (Figure 2-1):

Desire a position in the office management, accounting, or administrative assistant area. Prefer a position requiring responsibility and a variety of tasks.

This resume opens up more options for her than if she simply said "administrative assistant." Her improved resume (Figure 2-2) includes a brief summary that positions her just as clearly for a variety of related roles but does so in a way that is more employer-oriented:

Administrative professional with eight years of experience managing a high volume of complex insurance, accounting, and customer transactions. Problem solver who developed new processes and systems that increased efficiency and reduced costs. Effective supervisor and team member.

A good job objective allows you to be considered for more responsible jobs than you have held in the past or to accept jobs with different titles that use similar skills.

I see many objectives that emphasize what the person wants but that do not provide information on what he or she can do. For example, an objective that says "Interested in a position that allows me to be creative and that offers adequate pay and advancement opportunities" is not good. Who cares? Your objective should emphasize what you can do, your skills, and where you want to use them.

Use the following worksheet to help you construct an effective and accurate Job Objective statement for your resume.

THE JOB OBJECTIVE WORKSHEET

1. **What sort of position, title, and area of specialization do you want?** Write the type of job you want, just as you might explain it to someone you know.

_____

_____

_____

2. **Define your bracket of responsibility.** Describe the range of jobs you would accept, from the minimum up to those you think you could handle if you were given the chance.

_____

_____

_____

3. **Name the key skills you have that are important in this job.** Describe the two or three key skills that are particularly important for success in the job that you are seeking. Select one or more of these that you are strong in and that you enjoy using. Write it (or them) here.

_____

_____

_____

4. Name any specific areas of expertise or strong interest that you want to use in your next job. If you have substantial interest, experience, or training in a specific area and want to include it in your job objective (remembering that it might limit your options), write it here.

_____

_____

_____

5. What else is important to you? Is there anything else you want to include in your job objective? This could be a value that is particularly important to you (such as "a position that allows me to help families" or "employment in a fast-paced environment"), a preference for the size or type of organization ("a small- to mid-size business"), or something else.

_____

_____

_____

Refer to the examples of simple but useful job objectives in the following box. Most provide some information on the type of job the candidate seeks as well as on the skills he or she offers.

Sample Job Objectives

A responsible general-office position in a busy, medium-sized organization.

A management position in the warehousing industry. Position should require supervisory, problem-solving, and organizational skills.

Computer programming or systems analysis. Prefer an accounting-oriented emphasis and a solution-oriented organization.

Medical assistant or coordinator in a physician's office, hospital, or other health services environment.

Responsible position that requires skills in public relations, writing, and reporting.

An aggressive and success-oriented professional seeking a sales position offering both challenge and growth.

A technical sales or sales support position in which my knowledge of enterprise-wide systems integration will be of value.

Most of the sample resumes throughout this book include summaries rather than objectives. Browse these for ideas as you work on improving your simple resume when you have the time.

> **TIP:** *The best objectives and summaries avoid a narrow job title and keep your options open to a wide variety of possibilities within a range of appropriate jobs.*

Now jot down your own draft job objective and refine it until it "feels good." Then rewrite it on the Instant Resume Worksheet on page 27.

Education and Training

Lead with your strengths. Recent graduates or those with good credentials but weak work experience should put their education and training toward the top because it represents a more important part of their experience. More experienced workers with work experience related to their job objective can put their education and training toward the end.

You can drop the Education and Training section if it doesn't support your job objective or if you don't have the credentials typically expected of those seeking similar positions. This is particularly true if you have lots of work experience in your career area. Usually, though, you should emphasize the most recent or highest level of education or training that relates to the job.

If you have a college degree or post–high school certification or training, it's not necessary to include high school on your resume.

> **TIP:** *Drop or downplay details that don't support your job objective. For example, if you possess related education but not a degree, tell employers what you do have. Include details of related courses, good grades, related extracurricular activities, and accomplishments.*

Depending on your situation, your education and training could be the most important part of your resume, so beef it up with details if you need to.

Look at the sample resumes in Chapter 7 for ideas. Then, on a separate piece of paper, rough out your Education and Training section. Then edit it to its final form and write it on pages 27–30 of the Instant Resume Worksheet.

Use Action Words and Phrases

Use active rather than passive words and phrases throughout your resume. Here is a short list of active words to give you some ideas:

Achieved	Established priorities	Organized
Administered	Expanded	Planned
Analyzed	Implemented	Presented
Controlled	Improved	Promoted
Coordinated	Increased productivity	Reduced expenses
Created	(or profits)	Researched
Designed	Initiated	Scheduled
Developed	Innovated	Solved
Diagnosed	Instructed	Supervised
Directed	Modified	Trained
Established policy	Negotiated	Transformed

Work and Volunteer History

This resume section provides the details of your work history, starting with the most recent job. List each job along with details of what you accomplished and special skills you used. Emphasize skills that directly relate to the job objective on your resume.

Treat volunteer or military experience the same way as other job experiences. This can be very important if this is where you got most of your relevant experience.

Job Titles

As a rule you should use the job title you held, but sometimes a title can be misleading. For example, if your title was sales clerk but you frequently opened and closed the store and were often left in charge, you might add the more descriptive title of night sales manager, perhaps in parentheses after your formal title.

If you were promoted, you can handle the promotion as a separate job if it is to your advantage. Also make sure your resume mentions that you were promoted.

TIP: *Look up the descriptions of jobs you have held in the past and jobs you want now in a book titled the* Occupational Outlook Handbook. *This book is available in most libraries. You can also find it online at the Department of Labor's website: www.bls.gov/oco. These descriptions will tell you the skills needed to succeed in the new job. Emphasize these and similar skills in your resume.*

Previous Employers

Provide the organization's name and list the city and state or province in which it was located. A street address or supervisor's name is not necessary.

Employment Dates

If you have large employment gaps that are not easily explained, use full years instead of months and years to avoid emphasizing the gaps. In fact, most people with many years of experience do not include months on their resumes even if their employment history has no gaps. Omitting months helps reduce clutter on the resume as well as disguise any short periods of unemployment.

If there was a significant period when you did not work, did you do anything that could explain it in a positive way? School? Travel? Raise a family? Self-employment? Even if you mowed lawns and painted houses for money while you were unemployed, that could count as self-employment.

In most cases it's better to include these experiences rather than to leave large gaps on your resume. You don't have to make a big deal out of them—if you were caring for your family, for example, you don't need to try to make yourself look like a "household manager" with budget and scheduling responsibilities. Just briefly list what you were doing so employers aren't wondering.

Duties and Accomplishments

In writing about your work experience, be sure to use action words and emphasize what you accomplished. Quantify what you did, and provide evidence that you did it well. Take particular care to mention skills that would directly relate to doing well in the job you want now.

If your previous jobs are not directly related to what you want to do now, emphasize skills you used in previous jobs that could be used in the new job. For example, someone who waits on tables has to deal with people and work quickly under pressure—skills that are needed in many other jobs such as accounting and managing.

Begin with a rough draft of your resume, and then edit it so that every word contributes something. You will probably go through several versions. When you're done, transfer your statements to pages 30–33 of the Instant Resume Worksheet.

Professional Organizations

This is an optional section where you can list job-related professional, humanitarian, or other groups with which you've been involved. These activities might be worth mentioning, particularly if you were an officer or were active in some other way. Mention accomplishments or awards. Many of the sample resumes in Chapter 7 include statements about accomplishments.

Now go to page 33 of the Instant Resume Worksheet and list your job-related efforts in professional organizations and other groups.

> **TIP:** *Emphasize accomplishments! Think about the things you accomplished in jobs, school, the military, and other settings. Make sure that you emphasize these things in your resume, even if it seems like bragging. Your accomplishments will set you apart from others and let future employers know what you can and will do for them.*

Recognition and Awards

If you have received any formal recognition or awards that support your job objective, consider mentioning them. You might create a separate section for them; or you can put them in the Work Experience, Skills, Education, or Personal section.

Personal Information

Years ago, resumes included personal details such as height, weight, marital status, hobbies, leisure activities, and other trivia. Please do not do this. Current laws do not allow an employer to base hiring decisions on certain points, so providing this information can cause some employers to toss your resume. For the same reason, do not include a photo of yourself.

Although a Personal section is optional, I sometimes like to end a resume on a personal note. Some resumes provide a touch of humor or playfulness as well as selected positives from outside school and work lives. This section is also a good place to list significant community involvements, a willingness to relocate, or personal characteristics an employer might like. Keep it short.

Turn now to page 33 of the Instant Resume Worksheet and list any personal information you feel is appropriate.

References

It is not necessary to include the names of your references on a resume. You can do better things with the precious space. It's not even necessary to state "references available on request" at the bottom of your resume, because that is obvious. If an employer wants your references, he or she knows to ask you for them.

It is helpful to line up references in advance. Pick people who know your work as an employee, volunteer, or student. Make sure they will express nice things about you by asking what they would say if asked. Push for negatives, and don't feel hurt if you get some. Nobody is perfect, and it gives you a chance to delete references before they do you damage.

> **TIP:** Some employers have policies against giving references over the phone. If this is the case with a previous employer, ask the employer to write a letter of reference for you to photocopy as needed. This is a good idea in general, so you might want to ask employers for one even if they have no rules against phone references.

Your references do *not* have to be your prior supervisors. You can choose anyone you like—anyone who can speak about your work, your skills, and your personal attributes. Of course, some employers will pursue your past supervisors anyway, but don't feel you must limit your list just to those who managed you. Choose a variety of people so that future employers get a broad picture.

When you know who to include, type a clean list of references on a separate sheet. Include names, addresses, phone numbers, email addresses, and details of why they are on your list. You can give this to employers who want it.

The Final Draft

At this point, you should have completed the Instant Resume Worksheet at the end of this chapter. Carefully review dates, addresses, phone numbers, spelling, and other details. You can now use the worksheet as a guide for preparing a better-than-average chronological resume.

Use the sample chronological resumes from this chapter as the basis for creating your resume. Additional examples of resumes appear in Chapters 3 and 7. Look them over for writing and formatting ideas. The sample resumes in Chapter 3 tend to be simpler and easier to write and format than some found in Chapter 7 and will provide better models for creating a resume quickly.

You will need to create your final draft using word-processing software, preferably Microsoft Word. Some programs have resume templates or "wizards," but these are not always the best or easiest choice because they force you to conform to their pre-set structures. Especially for a simple resume with basic formatting, you can just as easily create it on your own and get a cleaner format and easier-to-manage file.

Carefully review your final draft for typographical or other errors that may have slipped in. Then, when you are certain that everything is correct, save the file as your "final" version and print copies to use in your job search.

Instant Resume Worksheet

Identification

Name _____

Home address _____

City, state, and ZIP code _____

Phone number and description (if any) _____

_____

Alternative phone number and description _____

_____

Email address _____

Your Job Objective

_____

_____

_____

_____

_____

Education and Training

Highest Level/Most Recent Education or Training _____

Institution name _____

(continued)

(continued)

City, state/province (optional) _____

Certificate or degree _____

Specific courses or programs that relate to your job objective _____

_____

_____

Related awards, achievements, and extracurricular activities _____

_____

_____

Anything else that might support your job objective, such as good grades

_____

_____

_____

_____

College/Post High School

Institution name _____

_____

City, state/province (optional) _____

Certificate or degree _____

_____

Specific courses or programs that relate to your job objective _____

_____

_____

Related awards, achievements, and extracurricular activities _____

_____

_____

Anything else that might support your job objective, such as good grades

_____

_____

_____

_____

High School

Institution name _____

City, state/province (optional) _____

Certificate or degree _____

Specific courses or programs that relate to your job objective _____

_____

_____

Related awards, achievements, and extracurricular activities _____

_____

_____

Anything else that might support your job objective, such as good grades

_____

_____

_____

_____

**Armed Services Training
and Other Training or Certification**

Institution name _____

Specific courses or programs that relate to your job objective _____

_____

_____

(continued)

(continued)

Related awards, achievements, and extracurricular activities _____

_____

_____

Anything else that might support your job objective, such as good grades

_____

_____

_____

_____

Related Workshops, Seminars, Informal Learning, or Any Other Training

_____

_____

_____

_____

_____

_____

Work Experience

Most Recent Position

Dates (month/year) from _____ to _____

Organization name _____

City, state/province _____

Your job title(s) _____

Duties _____

_____

_____

Skills _____

_____

_____

Equipment or software you used _____

_____

_____

Promotions, accomplishments, and anything positive _____

_____

_____

Next Most Recent Position

Dates (month/year) from _____ to _____

Organization name _____

City, state/province _____

Your job title(s) _____

Duties _____

_____

_____

Skills _____

_____

_____

Equipment or software you used _____

_____

_____

Promotions, accomplishments, and anything positive _____

_____

_____

(continued)

(continued)

Next Most Recent Position

Dates (month/year) from_____ to_____

Organization name _____

City, state/province _____

Your job title(s) _____

Duties _____

_____

_____

Skills _____

_____

_____

Equipment or software you used _____

_____

_____

Promotions, accomplishments, and anything positive _____

_____

_____

Next Most Recent Position

Dates (month/year) from_____ to_____

Organization name _____

City, state/province _____

Your job title(s) _____

Duties _____

_____

_____

Skills _____

_____

_____

Equipment or software you used _____

_____

_____

Promotions, accomplishments, and anything positive _____

_____

_____

Any Other Work or Volunteer Experience

_____

_____

_____

_____

Professional Organizations

_____

_____

_____

_____

Personal Information

_____

_____

_____

_____

Chapter 3

Write a Skills Resume in Just a Few Hours

Although it takes a bit longer to do a skills resume than it does a chronological resume, you might find that it is a better choice for you. This chapter will show you why you might consider a skills resume and how to write one.

Be sure to read Chapter 1 and do the activities in Chapter 2 (particularly the Instant Resume Worksheet on pages 27–33) before completing the skills resume described here.

The Skills Resume

This chapter shows you how to write a resume that is organized around the key skills you have that the job you want requires.

The focus of a chronological resume is your work history—job titles, where you've worked, and when you've worked there. Employers often look for candidates with a work history that fits the position. If they want to hire a cost accountant, they will look for someone who has done this work. If you are a recent graduate or have little experience in the career or at the level you now want, you will find that a simple chronological resume emphasizes your *lack* of related experience rather than your ability to do the job.

A skills resume avoids these problems by highlighting what you have done under specific skills headings rather than under past jobs. If you hitchhiked across the country for two years, a skills resume won't necessarily

> **TIP:** Because skills resumes can hide your problems, some employers do not like them—or, when employers receive them, they try to figure out what you're "hiding." For these reasons, I don't often write or recommend a skills resume; I think a chronological resume, if written well, can highlight your relevant strengths and will be better received by employers. However, for some people the skills resume is truly the best choice. If you use one, be aware that you might get some negative feedback, but be confident that you have presented yourself in the best possible way.

display this as an employment gap. Instead, you could say "Traveled extensively throughout the country and am familiar with most major market areas." That could be very useful experience for certain positions.

A Sample Skills Resume

Following is a basic skills resume (see Figure 3-1). The example is for a recent high school graduate whose only paid work experience has been in a hamburger place. Read it, and ask yourself whether you would consider interviewing Lisa if you were an employer. For most people, the answer is yes.

This resume presents a good example of how a skills resume can help someone who does not have the best credentials. It allows the job seeker to present school and extracurricular activities to good effect. It is a strong format choice because it lets her highlight strengths without emphasizing her limited work experience. It doesn't say where she worked or for how long, yet it gives her a shot at many jobs.

TIP: You might have more work experience than shown in this sample. If so, look at the end of this chapter to find sample skills resumes written for people with more education and experience.

Although the sample resume is simple, it presents Lisa in a positive way. She is looking for an entry-level job in a nontechnical area, so many employers will be more interested in her skills than in her job-specific experience. What work experience she does have is presented as a plus. And notice how she listed her gymnastics experience next to "Work Ethic."

The skills format can work well for a variety of situations and might be right for you.

Figure 3-1: A Basic Skills Resume

Lisa M. Rhodes

813 Lava Court • Denver, CO 81613
(303) 442-1659
lisa.rhodes@yahoo.com

Position Desired

Sales-oriented position in a retail sales or distribution business.

Skills and Abilities

Communications	Good written and verbal presentation skills. Use proper grammar and have a good speaking voice.
Interpersonal	Able to get along well with coworkers and accept supervision. Received positive evaluations from previous supervisors.
Flexibility	Willing to try new things and am interested in improving efficiency on assigned tasks.
Attention to Detail	Concerned with quality. My work is typically orderly and attractive. Like to see things completed correctly and on time.
Work Ethic	Throughout high school, worked long hours in strenuous activities while attending school full-time. Often handled as many as 65 hours a week in school and other structured activities while maintaining above-average grades.
Customer Contact	Routinely handled as many as 500 customer contacts a day (10,000 per month) in a busy retail outlet. Averaged a lower than .001% complaint rate and was given the "Employee of the Month" award in my second month of employment. Received two merit increases.
Cash Sales	Handled more than $2,000 a day ($40,000 a month) in cash sales. Balanced register and prepared daily sales summaries and deposits.
Reliability	Never absent or late. Trusted to deliver daily cash deposits totaling more than $40,000 a month.

Education

Graduated from Franklin High School in top 30% of class. Took advanced English classes. Member of award-winning band. Superior attendance record and communication skills.

Other

Active gymnastics competitor for four years. This taught me discipline, teamwork, how to follow instructions, and how to work hard to achieve a goal. I am ambitious, outgoing, reliable, and willing to work.

Writing Your Skills Resume

The skills resume format uses a number of sections similar to those in a chronological resume. Here I will discuss only those sections that are substantially different—the job objective and skills sections. Refer to Chapter 2 for information on sections that are common to both resume types. The samples at the end of this chapter give you ideas on skills resume language, organization, and layout, as well as how to handle special problems.

Don't be afraid to use a little creativity in writing your skills resume. Remember, you are allowed to break some rules if it makes sense.

Job Objective

Although a simple chronological resume does not require a career objective, a skills resume does. Without a reasonably clear job objective, you can't select and organize the key skills you have to support that job objective. The job objective statement on a skills resume should answer the following questions:

- **What sort of position, title, or area of specialization do you seek?** After reading the information on job objectives in Chapter 2, you should know how to present the type of job you are seeking. Is your objective too narrow and specific? Is it so broad or vague that it's meaningless?

- **What level of responsibility interests you?** Job objectives often indicate a level of responsibility, particularly for supervisory or management roles. If in doubt, always try to keep open the possibility of getting a job with a higher level of responsibility (and, often, salary) than your previous or current one. Write your job objective to include this possibility.

> **TIP:** Review the "Sample Job Objectives" box on page 21 in the preceding chapter and look at the sample resumes at the end of this chapter. Notice that some resumes use headings such as "Position Desired," "Career Objective," or "Profile" to introduce the job objective section. Many people think that these headings sound more professional than "Job Objective." It's your decision.

- **What are your most important skills?** What are the two or three most important skills or personal characteristics needed to succeed in the job you're targeting? These are often mentioned in a job objective.

The Skills Section

This section can be called Areas of Accomplishment, Summary of Qualifications, Areas of Expertise and Ability, and so on. Whatever you choose to call it, this section is what makes a skills resume. To construct it, you must carefully consider which skills you want to emphasize.

Your task is to feature the skills that are essential to success on the job you want *and* that you have and want to use. You probably have a good idea of which skills meet both criteria.

Note that some resumes in this book emphasize skills that are not specific to a particular job. For example, "work ethic" and "organizational skills" are important for many jobs. In your resume, you should provide specific examples of situations or accomplishments that show you possess such skills. You can do this by including examples from previous work or other experiences.

The Key Skills List

On the next page is a list of skills that are considered key for success on most jobs. It is based on research with employers about the skills they look for in employees. So if you have to emphasize some skills over others, include these—assuming you have them, of course.

Key Skills Needed for Success in Most Jobs	
Basic Skills Considered the Minimum to Keep a Job	*Key Transferable Skills That Transfer from Job to Job and Are Most Likely Needed in Jobs with Higher Pay and Responsibility*
Basic academic skills	Instruct others
Accept supervision	Manage money and budgets
Follow instructions	Manage people
Get along well with coworkers	Meet the public

Basic Skills Considered the Minimum to Keep a Job	Key Transferable Skills That Transfer from Job to Job and Are Most Likely Needed in Jobs with Higher Pay and Responsibility
Meet deadlines	Work effectively as part of a team
Good attendance	Negotiating
Punctual	Organize/manage projects
Hard worker	Public speaking
Productive	Written and oral communication
Honest	Organizational effectiveness and leadership
	Self-motivation and goal setting
	Creative thinking and problem solving

In addition to the skills in the list, you will want to emphasize skills specific to the particular jobs you are pursuing. For example, an accountant needs to know how to set up a general ledger, use accounting software, and develop income and expense reports. These job-specific skills are called *job-content skills* and can be quite important in qualifying for a job.

IDENTIFY YOUR KEY TRANSFERABLE SKILLS

Look over the preceding key skills list, and write down any skills you have that are particularly important for the job you want. Add other skills you possess that you feel must be communicated to an employer to get the job you want. Write at least three, but no more than six, of these most important skills:

1. _____

2. _____

3. _____

4. _____

5. _____

6. _____

Prove Your Key Skills with a Story

Now write each skill you listed in the preceding box on a separate sheet. For each skill, write several detailed examples of when you used it. If possible, you should use work situations, but you can use other situations such as volunteer work, school activities, or other life experiences. Try to quantify the examples by giving numbers such as money saved, sales increased, or other measures to support those skills. Emphasize results you achieved and any accomplishments.

The following is an example of what one person wrote for a key skill. It might give you an idea of how to document your own skills.

Key skill: Meeting deadlines

I volunteered to help my social organization raise money. I found out about special government funds, but the proposal deadline was only 24 hours away. So I stayed up all night and submitted it on time. We were one of only three groups whose proposals were approved, and we were awarded more than $100,000 to fund a youth program for a whole year.

Edit Your Key Skills Proofs

If you carefully consider the skills needed in the preceding story, there are quite a few. Here are some I came up with:

- Work ethic
- Ability to meet deadlines
- Willingness to help others
- Good written communication skills
- Persuasive communication
- Problem solving

Review each "proof sheet" and select the proofs that are particularly valuable in supporting your job objective. You should have at least two proof stories for each skill area. After you select your proofs, rewrite them using action words and short sentences. In the margins, write the skills you needed to do these things. When you're done, write statements you can use in your resume. Rewrite your proof statements, and delete anything that does not reinforce the key skills you want to support.

Following is a rewrite of the proof story example. Do a similar editing job on each of your own proofs until they are clear, short, and powerful. You can then use these statements in your resume, modifying them as needed.

Key skill: Ability to meet deadlines

On 24-hour notice, submitted a complex proposal that successfully obtained more than $100,000 in funding.

You could easily use this same proof story to support other skills I listed earlier, such as work ethic. So, as you write and revise your proof stories, consider which key skills they best support. Use the proofs to support those key skills in your resume.

Tips for Editing Your Draft Resume into Final Form

Before you make a final draft of your skills resume, look over the samples at the end of this chapter for ideas on content and format. Several show interesting techniques that might be useful for your situation. For example, if you have a good work history, you can include a brief chronological listing of jobs. This jobs list could be before or after your skills section. If you have substantial work history, you could begin your skills resume with a summary of experience to provide the basis for details that follow.

When you have the content from the proof stories you need for your skills resume, word-process your first draft. Rewrite and edit it until the resume communicates what you really want to say about yourself. Cut anything that does not support your objective. When you are done, ask someone to *very carefully* review it for typographical and other errors. When you are certain that your resume contains no errors, prepare the final version.

Remember that this is your resume, so do it in a way you think presents you best. Trust your own good judgment.

Your objective is to get a good job, not to keep working on your resume. So avoid the temptation to make a "perfect" resume; instead, get this one done. Today. Then use it tomorrow.

> **TIP:** Chapter 5 provides information on modifying your resume for online use.

If the urge to improve your resume comes to you, don't resist. Just work on your next resume on weekends—Chapter 6 will help you. In the meantime, use the one you finished today in your job search. If all goes well, you might never need a "better" resume.

More Sample Skills Resumes

Look over the sample resumes that follow to see how others have adapted the basic skills format to fit their situations. These examples are based on real resumes (although the names and other details have been changed), and I have included comments to help you understand details that might not be apparent.

The formats and designs of the resumes are intentionally basic and can be done with any word processor. Chapter 7 includes a wide variety of resumes, many with fancier graphics and designs. But remember that it is better to have a simple and error-free resume—and be out there using it—than to be at home working on a more elaborate one.

Darrel Craig's Resume

This is a resume (Figure 3-2) of a career changer with substantial work experience, but in another occupation. After working for an alarm and security systems company and at a variety of other jobs, Darrel went back to school and learned computer programming. The skills format allows him to emphasize his past business experience to support his current job objective. His resume includes no chronological jobs listing and no education dates, so it is not obvious that he is a recent graduate with little formal work experience as a programmer.

Darrel does a good job of presenting previous work experience and includes numbers to support his skills and accomplishments. Even so, the relationship between his previous work and current objective could be improved. For example, collecting bad debts requires discipline, persistence, and attention to detail—the same skills required in programming. And, although he is good at sales, his resume does not relate the skills required for sales to his new job objective of programming.

Darrel's job objective could be improved. If Darrel were here to discuss it, I'd ask him if he wants to use his selling skills *and* his programming skills in a new job. If so, he could modify his job objective to include jobs such as selling technology or computer consulting services. Or, if he wants to be a programmer, I would suggest he emphasize other transferable skills that directly support his programming objective, such as his history of meeting deadlines. Still, this resume is effective in relating his past business experience to his ability to be a programmer in a business environment.

Figure 3-2: Darrel Craig's Resume

Darrel Craig

(412) 437-6217
Dcraig1273@aol.com
2306 Cincinnati Street, Kingsford, PA 15171

Career Objective

Challenging position in programming or related areas that would best use expertise in the business environment. Position should have opportunities for a dedicated individual with leadership abilities.

Programming Skills

Experienced in business program design including payroll, inventory, database management, sales, marketing, accounting, and loan amortization reports. Knowledgeable in program design, coding, implementation, debugging, and file maintenance. Familiar with distributed PC network systems (LAN and WAN) and have working knowledge of DOS, UNIX, BASIC, FORTRAN, C, and LISP plus UML, Java, C++, and Visual Basic.

Applications and Network Software

Microsoft Certified Systems Engineer familiar with a variety of applications programs including Lotus Notes, Novell and NT network systems, database and spreadsheet programs, and accounting and other applications software.

Communication and Problem Solving

Interpersonal communication strengths, public relations capabilities, innovative problem solving, and analytical talents.

Sales

A total of eight years of experience in sales and sales management. Sold security products to distributors and burglar alarm dealers. Increased company's sales from $36,000 to more than $320,000 per month. Organized creative sales and marketing concepts. Trained sales personnel in prospecting techniques and service personnel in more efficient and consumer-friendly installation methods. Result: Generated 90% of new business through referrals from existing customers.

Management

Managed security systems company for four years and increased profits yearly. Supervised 20 office, sales, accounting, inventory, and installation staff. Worked as assistant credit manager, responsible for $2 million in annual sales. Handled semi-annual inventory of five branch stores totaling millions of dollars.

Accounting

Balanced all books and prepared tax-return forms for security systems company. Four years of experience in credit and collections. Exceeded 98% collection rate each year, and collected a bad debt in excess of $250,000 deemed "uncollectible."

Education

School of Computer Technology, Pittsburgh, PA
Graduate of two-year Business Application Programming/TECH EXEC Program—3.97 GPA

Robert Morris College, Pittsburgh, PA
Associate degree in Accounting, Minor in Management

Thomas Marrin's Resume

This resume (Figure 3-3) combines elements of the chronological and skills formats. Thomas's resume breaks some "rules," but for good reasons. He has kept his job objective quite broad and does not limit it to a particular industry or job title. Because he sees himself as a business manager, it does not matter to him in what kind of business or industry he works. He prefers a larger organization, as his job objective indicates. His education is near the top because he thinks it is one of his strengths.

Thomas has worked with one employer for many years, but he presents each job there as a separate one. This allows him to provide more details about his accomplishments within each position and more clearly indicate that these were promotions to jobs with increased responsibility. His military experience, although not recent, is listed under a separate heading because he thinks it is important. Note how he presented his military experience using civilian language. This is very important because most hiring managers are unfamiliar with military jargon. (See Chapter 7 for more examples of civilian resumes for former military personnel.)

Notice how concise his description of his job at Hayfield Publishing is. This was a lower-level job, and therefore it's not necessary to elaborate. Keeping it short allowed him to fit his resume on one page and keep the focus on his more recent and relevant experience.

Figure 3-3: Thomas Marrin's Resume

THOMAS P. MARRIN
80 Harrison Avenue • Baldwin, NY 11563
716-223-4705 • tmarrin@techconnect.com

POSITION DESIRED
Mid- to upper-level management position emphasizing problem solving, planning, budget management, and cost reduction/efficiency improvement.

EDUCATION
University of Notre Dame, BS in Business Administration
Course emphasis on accounting, supervision, and marketing. Upper 25% of class.

Additional: Advanced training in time management, organizational behavior, and cost control.

BUSINESS EXPERIENCE

Wills Express Transit Co., Inc., Mineola, NY   **2002 to Present**
Promoted to Vice President, Corporate Equipment—2006 to Present
Control purchase, maintenance, and disposal of 1,100 trailers and 65 company cars with more
than $8 million operating and $26 million capital expense responsibilities. Schedule trailer
purchases for six divisions.

- Operated 2.3% under planned maintenance budget in company's second-best profit year
  while operating revenues declined 2.5%.
- Originated schedule to correlate drivers' preferences with available trailers, decreasing
  driver turnover 20%.
- Developed systematic Purchase and Disposal Plan for company car fleet.
- Restructured company-car policy, saving 15% on per-car cost.

Promoted to Assistant Vice President, Corporate Operations—2004 to 2006
Coordinated activities of six sections of Corporate Operations with an operating budget of more
than $10 million.

- Directed implementation of zero-base budgeting.
- Developed and prepared executive officer analyses detailing achievable cost-reduction
  measures. Resulted in cost reduction of more than $600,000 in first two years.
- Designed policy and procedure for special equipment leasing program during peak seasons.
- Cut capital purchases by more than $1 million.

Promoted to Manager of Communications—2002 to 2004
Directed and managed $1.4 million communication network involving 650 phones, three
switchboards, and 15 employees.

- Installed new communications control system that directed calls to lowest-cost options and
  pinpointed personal abuse. Achieved 100% system payback six months earlier than
  projected.
- Devised procedures that allowed simultaneous 20% increase in calls and a $75,000/year
  savings.

Hayfield Publishing Company, Hempstead, NY   **2000 to 2002**
Communications Administrator
Managed operations of a large Communications Center. Cut costs 12% and improved services.

MILITARY EXPERIENCE

U.S. Army—2nd Infantry Division, 1992 to 1994.
First Lieutenant and platoon leader stationed in Korea and Ft. Knox, KY. Supervised an annual
budget equivalent of nearly $9 million and equipment valued at more than $60 million.
Responsible for training, scheduling, supervision, mission planning, and activities of as many as
40 staff. Received several commendations. Honorable discharge.

Peter Neely's Resume

Peter lost his factory job when the plant closed. He got a survival
job as a truck driver and now wants to make truck driving his career
because it pays well and he likes the work.

Notice how his resume (Figure 3-4) emphasizes skills from previous
jobs and other experiences that are essential for success as a truck driver. This resume uses a combination format that includes elements from
both skills and chronological resumes. The skills approach allows him
to emphasize specific skills that support his job objective; the chronological list of jobs allows him to display a stable work history.

The jobs he had years ago are clustered under one grouping because they are not as important as more recent experience. Also, doing so does not show that he is older. Yes, I realize employers are not supposed to discriminate based on age, but Peter figures, "Why take chances?" For the same reason, Peter does not include dates for his military experience or high school graduation, nor does he separate them into categories such as Military Experience or Education. They just aren't as important in supporting his job objective as they might be for a younger person.

Unusual elements are comments about not smoking or drinking and a stable family, although these comments work. Peter figures that an employer will think that a stable, healthy, and sober truck driver is better than the alternative. Also note how Peter presented his military experience as another job, with an emphasis on the truck driving and diesel experience.

Figure 3-4: Peter Neely's Resume

Peter Neely
203 Evergreen Road, Houston, TX 39127
237-649-1234   pneeley@mac.com

POSITION DESIRED: Short- or Long-Distance Truck Driver

Summary	More than 15 years of stable work history, including substantial experience with diesel engines, electrical systems, and driving all sorts of trucks and heavy equipment.

SKILLS

Driving Record/ Licenses:	Current Commercial Driving License and Chauffeur's License; qualified and able to drive anything that rolls. No traffic citations or accidents in more than 20 years.
Vehicle Maintenance:	I maintain correct maintenance schedules and avoid most breakdowns as a result. Substantial mechanical and electrical systems training and experience enable me to repair many breakdowns immediately and avoid towing.
Record Keeping:	Excellent attention to detail. Familiar with recording procedures and submit required records on a timely basis.
Routing:	Thorough knowledge of most major interstate routes, with good map-reading and route-planning skills. I get there on time and without incident.
Other:	Not afraid of hard work, flexible, get along well with others, meet deadlines, excellent attendance, responsible.

WORK EXPERIENCE

2006–Present	CAPITAL TRUCK CENTER, Houston, TX: Pick up and deliver all types of commercial vehicles from across the United States. Trusted with handling large sums of money and complex truck-purchasing transactions.
1998–2006	QUALITY PLATING CO., Houston, TX: Promoted from production to Quality Control. Developed numerous production improvements that resulted in substantial cost savings.
1993–1998	BLUE CROSS MANUFACTURING, Houston, TX: Received several increases in salary and responsibility before leaving for a more challenging position.
Prior to 1993	Truck delivery of food products to destinations throughout the South. Also responsible for up to 12 drivers and equipment-maintenance personnel.

OTHER

Four years of experience in the U.S. Air Force, driving and operating truck-mounted diesel power plants. Responsible for monitoring and maintenance on a rigid 24-hour schedule. Stationed in Alaska, California, Wyoming, and other states. Honorable discharge.

High school graduate plus training in diesel engines and electrical systems. Excellent health, love the outdoors, stable family life, nonsmoker and nondrinker.

Andrea Atwood's Resume

This resume (Figure 3-5) uses a simple format with few words and lots of white space. I would like to see more numbers used to indicate performance or accomplishments. For example, what was the result of the more efficient record-keeping system she developed? And why did she receive the employee-of-the-month awards?

As a recent high school graduate, Andrea does not have substantial experience in her field, having had only one full-time job since graduation. This resume's skills format allows her to present her strengths better than a chronological resume would. Because she has formal training in retail sales, she could have given more details about specific courses she took or other school-related activities that would support her objective. Even so, her resume does a good job of presenting her basic skills to an employer in an attractive format.

Figure 3-5: Andrea Atwood's Resume

ANDREA ATWOOD
3231 East Harbor Road
Grand Rapids, Michigan 41103
616-447-2111
andrea.atwood@aol.com

Objective: A responsible position in retail sales or marketing.

Areas of Accomplishment:

Customer Service
- Communicate well with all age groups.
- Able to interpret customer concerns to help them find the items they want.
- Received 6 Employee-of-the-Month awards in 3 years.

Merchandise Display
- Developed display skills via in-house training and experience.
- Received Outstanding Trainee Award for Christmas toy display.
- Dress mannequins, arrange table displays, and organize sale merchandise.

Inventory Control
- Maintained and marked stock during department manager's 6-week illness.
- Developed more efficient record-keeping procedures.

Additional Skills
- Operate cash register and computerized accounting systems.
- Willing to work evenings and weekends.
- Punctual, honest, reliable, and hardworking.

Experience:
Harper's Department Store
Grand Rapids, Michigan
2000 to present

Education:
Central High School
Grand Rapids, Michigan
3.6 grade-point average (4.0 scale)
Honor Graduate in Distributive Education
Two years of retail sales training in Distributive Education
Courses in Business Writing, Computerized Accounting, and Word Processing

Chapter 4

The 15-Minute Cover Letter and Other Job Search Correspondence

This chapter provides advice on writing cover letters, JIST Cards®, and thank-you notes. It includes various samples of each type of correspondence.

Cover Letters

Writing a simple cover letter *is* pretty simple. Once you know how it's done, you should be able to write one in about 15 minutes or so.

It is not appropriate to send a resume to someone without explaining why. It is traditional to provide a letter—a cover letter—along with your resume. Depending on the circumstances, the letter would explain your situation and ask the recipient for some specific action, consideration, or response.

Entire books discuss the art of writing cover letters. My objective here is to give you a simple, quick review of cover letter basics that will meet most needs.

If you think about it, you will send a resume and cover letter to only two groups of people:

- People you know.

- People you don't know.

Although I realize this sounds simple, it's true. And this observation makes it easier to understand how you might structure your letters to each group. First let's review some basics regarding writing cover letters in general.

> **TIP:** *Although many situations require a formal letter, a simple note will do in many instances (for example, when you know the person you are writing to). You'll find examples of informal notes later in this chapter.*

Seven Quick Tips for Writing a Superior Cover Letter

No matter who you are writing to, virtually every good cover letter should follow these guidelines.

Write to Someone in Particular

Try *never* to send a cover letter to "To whom it may concern" or use some other impersonal opening. We all get enough junk mail and email. If you don't send your letter to someone by name, it will be treated like junk mail.

Make Absolutely No Errors

One way to offend people quickly is to misspell their names or use incorrect titles. If you have any question, call to verify the correct spelling of the name and other details before you send the letter. Also, review your letters carefully to be sure that they contain no typographical, grammatical, or other errors.

Personalize Your Content

If you can't personalize your letter in some way, don't send it. I've never been impressed by form letters, and you should not use them. Those computer-generated letters that automatically insert a name never fool anyone, and I find cover letters done in this way offensive. Although some resume and cover letter books recommend that you send out lots of these "broadcast letters" to people you don't know, I suggest that doing so wastes time and money.

Present a Good Appearance

Your contacts with prospective employers should always be professional. If you are sending cover letters and resumes by mail, print them on good-quality stationery and use matching envelopes. Follow a standard format for a business letter—you can model your letter on samples found later in this chapter.

If sending your letter by email, use a descriptive subject line that helps readers identify your email. Create—and always use—a standard signature that includes your contact information. Even people who know you well might not have your phone number and email address handy, so make it easy on them by providing it every time you write.

Provide a Friendly Opening

Begin your letter with a reminder of any prior contacts and the reason for your correspondence now. The examples later in this section will give you some ideas on how to handle this.

Target Your Skills and Experiences

To do this well, you must know something about the organization, the person you're writing to, or the job you are writing about. Present any relevant background information that might be of particular interest.

Close with an Action Statement

Don't close your letter without clearly identifying what you will do next. I do not recommend that you leave it up to the employer to contact you, because that doesn't guarantee a response. Close on a positive note, and let the employer know you will make further contact.

Writing Cover Letters to People You Know

It is always best if you know the person you are writing to. Written correspondence is less effective than personal contact, so the ideal circumstance is to send a resume and cover letter after having spoken with the person directly.

For example, it is far more effective to first call someone who has posted a job opening than to simply send a letter and resume. You will immediately differentiate yourself from "one of the crowd." You can get to know all kinds of people who can help you with your job search. You might not have known them yesterday, but you can get to know them today.

So I'll assume you have made some sort of personal contact before sending your resume. Within this assumption are hundreds of possible situations, but I will review the most important ones in the following box and let you adapt your approach to your own situation.

The Four Types of Cover Letters to People You Know

You will be in one of four basic situations when you send cover letters to people you know. Each situation requires a different approach.

1. **An interview is scheduled, and a specific job opening might interest you.** In this case, you have already arranged an interview for a job opening that interests you. The cover letter should provide details of your experience that relate to the specific job.

2. **An interview is scheduled, but no specific job is available.** In essence, you will send this letter for an interview with an employer who does not have a specific opening for you now but who might in the future. This is fertile ground for finding job leads where no one else might be looking.

3. **An interview has taken place.** Many people overlook the importance of sending a letter after an interview. This is a time to say that you want the job (if that is the case, your letter should say so) and add any details on why you think you can do the job well.

4. **No interview is scheduled yet.** In some situations, you just can't arrange an interview before you send a resume and cover letter. For example, you might be trying to see a person whose name was given to you by a friend, but that person is on vacation. In these cases, sending a good cover letter and resume will allow any later contacts to be more effective.

In this chapter you will find sample cover letters for each situation.

The following are sample cover letters for the most common situations. Note that they use different formats and styles to show you the range of styles that are appropriate. Each addresses a different situation, and each incorporates all of the cover letter writing guidelines presented earlier in this chapter.

Sample Cover Letter: Pre-Interview, for a Specific Job Opening

Comments: This writer called first and arranged an interview, which is the best approach of all. In his letter, he conveys both the hard skills and the intangibles that make him a great mechanic and a great employee.

Matt Young   249 Maple Grove Road ▪ East Haven, CT 06512
                                   203-467-1276 ▪ mattyoung@gmail.com

---

December 2, 20XX

Stanley Cohen
President
Savin Industrial
2590 East Haven Parkway
New Haven, CT 06510

Dear Mr. Cohen:

Thanks for taking my call and discussing your available mechanic position. I am very interested.

People say that I can fix anything. While that might not be true, I do have a wide range of skills and experience that can help keep your equipment and your facility running smoothly and safely.

I have spent my career building, fixing, and maintaining equipment for manufacturing and construction companies. I have a strong natural mechanical aptitude and the resourcefulness to solve any number of equipment problems, and I have continuously added to my skills through training, team projects, and the willingness to tackle just about anything.

The enclosed resume describes the breadth of my experience, but it cannot convey the creativity and energy I bring to every job nor the satisfaction I get from making machinery and equipment run well.

I look forward to our interview at 8:30 a.m. on the 8th. It will be a pleasure to meet you.

Sincerely,

Matt Young

enclosure: resume

Sample Cover Letter: Pre-Interview, No Specific Job Opening

Comments: Written to a recruiter, this letter is presented as an e-letter (email format). Notice the specific subject line that will help the recruiter quickly identify the reason he is receiving this email. In the body of the letter, this job seeker tells a short success story that is very relevant to the recruiter's area of specialization. She closes with a signature line that makes her correspondence appear very professional.

To: Richard.Talmadge@recruitsmart.com
From: eviepepper@gmail.com
Subject: In advance of our meeting next week – sending resume as you requested

Dear Mr. Talmadge:

Thank you for your time on the phone and your suggestion to forward my resume for potential opportunities through RecruitSmart. I was excited to learn of the depth of your expertise in the fashion industry — which, as we discussed, is my area of expertise as well.

The attached resume highlights my background and qualifications as a Showroom Designer/Visual Merchandiser. For the past six years I managed the start-to-finish design of ModCom's 2300-sq.ft. New York showroom several times yearly. The results have been consistently positive: on-time, on-budget completion, excellent customer feedback, and strong sales performance. My experience and track record should be of particular interest to your clients seeking to revitalize their showroom displays.

My entire career has been spent in the fashion industry, specifically home décor, and I have excellent sales and marketing qualifications as well as visual design skills. I would be very interested in being considered for any number of positions that cross your desk that might benefit from my industry knowledge and proven capabilities.

I look forward to meeting you in person next week; I'll be there at 9 am on the 6th. Thank you.

Sincerely,

Evelyn Pepper
****
555-555-5555
eviepepper@gmail.com
http://www.linkedin.com/in/evelynpepper

Sample Cover Letter: After an Interview

Comments: This letter shows how you might follow up after an interview and make a pitch for the company to hire you. It is a strong letter, to match the personality of the candidate and the position in financial sales. Notice how she refers to the conversation held during the interview—this is in no way a "form letter" but is customized to the circumstances.

KATHY MILLER

2943 Hillside Street, Unit 2-B ▪ Oakland, CA 94624 ▪ 510-245-7450 ▪ kathymiller@verizon.net

December 2, 20XX

Steve Rostakoff
Western Regional Manager
NuTraders Network
9090 Mile High Drive
Denver, CO 80209

Dear Steve:

NuTraders has an exciting future, and I would like to help the Institutional Services division skyrocket to a market-dominant position in the West.

NuTraders' new offerings put the company in a short-term position of market advantage. To seize this advantage requires a "hit the ground running" sales approach. As we discussed, my experience with Schwab closely parallels your new Western Sales Manager position. I know the market... I know the key players... I know the industry and the products... and I have the experience and track record to deliver both immediate revenue results and sustainable long-term growth.

With the right person at the helm, the first-year goal of $100 million in sales is easily reachable. I believe I am that person. I hope you agree.

As you requested, I am attaching a list of professional references, and I will follow up with you on April 6 to see if you have any additional questions. Thank you for sharing so much time and information with me this week; I am inspired by your enthusiasm and eager to play a part in building a strong Western Region for NuTraders.

Sincerely,

Kathy Miller

enclosure

Sample Cover Letter: No Interview Is Scheduled

Comments: This letter starts with a quotation from a newspaper interview and goes on to clearly tie this job seeker's skills and attributes to the company he's approaching. Notice that he did phone prior to writing the letter, and he references his contact in the last paragraph.

Dion Maxwell

119 Old Possum Way, Middlefield, CT 06455 — 860-247-0904 — dionmaxwell@aol.com

---

December 2, 20XX

Mr. Curtis Sanderson
President, Oxbow Industries
25 Main Street
Middletown, CT 06457

Dear Mr. Sanderson:

> **"We're always looking for employees who have a good attitude and a great work ethic."**—*Curtis Sanderson, Connecticut Business Journal 11/19/XX*

When I read this quotation from your recent interview, I knew that I had what you are looking for—the qualities you seek in your best employees, plus skills that are a great fit for your growing Middletown distribution center.

I have more than 20 years of experience at a small milling plant where I filled a variety of roles—changing job duties and pitching in where needed to keep our products moving out the door. I am a licensed forklift operator, capable machinery operator, experienced shift supervisor, and leader in the areas of quality and safety. My work ethic and reliability are second to none.

When I spoke with Adelyn in your office this week, she suggested that I forward my resume directly to your attention. I will call again in a few days to determine the next steps. Thank you for your consideration.

Sincerely,

Dion Maxwell

enclosure

Writing Cover Letters to People You Don't Know

If it is not practical to directly contact a prospective employer by phone or some other method, it is acceptable to send a resume and cover letter. This approach makes sense in some situations, such as if you are moving to a distant location or responding to a blind ad that does not include a company or contact name.

I do not recommend the approach of sending out "To Whom It May Concern" letters by the basketful. However, sending an unsolicited resume can make sense in some situations, and there are ways to modify this "shotgun" approach to be more effective. Try to find something you have in common with the person you are contacting. By mentioning this link, your letter then becomes a very personal request for assistance. Look at the two following letters for ideas.

Sample Cover Letter: Response to a Want Ad

Comments: Responding to a want ad puts you in direct competition with the many others who will read the same ad, so the odds are not good that this letter would get a response. The fact that the writer does not yet live in the area is another negative. Still, I believe that you should follow up on any legitimate lead you find. You can boost your chances if you do as this job seeker did and include some strong and relevant accomplishments in your letter.

TRICIA BILLINGS

London, England (through January 20XY)
TriciaBillings@yahoo.com

December 2, 20XX

Re: Market Development Manager: Posting #794-MDM

Your advertised opening for a Market Development Manager describes interesting challenges. My background and accomplishments seem to be a good match for your needs, and I'd like to explore this opportunity with you.

For 12 years I have delivered strong business results for company operations in Europe and the U.S. Most recently, I took on the challenge of rapidly growing Standard Tool's business in the U.K. In two years, we increased sales nearly four-fold through highly effective market-entry strategies, brand repositioning, and organizational restructuring.

Previously, with Global Supplies, I was instrumental in successful market entry into Western and Eastern Europe, with results that outperformed goals for both sales and profits.

May we schedule a time to talk? I am always accessible via e-mail and can arrange a phone call immediately or an in-person visit during one of my frequent trips to the U.S.

Thank you.

Sincerely,

Tricia Billings

enclosure: resume

Sample Cover Letter: Unsolicited Resume Sent to Obtain an Interview

Comments: This is an example of a person conducting a long-distance job search using names obtained from a professional association. In this letter, Miguel explains why he is leaving his old job and asks for an interview even though there might not be any jobs open now. Notice that he also asks for "ideas or referrals" to build his network in his new location.

Miguel Francisco, D.V.M.

2390 Cherry Lane, Des Moines, IA 50312
mfvet@gmail.com • 515-990-1210

December 2, 20XX

Eleanor Gentile, D.V.M.
North Shore Animal Care, Inc.
491 Peabody Pike
Salem, MA 01960

Dear Dr. Gentile:

Are you considering adding an associate to your practice? If so, I would like to speak with you about how my blend of qualifications and capabilities can benefit your patients, your clients, your team, and your practice.

I have had a satisfying 10-year career as an associate with a thriving practice near Des Moines, Iowa. As small-animal practitioners in a rural area, we see a diverse caseload, perform surgery daily at our facility, and work collaboratively with veterinary specialists for complex cases. I have built excellent relationships with our clients while caring for their pets.

Because I will be relocating to my hometown of Salem in the fall, I am seeking a new veterinarian position, preferably with a multi-doctor small-animal practice. I'm eager to find a new opportunity to contribute my professional capabilities.

I will call next week to see if it might be convenient for us to meet during my visit to Salem later this month; I would appreciate any ideas or referrals you can provide, even if you do not anticipate expanding your practice at this time. Thank you.

Sincerely,

Miguel Francisco, D.V.M.

enclosure: resume

The Hardworking JIST Card®

JIST Cards are a job search tool that gets results. JIST Cards were developed by the late Mike Farr (former president of JIST Publishing) in the early 1970s, almost by accident. They received very positive employer reaction and over the years have evolved into every imaginable format. Forms of JIST Cards are now being used in electronic media as well as traditional printed form.

Think of a JIST Card as a Very Small Resume

A JIST Card is carefully constructed to contain all the essential information most employers want to know—in a very short format:

- Name, phone number, and email address
- The type of position you seek
- Your experience, education, and training
- Key job-related skills, performance, and results
- Your good-worker traits
- Any special conditions you are willing to work under (optional)

A JIST Card typically uses a 3×5-inch card format but has been designed into many other sizes and formats, such as a business card. In fact, the business card might be the best possible size because you will want business cards to hand out during your job search, anyway—why not make them the useful JIST Card rather than a plain old business card?

You should create JIST Cards in addition to a resume because you will use your JIST Cards in a different way.

JIST Cards Get Results

What matters is what JIST Cards accomplish—they get results. In a survey of employers, more than 90 percent of employers formed a positive impression of the JIST Card's writer within 30 seconds. More amazing is that about 80 percent of employers said they would be willing to interview the person behind the JIST Card, even if they did not have a job opening at the time.

How You Can Use Them

You can use a JIST Card in many ways, including the following:

- Attached to your resume or application

- Enclosed in a thank-you note

- Given to your friends, relatives, and other contacts—so they can give them to other people

- Sent out to everyone who graduated from your school or who are members of a professional association

- Put on car windshields or posted on the coffee shop bulletin board

- Included as your brief bio on various online sites

JIST Card Paper and Format Tips

Many office-supply stores have perforated light card stock sheets that you can run through your computer printer. You can then tear them apart into 3×5-inch cards. Many word-processing programs have templates that allow you to format a 3×5-inch card size. You can also use regular size paper, print several cards on a sheet, and cut it to the size you need. Print shops can also photocopy or print them in the size you need. Get a few hundred at a time. They are cheap, and the point is to get lots of them in circulation.

If you're challenged by design and are not sure you can produce a professional and attractive JIST Card, you can find services that will do it for you for a modest fee. Check your local print shop or go online. You'll find popular sites such as VistaPrint (http://www.vistaprint.com) that will produce cards in a variety of sizes, and you'll find specialty suppliers such as ResuMiniMe (http://www.resuminime.com) that are set up specifically to produce "mini resumes."

Your JIST Card does not have to be fancy, but it must look professional. And, just like your resume, it must be well written and without errors.

Sample JIST Cards

The following sample JIST Cards use a plain format, but you can make them as fancy as you want. So be creative. Look over the examples to see how they are constructed. Some are for entry-level jobs, and some are for more advanced ones.

Sandy Nolan

Position: General Office/ Administrative

Cell: (512) 232-9213

More than two years of work experience, plus one year of training in office practices. Trained in word processing (65 wpm), post general ledger, possess strong interpersonal skills, and get along with most people. Can meet deadlines and handle pressure well.

Willing to work any hours.

Organized, honest, reliable, and hardworking.

Joyce Hua   Cell: (214) 173-1659

                                                       E-mail: jhua@yahoo.com

Position: Programming/Systems Analyst

More than 8 years of combined education and experience in information systems and related fields. Competent programming in Visual Basic, C, C++, FORTRAN, and Java, and database management. Extensive PC network applications experience. Supervised a staff as large as 7 on special projects. Have a record of meeting deadlines.

Desire career-oriented position; will relocate.

Dedicated self-starter, creative problem solver.

Paul Thomas   Home: (301) 681-3922
                                        Cell: (301) 681-6966
                                        Email: PaulThomas33@gmail.com

Position: Research Chemist, Research Management
                 Small to Medium–Sized Company

Ph.D. in biochemistry plus more than 15 years of work experience. Developed and patented various processes with current commercial applications worth many millions of dollars. Experienced with all phases of lab work with an emphasis on chromatography, isolation, and purification of organic and biochemical compounds. Specialized in practical pharmaceutical and agricultural applications of chemical research. Teaching, supervision, and project-management experience.

Stable work history, results and task oriented, ambitious, and willing to relocate.

Richard Straightarrow   **Cell: (602) 253-9678**
                                    Email: RStraightarrow@yahoo.com

Objective: Electronics installation, maintenance, and sales

Four years of work experience plus two-year AA degree in Electronics Engineering Technology. Managed a $360,000/year business while going to school full time and earning grades in the top 25%. Familiar with all major electronic diagnostic and repair equipment. Hands-on experience with medical, consumer, communication, and industrial electronics equipment and applications. Good problem-solving and communication skills. Customer-service oriented.

Willing to do what it takes to get the job done.

Self motivated, dependable, learn quickly.

Juanita Rodriguez   (639) 361-1754
                                             juanitar@comast.net

Position: Warehouse Management

Six years of experience plus two years of formal business course work. Have supervised a staff as large as 16 people and warehousing operations covering more than two acres and valued at more than $14 million. Automated inventory operations, resulting in a 30% increase in turnover and annual savings of more than $250,000. Working knowledge of accounting, computer systems, time & motion studies, and advanced inventory-management systems.

Will work any hours.

Responsible, hardworking, and can solve problems.

Jonathan Michael   Cell phone: (614) 788-2434
                                        E-mail: jonn@pike.org

Objective: Management

More than 7 years of management experience plus a BS degree in business. Managed budgets as large as $10 million. Experienced in cost control and reduction, cutting more than 20% of overhead while business increased more than 30%. Good organizer and problem solver. Excellent communication skills.

Prefer responsible position in a medium-to-large business.

Cope well with deadline pressure, seek challenge, flexible.

Thank-You Notes

Although resumes and cover letters get the attention, thank-you notes often get results. That's right. Sending thank-you notes makes both good manners and good job search sense. Thank-you notes can help you stand out from other candidates and reinforce the points you made during your interview. They make you more memorable and create a very positive impression.

Three Times When You Should Definitely Send Thank-You Notes—and Why

Thank-you notes have a more intimate and friendly social tradition than formal business correspondence. I think that is one reason they work so well—people respond to those who show good manners and say thank you. Here are some situations when you should use them, along with some sample notes for each situation.

1. Before an Interview

In some situations, you can send a less formal note before an interview. For example, you can simply thank someone for being willing to see you. Depending on the situation, enclosing a resume could be a bit inappropriate. Remember, this is supposed to be sincere thanks for help and not an assertive business situation.

Sample Thank-You Note 1

April 5, 20XX

Ms. Kijek,

Thanks so much for your willingness to see me next Wednesday at 9 a.m. I know that I am one of many who are interested in working with your organization. I appreciate the opportunity to meet you and learn more about the position.

I've enclosed a JIST Card that presents the basics of my skills for this job and will bring my resume to the interview. Please call me if you have any questions at all.

Sincerely,

Bruce Vernon
(617) 555-5555

2. After an Interview

One of the best times to send a thank-you note is right after an interview. Here are several reasons why:

- Doing so creates a positive impression. The employer will assume you have good follow-up skills—and good manners.

- It creates yet another opportunity for you to remain in the employer's consciousness at an important time.

- If they buried, passed along, or otherwise lost your resume and previous correspondence, a thank-you note and corresponding JIST Card provide one more chance for employers to find your number and call you.

TIP: *Enclose a JIST Card with each thank-you note you send in the mail. They fit well into an envelope and provide key information an employer can use to contact you. JIST Cards also list key skills and other credentials that will help you create a good impression. And the employer could always forward the card to someone who might have a job opening for you.*

For these reasons, I suggest you send a thank-you note right after the interview—and certainly within 24 hours, when you are freshest in the employer's mind. You can send your note by email or by postal mail—either is acceptable. Email is more immediate, but postal mail is a bit more formal and permanent and allows you to enclose a JIST Card.

The following is an example of a post-interview thank-you note; you'll find a more detailed thank-you letter earlier in this chapter on page 55.

Sample Thank-You Note 2

December 2, 20XX

Dear Mr. O'Beel:

Thank you for the opportunity to interview for the position available in your production department. I want you to know that this is the sort of job I have been looking for and that I am enthusiastic about the possibility of working for you.

I believe that I have both the experience and skills to fit nicely into your organization and to be productive quickly.

Thanks again for the interview; I enjoyed the visit.

Sara Smith

(505) 665-0090

3. Whenever Anyone Helps You in Your Job Search

Send a thank-you note to anyone who helps you during your job search. This includes those who give you referrals, people who provide advice, or simply those who are supportive during your search. I suggest you routinely enclose one or more JIST Cards in these notes because recipients can give them to others who might be in a better position to help you.

Sample Thank-You Note 3

October 31, XXXX

Debbie Childs
2234 Riverbed Avenue
Philadelphia, PA 17963

Ms. Helen A. Colcord
Henderson and Associates, Inc.
1801 Washington Blvd., Suite 1201
Philadelphia, PA 17963

Dear Ms. Colcord,

Thank you for sharing your time with me so generously yesterday. I really appreciated talking to you about your career field.

The information you shared with me increased my desire to work in such an area. Your advice has already proven helpful—I have an appointment to meet with Robert Hopper on Friday.

In case you think of someone else who might need a person like me, I'm enclosing another resume and JIST Card.

Sincerely,

Debbie Childs

Six Quick Tips for Writing Thank-You Notes

Here are some brief tips to help you write your thank-you notes.

1. Avoid Handwritten Notes

Unless you are writing one- or two-sentence notes, it's best to word-process them so that recipients can read them quickly. Also, I recommend that you do more than just say "thank you." Make a case for yourself by reiterating key points from your interview, and mention any additional relevant information you forgot to disclose. Your thank-you note is a business letter and should have a professional and businesslike appearance.

However, a handwritten note is much better than no note at all! If you handwrite yours, use your best penmanship and strive to make your note very readable.

2. For Mailed Notes, Use High-Quality Paper and Envelopes

It's perfectly acceptable to email your thank-you note, but a traditional mailed letter may make more of an impression (and a very positive one at that!). Use the same paper you used for your resume, and copy the heading from your resume onto your letter to create a stationery look.

Whether emailed or mailed, proofread carefully and make no errors!

3. Use a Formal Salutation

Unless you know the person you are thanking, or were invited to call them by their first name, don't get too friendly. Write "Dear Ms. Smith" rather than the less formal "Dear Pam." Include the date.

4. Make it Personal

Keep your note friendly and personal. Make sure it doesn't sound like a form letter. The best way to do that is to refer to topics you discussed during the interview. Add some new information, or reinforce points you already made.

As appropriate, be specific about the next step—when and how you will contact the person or when (specifically) you expect to hear from them.

5. Sign It

If you're sending a paper letter, sign your first and last names. Avoid initials, and make your signature legible.

If emailed, use your standard email signature that includes your contact information.

6. Send It Right Away

Write and send your note no later than 24 hours after your interview or initial contact. Ideally, you should write it immediately after the contact, while the details are fresh in your mind.

Chapter 5

Use Your Resume Online and Off

A lthough the Internet has helped many people find job leads, far more have been disappointed. The problem is that many job seekers assume they can simply put resumes in online resume databases and zap out dozens of replies to job postings, with employers then lining up to hire them. It sometimes happens this way, but not often.

In this chapter, I'll give you advice for putting your new resume to work—online and offline. Looking for a job is neither simple nor easy, but by learning the basics you can make the best use of your time and have realistic expectations for what you'll need to do and what the Internet can (and can't) do for you.

Multiple Ways to Use the Internet in Your Job Search

Job seeking on the Internet involves more than simply posting your resume on one or more resume database sites or sending your resume in response to a job posting. Here are some other ways the Internet can help you in your job search:

- **Employer websites.** Many employers have websites that include career information and a process for applying to current job openings. Some employer career sites feature employee blogs or video interviews that let you gain a sense of the corporate culture. Some sites allow you to interact with staff online or via email to get answers to questions about working there.

- **Inside information.** You can use the Internet to find information on a specific employer or industry (see www.vault.com, www.wetfeet.com, and www.jobster.com); get detailed lists of job skills and requirements to emphasize in interviews and on your resume (see www.onetonline.org); find career counseling and job search advice (see www.certifiedcareercoaches.com and www.coachfederation.org); and look up almost anything else you need related to your job search.

(continued)

(continued)

- **Job boards and job aggregators.** Large national sites such as Monster and CareerBuilder let you search for openings based on specific criteria. Make your search more efficient by using job aggregators—sites that bring together numerous job postings from multiple sites—such as www.indeed.com and www.simplyhired.com.

- **Specialty sites.** You can find websites that specialize in the jobs that interest you (for example, www.dice.com for technology careers or www.healthcarejobs.org for—obviously!—jobs in healthcare). Many have job postings, useful information, and access to people in the know. Also, many geographic-specific sites for cities and towns list local openings.

- **Professional associations.** Professional associations can be a goldmine of information, contacts, and job leads in your specific field. You can find an association for just about any profession using an online directory such as the one at job-hunt.org.

- **Networking.** Create a profile on business networking sites such as LinkedIn, Ryze, and ecademy to organize your existing network and make new contacts for career research. When you are able to see the contacts that your contacts have, you can better tell them how they can be of help.

For suggestions on the best sites to help you in your job search, see the end of this chapter; for even more help, see the book *Best Career and Education Web Sites* from JIST.

Adapting Your Resume for Electronic Use

Employers and recruiters scan resume databases and applicant systems to find candidates with the right combination of keywords to match their requirments. In an Internet-based job search, your resume must first pass these "electronic gatekeepers" to give you a chance to speak with a real human (who can actually hire you).

So let's first discuss the realities of resume scanning.

Most resume databases, job boards, and employer career sites give you the option to upload your resume as a Word file. If your resume is very simply formatted—no fancy borders, tables, charts, graphs, shading, graphics, italic type, or very tight and precise positioning—go right ahead and upload it.

But if your resume does contain these extra elements that make your resume attractive to human eyes, you can't be certain it will upload smoothly and read perfectly on the receiving end. So it's better to use a separate, plain-text format for uploading.

Sample Text-Only Resume, with All Graphics and Formatting Removed

Look at the two versions of the sample resume that follow. The first version is a traditional resume, with appropriate formatting for human eyes. The second version of the resume has had all formatting and graphic elements removed for submission in electronic or scannable form. It has the following features:

- No graphics
- No lines (it uses equal signs instead)
- No bold, italic, or other text variations
- Only one easy-to-scan font (Courier)
- No tab indents
- No line or paragraph indents

Yes, this resume looks boring, but it has the advantage of being universally accepted into company databases or online job boards.

Figure 5-1: Sample Resume—Word Format

Gerald T. Clark   909 Main Street, Reading, MA 01867 • 781-942-0040 • geraldclark@mac.com

CAREER TARGET   **Human Resources/Employee Assistance Programs (EAP)**

SUMMARY OF QUALIFICATIONS

- **Education:** Earned advanced degree in Industrial and Organizational Psychology and Organizational Development; can diagnose and design remedies for organizational issues that affect productivity, employee retention and satisfaction, and bottom-line results.
- **Multicultural/international background:** From six-plus years living outside the U.S., appreciate diverse cultures and understand the challenges faced by relocating employees.
- **Communication skills:** Can build rapport with people at all levels of the organization, speak confidently before business and academic groups, and train and supervise employees.
- **Organization and leadership:** Can take ideas from concept to reality.
- **Adaptability:** Able to adapt quickly in new and changing business, social, and cultural environments.

EDUCATION

UNIVERSITY OF KANSAS, Manhattan, KS
Master of Science in Industrial/Organizational Psychology, 2011
Concentration: Organizational Development

- GPA 3.98/4.0 — Dean's List all quarters.
- Completed coursework in Organizational Development, Organizational Behavior, Counseling in the Work Environment, and Industrial/Organizational Psychology.
- Student Affiliate, Society for Industrial and Organizational Psychology (SIOP).
- Member, OD Network National Conference Committee: Worked with OD professionals to plan and manage 2010 national conference.

BOSTON UNIVERSITY, Boston, MA
Bachelor of Science in Psychology, 2009
Minor: Spanish

- GPA 3.27/4.0.

UNIVERSITAT DE BARCELONA, Barcelona, Spain
Semester Abroad, 1/08–5/08

- Attended college classes that emphasized European culture and heritage.
- Resided with a European family and traveled extensively throughout Europe.

WORK EXPERIENCE

Defrayed college expenses and gained problem-solving, decision-making, communication, and leadership skills through diverse customer service, training, and supervisory positions.

- **Security Guard,** CLUB MARDI GRAS, Manhattan, KS: 10/10–5/11
- **Crew Trainer and Supervisor,** WENDY'S, Manhattan, KS: 9/09–5/10
- **Ski Technician and Rental Clerk,** CANYONS SKI RESORT, Park City, UT: 11/08–3/09
- **Doorman/Crowd Control,** THE RATHSKELLAR, Boston, MA: 10/07–1/08; 5/08–6/08
- **Doorman,** BOSTON UNIVERSITY CLUB PUB, Boston, MA: 1/07–6/07
- **Sales Associate,** RADIO SHACK, Peabody, MA: Summers 2004, 2005, 2006

ADDITIONAL INFORMATION

- Fluent in Spanish; conversationally proficient in Italian.
- Lived overseas from 1994–2000: Japan (grades 3–4), Peru (grades 5–7), and Canary Islands (grade 8).
- Proficient in using Microsoft Office, SPSS, and SAS.
- Available for national or international relocation.

Figure 5-2: Sample Resume—Plain Text

```
Gerald T. Clark
909 Main Street, Reading, MA 01867
781-942-0040
geraldclark@mac.com

===================================
CAREER TARGET: Human Resources/Employee Assistance Programs (EAP)

===================================
SUMMARY OF QUALIFICATIONS

* Education: Earned advanced degree in Industrial and Organizational Psychology and Orga-
nizational Development; can diagnose and design remedies for organizational issues that
affect productivity, employee retention and satisfaction, and bottom-line results.

* Multicultural/international background: From six-plus years living outside the U.S., ap-
preciate diverse cultures and understand the challenges faced by relocating employees.

* Communication skills: Can build rapport with people at all levels of the organization,
speak confidently before business and academic groups, and train and supervise employees.

* Organization and leadership: Can take ideas from concept to reality.

* Adaptability: Able to adapt quickly in new and changing business, social, and cultural
environments.

===================================
EDUCATION

UNIVERSITY OF KANSAS, Manhattan, KS
-----------------------------------
Master of Science in Industrial/Organizational Psychology, 2011
Concentration: Organizational Development
* GPA 3.98/4.0 - Dean's List all quarters.
* Completed coursework in Organizational Development, Organizational Behavior, Counseling
in the Work Environment, and Industrial/Organizational Psychology.
* Student Affiliate, Society for Industrial and Organizational Psychology (SIOP).
* Member, OD Network National Conference Committee: Worked with OD professionals to plan
and manage 2010 national conference.

BOSTON UNIVERSITY, Boston, MA
-----------------------------------
Bachelor of Science in Psychology, 2009
Minor: Spanish
* GPA 3.27/4.0.

UNIVERSITAT DE BARCELONA, Barcelona, Spain
-----------------------------------
Semester Abroad, 1/08-5/08
* Attended college classes that emphasized European culture and heritage.
* Resided with a European family and traveled extensively throughout Europe.

===================================
WORK EXPERIENCE

Defrayed college expenses and gained problem-solving, decision-making, communication, and
leadership skills through diverse customer service, training, and supervisory positions.

* Security Guard, CLUB MARDI GRAS, Manhattan, KS: 10/10-5/11
* Crew Trainer and Supervisor, WENDY'S, Manhattan, KS: 9/09-5/10
* Ski Technician and Rental Clerk, CANYONS SKI RESORT, Park City, UT: 11/08-3/09
* Doorman/Crowd Control, THE RATHSKELLAR, Boston, MA: 10/07-1/08; 5/08-6/08
* Doorman, BOSTON UNIVERSITY CLUB PUB, Boston, MA: 1/07-6/07
* Sales Associate, RADIO SHACK, Peabody, MA: Summers 2004, 2005, 2006
```

(continued)

(continued)

```
ADDITIONAL INFORMATION
===================================
* Fluent in Spanish; conversationally proficient in Italian.
* Lived overseas from 1994-2000: Japan (grades 3-4), Peru (grades 5-7), and Canary Islands
(grade 8).
* Proficient in using Microsoft Office, SPSS, and SAS.
* Available for national or international relocation.
```

Converting Your Resume to Electronic Format

You can easily take your existing resume and reformat it for electronic submission. Here is a simple five-step process for doing so:

1. Open your existing resume and choose the "Save As" feature in your word processor. Choose "Text Only" as the file format and rename your document.

2. Close the file, open the renamed version, and you'll see that an automatic conversion has taken place—your resume now appears in Courier font, with most of the formatting stripped out.

3. Review the resume to fix any odd formatting glitches. If you've used tables, columns, or other unusual formatting, take extra time to be sure that all the text is in the right place.

4. Add extra blank lines before key sections, if necessary, and use lines of the available "typewriter symbols" to create graphic separators. (Typewriter symbols include ~, !, @, #, $, %, ^, &, *, (,), <, >, and /.)

5. Don't worry about how long your resume is or whether it breaks oddly between pages. It's not intended to be printed; rather, you will paste it into online applications or enter it into a resume database.

Close the document and reopen it in a text editor, such as Notepad or TextEdit, just to double-check that all of the characters have been converted correctly.

Now you are ready to upload your resume or paste it into a job board or employment website.

The Importance of Keywords

As mentioned, employers and recruiters use keywords to search for candidates. So it's important that you include all the right kewords in your resume to increase your chances of being selected.

You shouldn't have to rewrite your resume for every job, but you will want to adjust it as needed to include the right keywords to match the job requirements as closely as possible. Make this task quick and easy by creating a section on your resume called "Key Skills" or "Core Competencies" or something similar. Then edit this section as needed for each job you apply for.

> **TIP:** Having all the right keywords doesn't guarantee that your resume will be selected. But include as many as you can that are appropriate based on your background and the job you're applying for. Increase the odds in your favor!

Quick Tips for Selecting Keywords to Include in Your Resume

The main thing to realize when thinking about which keywords to put in your resume is that computers, although they let you do wonderful things, are just not very smart. They don't have the same power that people do to think and interpret. So your job here is to use keywords that give the computer exactly what it is looking for.

Let's say you see a job ad that asks for knowledge of Microsoft Access. You might have been working in an office for years and are familiar with Microsoft Access, Word, and all the other parts of the Microsoft Office software suite. The temptation is to just list "Microsoft Office" as a skill on your resume. The danger is that the computer might not know that Access is part of Microsoft Office and will toss out your resume. Therefore, if a job ad asks for a specific skill, use exactly the same words as in the job ad. Don't just write "Microsoft Office." Instead, write "Microsoft Office" followed in parentheses by the particular programs you have experience with, such as "Excel, Access, Word, and PowerPoint."

Here are some keyword tips for you to keep in mind:

- **Think like a prospective employer.** Think of the jobs you want, and then include the keywords you think an employer would use to find someone who can do what you can do.

- **Review job descriptions from major references** such as the *Occupational Outlook Handbook* or the *O*NET Dictionary of Occupational Titles.* These are available in both print and online formats. They will give you a variety of keywords you can use in your electronic resume.

- **Include all your important skill words,** such as those you documented in Chapter 3.

- **Look for additional sources of keywords to include.** You can identify keywords by reviewing the sample resumes in Chapter 7, job descriptions of jobs you want, want ads, employer websites, job board postings, and more.

Always be as specific as possible. Read each job ad carefully, and be ready and willing to adjust your resume for the precise needs of positions you're pursuing.

Sample Keyword Resumes

All of the sample resumes in Chapter 7 contain lots of keywords. Some provide a list of keywords in a separate section, in addition to the many keywords used throughout the resume. Look to them for inspiration on how to add more keywords to your own electronic resume.

Managing Your Online Identity

Now that you've seen how you can use the Internet to uncover opportunities and effectively distribute your resume, it's also important to understand that others will be using the Internet to find and research you.

More and more, you will be googled in your job search, and employers are looking at everything they find—and not necessarily just the things you want them to see. You might use social media sites such as Facebook and Twitter for personal messages and opinions, but these can be easily found and evaluated by employers looking to hire just the right candidate. It's clear that your online identity can impact your job search, so it's ultra important that you manage that identity.

Google Yourself

Have you googled yourself lately? Try typing your first and last names into Google, and then try it in quotes (such as "Louise Kursmark"). When you do, you could discover one of the following:

- You don't show up at all, making potential employers wonder how important you are.

- You have a common name, and it's hard to find anything relevant to you.

- There are negative results about you (arrests, firings, or other unflattering information).

- Your personal blog or family website comes up high in the search results and it isn't something that you would want potential employers to find as a first impression.

- There are quite a few professionally relevant and positive results about you, but these snippets of information make it difficult to get a comprehensive picture.

- You have a website that comes up highly ranked in the search results and paints a clear picture of your professional self.

You can surmise from these scenarios that everything that you post online or that is written about you becomes a part of your online identity. You'll want to consider the impact—positive or negative—that a comment on someone's blog or a review on epinions.com will have.

> **TIP:** *You can help employers find the right Google results about you—accurate and relevant information—by creating a "search me" button that aggregates the top relevant findings that you select. I highly recommend this tool, a free service from a company called Vizibility (http://vizibility.com), for people who have a common name or a great deal of irrelevant informationm about them on the Web. In fact, it's great for just about everyone because it helps you paint the right picture for employers and removes the clutter of the irrelevant.*
>
> *And if a search reveals negative information about you, do look into an online reputation service (such as www.reputation.com) to see if you can remove or reduce the harmful listings.*

LinkedIn and Other Professional Profiles

I think it's essential for every professional to create a profile on LinkedIn, which has become the most-used networking site for professionals and a valuable search tool for recruiters. Use your resume as a building block for creating a strong and relevant LinkedIn profile.

Then take the time to check out other online profile sites and add your information as appropriate. Top sites include Ryze, ecademy, Google Profile, and Plaxo.

A great benefit of having a LinkedIn or Google profile is that they are very search-engine friendly and often will come up first or near the top in a Google search.

Blogs and Tweets

One of the easiest and most economical ways to get an online presence that is well-designed and search-engine friendly is to create a professional blog. With easy-to-use applications such as WordPress, TypePad, or Blogger, you don't have to know HTML to start posting articles about your area of expertise. Just make sure that your posts are professional and relevant to your target audience. Use this vehicle to demonstrate your knowledge, experience, and current grasp on happenings in your industry. On your blog, you can make your resume available for download (include text, Word, and PDF versions), link to other relevant sites, and include your career bio on the "about" page.

In addition to or instead of your own blog, make it a habit to visit the blogs of other professionals in your field and leave well-thought-out comments. The purpose is to build your professional visibility and increase the positive and relevant references that come up in a Google search.

> **TIP:** Don't get fired for blogging! What goes in a career-management blog? There are no rules, but common sense and good writing apply. There have been cases where people have been fired for blogging about proprietary corporate information or making unflattering remarks about their work environment. Ninety percent of your posts should be relevant to your professional target audience. Because blogs are expected to reveal your personality, you should occasionally write about your interests—but only the ones that you'd also include on a resume.

Similarly, you might establish an account on Twitter and use it to share comments, ideas, and links to information related to your profession. It's perfectly okay—in fact, it's expected—that you'll also tweet personal information, but be careful to balance it out and never tweet something you'd be embarrassed for an employer to see.

Online Career Portfolios and Personal Websites

To go beyond the blog and create a more comprehensive picture of who you are and what you have done, you can create an online career portfolio or personal website. A Web portfolio is the traditional paper portfolio concept reinvented for the online medium with links and multimedia content. Portfolios are more than Web-based resumes in that they *must* contain tangible evidence of your past performance, including work samples, testimonials, articles, videoes, photographs, charts, and so on.

Providing this depth of information earlier in the career search process weeds out no-win situations and establishes virtual rapport with your interviewers. The portfolio concept also helps prove the facts on your resume because it shows and not just tells. Prospective employers and clients want to see that you have solved problems like theirs.

If you say that you have strong presentation skills, show a video clip! Articles, awards, graphs, audio references, white papers, case studies, press releases, and schedules of appearances are just some of the options you have to prove your expertise.

Consider using a free service such as VisualCV (www.visualcv.com) to create an outstanding online profile. You can view my VisualCV here: http://www.visualcv.com/louisekursmark.

The bottom line? You will be googled, and when the average job lasts only about 3.5 years, it certainly makes sense to constantly foster professional visibility both online and offline.

Resume Banks, Job Boards, and Online Information

The Internet abounds with career information, career services, and job opportunities. Some of the sites are genuine, helpful, low cost, or free. Others are time-wasters or scams. The landscape changes frequently as new players enter the field, new technologies arise, and established players struggle to adapt. For example, Google+ is currently a hot new opportunity to build personal and professional networks, and the once-dominant AOL is trying to stay relevant.

Rather than recommend specific sites, I am going to point you in the direction of one of the most helpful career sites on the Internet. Job-Hunt (www.job-hunt.org) is chock-full of good advice from reputable experts, a vast array of career-related resources, and direct links to employers. Every site that appears on Job-Hunt—whether a recommended resource or a sponsor—has been screened for quality and ethics. This is not to suggest that you don't have to do your own homework. You do. But at least start with reputable sites and take advantage of great, free resources.

Chapter 6

Write a Better Resume Now

After completing some or all of Chapters 1 and 2, you are ready to put together a "better" resume. By better, I mean one that is more carefully crafted than the simple version you have already done. This chapter will help you pull together what you have learned and create an effective resume. It also expands on tips in Chapter 2 on how to design, produce, and use your resume to best effect.

This chapter assumes that you have read and done the activities in Chapters 1, 2, and 3. I also assume that you have done a basic resume as outlined in those chapters, and I hope you have taken my advice to use your basic resume right away while you worked on creating a "better" one as time permitted.

If You Aren't Good at This, Get Some Help

If you are not particularly good at writing and designing a resume, consider getting help with various elements. Several sources of help are available.

Professional Resume Writers

I am a professional resume writer myself, so I am biased! But I truly believe an investment in your resume will have a positive effect on your career.

You can find resume writers who are generalists and those who specialize in certain professions or industries. Fee ranges are extremely wide, from a few hundred dollars to a few thousand! An inexpensive resume is not a bargain if it is done poorly. If you decide to work with a professional, you'll need to do your homework to be certain you choose the right partner for this very important document.

The following guidelines will help as you evaluate different resume services.

1. **Choose scope of service.** Do you want to work one-on-one with a specific writer and have in-depth conversations about your career? Or are you simply looking for someone to edit and polish the resume draft that you've written? Or do you fit somewhere in between?

   Additionally, are you interested in working with a coach or counselor who can help you decide on your career direction and support you throughout your job search?

   Evaluate the services offered by each resume writer, and decide whether he or she is a good fit for your needs. Expect to pay a higher fee for more in-depth and comprehensive services.

2. **See a sample.** Many resume writers post sample resumes on their websites; others have samples published in books (such as this one); some might send you a sample if you ask. When looking at the example resume, consider these factors:

   - **Presentation.** Does it make a good first impression? Is it easy to skim and read? Is the content clear and well written? Is it free from errors and typos?

   - **Message.** Can you quickly tell "who" the candidate is and what his or her areas of expertise are? Does the rest of the content support that image?

   - **Clarity.** Can you readily determine the story of this person's career? Is the chronology clear, are key skills highlighted, and are accomplishments prominent?

3. **Understand the process.** It takes two—you and your writer—to create your resume, so you'll need to know what is expected of you and what you can expect during the process. Be sure you are clear about timelines, information you need to supply, and the type of documents you can expect to receive.

4. **Speak directly to your writer.** Some services are entirely Web based— you input your payment information; forward your resume; and at some point hear back from a company representative, who might or might not be your writer. Other services manage initial phone or email contact through salespeople, who then pass you on to your writer. There's nothing wrong with either of these models, but I recommend that before you pay for services you ask to speak with the person who will actually be writing your resume. You want to establish rapport and feel comfortable that your writer has the expertise you need.

Typically the smaller companies (many of them one-person shops) will handle all contact from initial inquiry through writing and follow-up. The only time this isn't a great idea is when you have some disagreement with your resume writer and there's no one else in the company to help resolve it.

5. **Assess credentials, experience, and expertise.** Has your writer earned a resume-writing certification? Does he or she belong to a professional association for people in the careers industry? Does he or she write a blog or post articles that you can review? As a rule, you want to affiliate with someone who is serious about a career as a resume writer and who stays up to date with changes in the world of employment.

6. **Expect to pay up front.** Once you've chosen your writer, you'll most likely need to pay 100 percent of the fee at the start of the project. Resume writing is a customized service, so essentially you're paying for your writer's time and expertise.

> **TIP:** *If you're looking for a writer, I suggest you start with the writers who contributed the resumes in Chapter 7—you can choose someone whose work you like and who perhaps specializes in working with people like you. You can also find resume writers through a Web search or a professional association (see the sidebar later in this chapter). Perhaps the best source is through a referral by someone who has used a specific writer, so ask around.*

I said early in this book that writing a good resume creates structure that will help you clarify your career goals and communicate your value to an employer. That process is not simple, and you might benefit greatly from the help of a true career-counseling professional, a career coach, or an experienced resume writer. On the other hand, not every writer is a great writer and not every writer is right for you. Know exactly what you're getting into—and what you'll get out of it—before you commit to any resume-writing services.

Ask for Credentials

Three major associations of professional resume writers exist: Career Directors International (CDI; www.careerdirectors.com), the National Resume Writers' Association (NRWA; www.thenrwa.com), and the Professional Association of Résumé Writers and Career Coaches (PARW/CC; www.parw.com). The Resume Writing Academy (www.resumewritingacademy.com), although not an association, is a training organization for resume writers. (Note, I co-own the RWA, and I train and certify writers.) You can find member listings on each organization's website. Because each of these associations has a code of ethics, someone who belongs to one or more of these groups offers better assurance of legitimate services.

Better yet is someone who is an Academy Certified Resume Writer (ACRW), Certified Professional Resume Writer (CPRW), Nationally Certified Resume Writer (NCRW), Certified Resume Writer (CARW, CERW, or CMRW), Master Resume Writer (MRW), or similar designation that indicates the writer's skills have been tested and validated. In any situation, ask for the credentials of the person who will provide the service and see examples of the person's work before you agree to anything.

Career or Job Search Counselors and Transition Services

In your search for someone to help you with your resume, you might run into high-pressure efforts to sell you services. If so, buyer beware! Good, legitimate job search and career professionals are out there, and they are worth every bit of their reasonable fees. Many employers pay thousands of dollars for outplacement assistance to help those leaving find new jobs. But some career transition businesses prey on unsuspecting, vulnerable souls who are unemployed. Some "packages" can cost thousands of dollars and are not worth the price.

I have said for years that many job seekers would gain more from reading a few good job search books than they might get from the less-than-legitimate businesses offering these services. But how do you tell the legitimate from the illegitimate? One clue is

> **TIP:** *Low-cost services often are available from local colleges or other organizations as well as state-supported employment centers. Services might consist of workshops and access to reading materials, assessment tests, and other support at a modest or even no cost. Consider these as an alternative to higher-priced services, and be sure to compare and contrast what you're getting.*

high-pressure sales and fees that are beyond the range of every other service you're investigating. If this is the case, your best bet is to walk away quickly.

Improve Your Resume

You learned to create a basic chronological resume in Chapter 2 and a skills-based resume in Chapter 3. Now that you have more time, here are some ways to improve that basic resume.

Write or Expand Your Summary Section

A summary or introduction—the first section of the resume below your name and contact information—allows you to quickly and clearly establish important baseline information that will help employers. Your goal in this section is to communicate who you are, your special skills, and your uniqueness.

Look through the resumes in Chapter 7 to see the vast variety of ways this summary section can be written and presented. You'll get some good ideas for making your summary more interesting and more effective.

Quantify Your Accomplishments

Look back at how you have written your job descriptons or skills summaries in your simple resume. If your accomplishments are vague, now is the time to dig deep to find the details and specifics that will make them more meaningful.

Expand Your Education and Training Section

Let's say that you are a recent graduate who worked your way through school, earned decent grades (while working full time), and got involved in extracurricular activities. The standard listing of education would not do you justice, so consider expanding that section to include statements about your accomplishments while going to school.

Add New Sections to Highlight Your Strengths

There is no reason you can't add one or more sections to your resume to highlight something you think will help you. For example, let's say you have excellent references from previous employers. You might add a statement to that effect and even include one or more positive quotations. (Several resumes in Chapter 7 use this technique.) Or maybe you got exceptional performance reviews, wrote some articles, edited a newsletter, traveled extensively, or did something else that might support your job objective. If so, nothing prevents you from creating a special section or heading to highlight these activities.

Portfolios and Enclosures

Some occupations typically require a portfolio of your work or some other concrete example of what you have done. Artists, copywriters, advertising people, clothing designers, architects, radio and TV personalities, and many others know this and should take care to provide good examples of what they do.

Examples can include writing samples, photographs of your work, articles you have written, sample audio or video files, artwork, and so on. See Chapter 5 for more on developing an online version of your portfolio.

Gather Information and Emphasize Accomplishments, Skills, and Results

Chapter 2 included a worksheet designed to gather essential information for your resume. This chapter includes an expanded worksheet to help you gather the information that will help your resume stand out from the crowd. Some information is the same as that called for in the Instant Resume Worksheet in Chapter 2, but this new worksheet is considerably more thorough. If you complete it carefully, it will prepare you for the final step of writing a superior resume.

COMPREHENSIVE RESUME WORKSHEET

Use this worksheet to write a draft of the material you will include in your resume. Use a writing style similar to that of your resume, emphasizing skills and accomplishments. Keep your narrative as brief as possible, and make every word count.

You might find it helpful to use a separate sheet of paper for drafting the information for some worksheet sections. After you do that, go ahead and complete the worksheet in the book. Or, if you prefer, build your resume material in your word-processing program, following the worksheet questions and guidelines. The information you gather on the worksheet should be pretty close to the information you will use to write your resume, so write it carefully.

Personal Identification

Name_____

Home address _____

_____

City, state or province, ZIP or postal code_____

_____

Primary phone number _____

Comment _____

Alternative/cell phone number_____

Comment _____

Email address_____

Web portfolio or online profile URL_____

(continued)

(continued)

Job Objective Statement

Write your job objective here, as you would like it to appear on your resume. Writing a good job objective is tricky business and requires a good sense of what you want to do as well as the skills you have to offer.

Remember, in many cases you won't write an actual job objective on your resume, but it's absolutely essential that you have a clear objective before you start writing. A clear objective is the foundation for a great resume.

_____

_____

_____

In Just a Few Words, Why Should Someone Hire You?

A good resume will answer this question in some way. So, to clarify the essential reasons why someone should hire you over others, write a brief answer to the question in the following space. Then, in some way, make sure that your resume gets this across.

_____

_____

_____

_____

Key Adaptive Skills to Emphasize in Your Resume

Adaptive skills are skills you use every day to survive and get along, such as getting to work on time, honesty, enthusiasm, and getting along with others. What key adaptive skills do you have that support your stated job objective? List the skills that best support your job objective. After each, write the accomplishments or experiences that best support those skills—proof that you have these skills. Be brief and emphasize numbers and results when possible. Include some or all of these skills in your resume.

Adaptive skill _____

Proof of this skill _____

_____

_____

_____

_____

Adaptive skill _____

Proof of this skill _____

_____

_____

_____

_____

Adaptive skill _____

Proof of this skill _____

_____

_____

_____

_____

Key Transferable Skills to Emphasize in Your Resume

Transferable skills are general skills that can be useful in a variety of jobs, such as writing clearly, good language skills, and the ability to organize and prioritize tasks. Select your transferable skills that best support your stated job objective. List them, along with examples of when you used or demonstrated these skills. Use some or all of these in your resume.

(continued)

(continued)

Transferable skill _____

Proof of this skill _____

_____

_____

_____

_____

Transferable skill _____

Proof of this skill _____

_____

_____

_____

_____

Transferable skill _____

Proof of this skill _____

_____

_____

_____

_____

Transferable skill _____

Proof of this skill _____

_____

_____

_____

_____

Transferable skill _____

Proof of this skill _____

_____

_____

_____

_____

What Are the Key Job-Related Skills Needed in the Job You Want?

Job-related skills are those needed to perform a particular job or type of job, such as repairing brakes or using a computer accounting program. If you have selected an appropriate job objective, you should have the exact skills needed for that job. Write the most important job-related skills (more if you know them), along with examples to support these skills—and include them in your resume.

Job-related skill _____

Proof of this skill _____

_____

_____

_____

_____

Job-related skill _____

Proof of this skill _____

_____

_____

_____

_____

(continued)

(continued)

Job-related skill _____

Proof of this skill _____

_____

_____

_____

_____

Job-related skill _____

Proof of this skill _____

_____

_____

_____

_____

Job-related skill _____

Proof of this skill _____

_____

_____

_____

_____

What Specific Work or Other Experiences Do You Have That Support Your Doing This Job?

If you are doing a chronological resume, you should organize the information in order of the jobs you have held. If you are doing a skills resume, you will ultimately organize the information within major skill areas. But I suggest you start with the chronological format because then you'll have a clear record of when and where you did each thing. Write the content as if you were writing it for use on your resume. You can, of course, further edit what you write here into its final form, but try to approximate the writing style you will use in your resume. Use short sentences. Include action words. Emphasize key skills. Include numbers to support your skills, and emphasize accomplishments and results instead of simply listing your duties.

In previous jobs that don't relate well to what you want to do next, emphasize adaptive and transferable skills and accomplishments that relate to the job you want. Mention promotions, raises, or positive evaluations as appropriate. If you did more than your job title suggests, consider a title that is more descriptive (but not misleading) such as "head waiter and assistant manager," if that is what you were, instead of "waiter." If you had a number of short-term jobs, consider combining them all under one heading such as "Various Jobs While Attending College."

You might need to complete several drafts of this information before it begins to "feel good," so use additional sheets of paper or edit your word-processing file as needed.

Experiences Organized by Chronology

Most recent or present job title _____

Dates (month/year) from _____ to _____

Organization name _____

City, state or province, ZIP or postal code_____

_____

Duties, skills, responsibilities, accomplishments_____

_____

_____

_____

_____

_____

(continued)

(continued)

Next most recent job title _____

Dates (month/year) from _____ to _____

Organization name _____

City, state or province, ZIP or postal code _____

_____

Duties, skills, responsibilities, accomplishments _____

_____

_____

_____

_____

Next most recent job title _____

Dates (month/year) from _____ to _____

Organization name _____

City, state or province, ZIP or postal code _____

_____

Duties, skills, responsibilities, accomplishments _____

_____

_____

_____

_____

Next most recent job title _____

Dates (month/year) from _____ to _____

Organization name _____

City, state or province, ZIP or postal code _____

_____

Duties, skills, responsibilities, accomplishments_____

_____

_____

_____

Experience Organized by Skills

Skills resumes often include statements regarding accomplishments and results as well as duties. They also often mention other skills that are related to or support the key skill as well as specific examples. These can be work-related experiences or can come from other life experiences.

Begin by listing the three to six skills you consider to be most important to succeed in the job you want. When you decide which ones to list, write in examples of experiences and accomplishments that directly support these skills. Write this just as you want it to appear in your resume.

Key skill 1 _____

Resume statement to support this skill_____

_____

_____

_____

_____

Key skill 2 _____

Resume statement to support this skill_____

_____

_____

_____

_____

(continued)

(continued)

Key skill 3 _____

Resume statement to support this skill_____

_____

_____

_____

_____

Key skill 4 _____

Resume statement to support this skill_____

_____

_____

_____

_____

Key skill 5 _____

Resume statement to support this skill_____

_____

_____

_____

_____

Key skill 6 _____

Resume statement to support this skill_____

_____

_____

_____

_____

What Education or Training Supports Your Job Objective?

In writing your education and training section, be sure to include any additional information that supports your qualifications for your job objective. New graduates should emphasize their education and training more than experienced workers and include more details in this section.

Use the space that follows to write what you want to include on your resume under the Education and Training heading.

School or training institution attended _____

Dates attended or graduated _____

Degree or certification obtained_____

Anything else that should be mentioned _____

_____

_____

_____

_____

School or training institution attended _____

Dates attended or graduated _____

Degree or certification obtained_____

Anything else that should be mentioned _____

_____

_____

_____

School or training institution attended _____

Dates attended or graduated _____

Degree or certification obtained_____

(continued)

(continued)

Anything else that should be mentioned _____

_____

_____

_____

Other Formal or Informal Training That Supports Your Job Objective

_____

_____

_____

Other Resume Sections

If you want to include other sections on your resume, write their headings and whatever you want to include. Examples might be "Core Competency List," "Special Accomplishments," "Technical Skills," "International Travel," or many other things. For inspiration, see the headings of this kind among the sample resumes in Chapter 7.

_____

_____

_____

_____

_____

_____

More Quick Resume-Writing Tips

Chapters 1 through 3 covered the basics of writing a resume, but here are some additional tips and information you might find helpful.

As Much as Possible, Write Your Resume Yourself

I have come to realize that some people, even very smart people who are good writers, can't write or design a good resume. And there is no good reason to force them to write one from start to finish. If you are one of these people, just decide that your skills are in other areas and don't go looking for a job as a resume writer. Get someone else, preferably a professional resume writer, to write your resume for you.

But even if you don't write your own resume, you should be involved in the process as much as possible. If you aren't, your resume won't be truly yours. Your resume might present you well, but it won't be *you*. Not only might your resume misrepresent you to at least some extent, you also will not have learned what you need to learn by going through the process of writing your resume. You would not have struggled with your job objective statement in the same way and might not have as clear a sense of what you want to do as a result. You would not have the same understanding of the skills you have to support your job objective. As a result, you probably won't do as well in an interview.

So, even though I encourage you to "borrow" ideas from this book's sample resumes, your resume must end up being yours. You have to be able to discuss its content and prove every statement you've made. Even if you end up hiring someone to help with your resume, you must provide this person with what to say and let him or her help you with how to say it. If you don't agree with something the writer does, ask the person to change it to your specifications. However you do it, make sure that your resume is *your* resume and that it represents you accurately.

Don't Lie or Exaggerate

Some job applicants misrepresent themselves. They lie about where they went to school or say that they have a degree that they do not have. They state previous salaries that are higher than they really were. They present themselves as having responsibilities and titles that are not close to the truth.

I do not recommend you do this. For one reason, it is simply not right, and that is reason enough. But there are also practical reasons for not doing so. The first is that you might get a job that you can't handle. If that were to happen, and you fail, it would serve you right. Another reason is that some employers check references and backgrounds more thoroughly than you might realize. Sometimes this can occur years after you are employed and, if you are caught, you could lose your job, which would not be a pleasant experience.

So my advice is this: Honesty is the best policy.

Never Include a Negative

Telling the truth does not mean you have to tell *everything*. Some things are better left unsaid, and a resume should present your strengths and not your weaknesses. In writing your resume, you should *never* include anything employers might interpret as a negative. For example, if you are competing with people who have a degree and you don't, it is better to not mention your education (or, in this case, lack of it). Instead, emphasize your skills and accomplishments. If you can do the job, it really shouldn't matter, and many employers will hire based on what you can do rather than on what you don't have.

Trust me on this: If you can honestly and convincingly tell employers why they should hire you over someone else, they probably will.

This Is No Place to Be Humble

Being honest on your resume does not mean you can't present the facts in the most positive way. A resume is not a place to be humble. So work on *what* you say and *how* you say it, so that you present your experiences and skills as positively as possible.

Use Short Sentences and Simple Words

Short sentences are easier to read. They communicate better than long ones. Simple words also communicate more clearly than long ones. So use short sentences and easy-to-understand words in your resume (like I've done in this paragraph).

Good writing is easy to read and understand. It is harder to do, but it's worth the time.

If It Doesn't Support Your Job Objective, Cut It Out

A resume is only one or two pages long, so you have to be careful what you do and do not include. Review every word and ask yourself, "Does this support my ability to do the job in some clear way?" If that item does not support your job objective, it should go.

Include Numbers

Most of the sample resumes in Chapter 7 include numbers. Numbers communicate in a special way, and you should include numbers that support key skills you have or that reflect your accomplishments or results.

Numbers make your resume more credible and your accomplishments and experiences easier to grasp. They also help employers better understand the scope of your various jobs and the size of your contribution. Get in the habit of including numbers in as many accomplishment and position statements as possible. You'll be very glad you did!

Emphasize Skills

It should be obvious by now that you should emphasize skills in your resume. Besides listing the key skills needed to support your job objective in a skills resume, you should include a variety of skill statements in all narrative sections of your resume. In each case, select skills you have that support your job objective.

Highlight Accomplishments and Results

Anyone can go through the motions of doing a job, but employers want to know how well you have done things in the past. Did you accomplish anything out of the ordinary? What results did you achieve?

The Importance of Doing Drafts

It will probably take you several rewrites before you are satisfied with your resume's content. And it will take even more changes before you are finished. Writing, modifying, editing, changing, adding to, and subtracting from content are important steps in writing a good resume. Expect to produce several drafts and you won't feel discouraged as you work through the process.

Edit, Edit, Edit

Every word has to count in your resume, so keep editing until it is right. This might require you to make multiple passes and to change your resume many times. But, if you did as I suggested and first created a simple but acceptable resume, fretting over your "better" resume shouldn't delay your job search one bit. Right?

Get Someone Else to Review Your Resume for Errors

After you have finished writing your resume, ask someone with good spelling and grammar skills to review it once again. It is simply amazing how errors creep into the most carefully edited resume.

More Tips to Improve Your Resume's Design and Appearance

Just as some people aren't good at resume writing, others are not good at design. Many resumes use simple designs, and this is acceptable for most situations. But you can do other things to improve your resume's appearance.

> **TIP:** When looking at the sample resumes in Chapter 7, note how some have a more distinctive appearance than others. Some have rules and bullets; others do not. Some include more white space, whereas others are quite crowded. Compromises are made in most resumes, but some clearly look better than others. Note the resumes with the appearances you like, and try to incorporate those design principles in your own resume.

Increase Readability with Some Simple Design Principles

People who design advertising know what makes something easy or hard to read—and they work very hard to make things easy. Here are some things they have found to improve readability. You can apply these same principles in writing your resume.

- Short sentences and short words are better than long ones.

- Short paragraphs are easier to read than long ones.

- Narrow columns are easier to read than wide ones.

- Put important information on the top and to the left because people scan materials from left to right and top to bottom.

- Using plenty of white space increases the text's readability. And it looks better.

- Don't use too many type styles (fonts) on the same page. Using one or two fonts is ideal; three is pushing it.

- Use underlining, bold type, and bullets to emphasize and separate— but use them sparingly.

Avoid "Packing" Your Resume with Small Print

Sometimes it's hard to avoid including lots of detail, but doing so can make your resume appear crowded and hard to read. In many cases, you can shorten a crowded resume with good editing, which would allow for considerably more white space.

Use Two Pages at the Most

One page is often enough if you are disciplined in your editing, but two uncrowded pages are far better than one crowded one. Those with considerable experience or high levels of responsibility often require a two-page resume, but very, very few justify more than two.

Use Type Fonts Sparingly

Just because you have many type fonts on your computer does not mean you have to use them all on your resume. Doing so creates a cluttered, hard-to-read look and is a sure sign of someone without design skills. Good resume design requires relatively few and easy-to-read fonts in limited sizes. Look at the sample resumes in Chapter 7—few use more than one or two type fonts. They also use bold and different-sized fonts sparingly.

Consider Graphics

I have included some sample resumes in Chapter 7 that use graphic elements to make them more interesting. Although resumes with extensive graphic design elements are not the focus for this book, some resumes clearly benefit from this. Good graphic design is more important for those in creative jobs such as advertising, art, and media.

Edit Again for Appearance

Just as your resume's text requires editing, you should be prepared to review and make additional changes to your resume's design. After you have written the content just as you want it, you will probably need to make additional editing and design changes so that everything looks right.

Select Top-Quality Paper and Matching Envelopes

Don't use cheap copy-machine paper. After all your work, you should use only high-quality paper. Most print shops and office supply stores will have appropriate paper selections. The better-quality papers often contain a percentage of cotton or other fibers. I prefer an off-white or light cream color because it gives a professional, clean appearance.

Buy matching envelopes at the time you choose your resume paper.

Use your good resume paper and envelopes for all cover letters and thank-you letters that you are printing and sending by mail or hand-delivering.

Final Comments

The best use of your resume is to get it into circulation early and often. Have enough so that you don't feel like you need to "save" them. Plan on giving multiple copies to friends, relatives, and acquaintances and sending out lots prior to and after interviews.

Chapter 7

A Stupendous Collection of Professionally Written and Designed Resumes

The resumes in this section were written by professional resume writers. As a result, they present a wonderful variety of writing and design styles and techniques. Each was written with great care and skill to present a real (but fictionalized) person in the best way possible. This approach is much more helpful than showing you lots of resumes by the same writer, using the same format.

I want to thank the writers who submitted resumes, all of them graduates of the Resume Writing Academy who have earned the Academy Certified Resume Writer (ACRW) credential. I am constantly inspired by their excellent work!

How to Use the Sample Resumes in This Section

I've never felt that there was one right way to do a resume. Each person has unique information to present, and each resume can look and be different. Often there are good reasons for this. For example, some occupations (such as accounting or law) have more formal traditions, so those resumes typically are more formal. Someone looking for a job in graphic design or marketing might have a more colorful, graphic, and nontraditional resume.

There are many reasons to use different writing and design styles, and the resumes in this section show wide variety in all their elements. You will find resumes for all sorts of people looking for all sorts of jobs. Some resumes include interesting graphic elements, and others are quite plain.

This variety will give you ideas for writing and creating your own resume. Feel free to experiment and use whatever style best suits you.

Resumes for All Types of Jobs

I have organized the resumes into groups that should be helpful to you:

- Health care. . . pages 107–111

- Science, engineering, and technology. . . pages 112–118

- Education. . . pages 119–122

- Clerical, administration, and human resources. . . pages 123–129

- Sales and marketing. . . pages 130–143

- Logistics and operations. . . pages 144–146

- Accounting and finance. . . pages 147–152

- Media. . . pages 153–155

- Hospitality and services. . . pages 156–158

- Executives. . . pages 159–162

- New grads. . . pages 163–169

- Career changers. . . pages 170–173

- Military-to-civilian transitions. . . pages 174–177

One obvious way to use the samples is to turn to the section that seems most compatible with your career goals. You can see how others in similar situations or seeking similar jobs have handled their resumes. But I also encourage you to look at all the samples for formats, presentation styles, and other ideas to use in your resume. For example, some resumes have superior graphic design elements that might inspire you, even though your job objective lies in a different area.

The "Key Points" box at the bottom of each resume points out features, strategies, structures, and other insights into how (and why) each resume was written and designed to present each candidate in the best possible light.

Juanita P. Morales

3482 McCandlish Road
Grand Blanc, MI 48439
810-555-2396 • jpmsmiles@home.net

Profile	❖ Certification and training as **Dental Hygienist.**
	❖ Experience as chair-side **Dental Assistant** in general and periodontal practices.
	❖ Ability to earn **trust** and develop **rapport** with patients.
	❖ Strong patient **assessment** and **education** skills.
	❖ Training and experience in using **Prophy Jet** and **ultrasonic scalers.**

Dental Experience	CARO PERIODONTAL ASSOCIATES • Caro, MI	2011–Present
	FAMILY DENTAL • Clarkston, MI	2007–2011
	DR. ROGER ANDERSON • Rochester, MI	2006–2007
	MACKIN ROAD DENTAL CLINIC • Lapeer, MI	2002–2006

Education	MOTT COMMUNITY COLLEGE • Flint, MI	
	Certificate in Dental Hygiene	2011
	— Graduated in Top 10% of class	
	— Passed state and national exams	
	— Past President, MCC Dental Students Association	

Selected Classes & Training	❖ "Infection Control in a Changing World"
	❖ "Advanced Techniques in Root Planing and Instrument Sharpening"
	❖ "AIDS: Oral Signs, Symptoms, and Treatments"
	❖ "Periodontal Diseases in Children and Adolescents"
	❖ "Periodontal Screening Record"
	❖ "Strategies for Teamwork and Communication Skills"

Community Involvement	❖ International Institute — Event Assistant
	❖ Spanish-Speaking Information Center — Volunteer Tutor
	❖ Big Brothers Big Sisters of Greater Flint — Big Sister

KEY POINTS: Effective profile for a new grad • Simple table format • Ample white space • Easy-to-skim listings

Submitted by Janet Beckstrom

Miranda P. Oswald

2735 Magnolia Lane
Coralville, IA 52241

319-555-8511
mposwald@isp.com

— **Women's Health Nurse Practitioner** —

*Combining passion for women's health and 12+ years of clinical experience
to provide superior service to women*

Areas of expertise…
Patient Education | Patient Care | Health Promotion

Highly motivated, accomplished health care professional with acute and intensive care experience. Cross-functional knowledge in multiple specialties, demonstrating adaptability and eagerness to learn. Always a patient advocate; key strength is gaining trust and putting patients at ease with calming manner. Effectively communicate with physicians, colleagues, and ancillary care providers.

Selected for highly visible position requiring medical expertise, collaborative skills, and assertiveness in crisis situations.

Education

UNIVERSITY OF IOWA • Iowa City
Master of Science in Nursing (2012)
Women's Health Nurse Practitioner

IOWA STATE UNIVERSITY • Ames
Bachelor of Science in Nursing (2000)
Minor: Biology

Licensure & Certifications

State of Iowa Registered Nurse

SANE [Sexual Assault Nurse Examiner]
Pursuing certification through Coe College. Completed 40-hour classroom course. In process of completing clinical and field work. Projected completion: September 2012.

ACLS and BLS

Women's Health Clinical Experience

OB-GYN ASSOCIATES • Cedar Rapids, Iowa — January–April 2012
GENESIS MEDICAL CENTER • Davenport, Iowa — September–December 2011
Provided routine prenatal care; contraceptive management; STI screening, education, and treatment; and gynecological education regarding peri-menopause, menopause, and irregular bleeding. Conducted annual exams on women across the life span. Supported 2 physicians and 1 women's health nurse practitioner in providing care to diverse population.

MERCY MEDICAL CENTER OB/GYN CLINIC • Cedar Rapids, Iowa — April–July 2011
Performed STI screening and prevention education, contraception management (including IUD insertion), patient education, and health promotion. Served women ages 16–40 in family planning clinic.

Continued

Submitted by Janet Beckstrom

Miranda P. Oswald   319-555-8511 | mposwald@isp.com   Page 2

Career Progression

UNIVERSITY OF IOWA HOSPITALS & CLINICS • Iowa City, Iowa   1999–Present
Named one of "America's Best Hospitals" by U.S. News & World Report.

Clinical Nurse II – Surgical Intensive Care Unit [SICU] (2009–Present)
Provide specialty nursing care and close monitoring of critically ill patients requiring infusion, ventilary support, oscillation, and CRRT on unit serving liver transplant patients, ARDS patients, and labor and delivery patients with complications following cesarean sections.

> *Special Assignments:*
> **STAT Team** — Recommended by nurse manager for assignment to team supporting 734 adult beds, outpatient clinics, and procedure areas. Provide critical care resource to charge nurses, assistive care providers, and physicians in emergency situations, including direct patient care and facilitation of transport to ICU. Carry out STAT responsibilities an average of 2 days/month in lieu of SICU duties.
>
> **Code team** — Respond to adult cardiac/respiratory arrests not occurring in ICU.
>
> **Preceptor** — Frequently requested to precept student nurses and newly hired staff nurses.

Clinical Nurse II – Labor & Delivery Unit (2003–2009)
Delivered quality nursing care for high- and low-risk patients during all facets of birth process: labor and delivery, recovery, post-partum, and newborn care. Educated patients about breast feeding and post-partum care. Circulated in OR during obstetrical procedures.

Clinical Nurse I – Burn Treatment Center (2001–2003)
Delivered compassionate intensive, acute, and rehabilitative care to adult and pediatric patients. Managed pain control and conscious sedation. Performed dressing changes and wound care. Instructed patients and families in post-discharge wound care.

Critical Care Nurse Extern – Heart & Vascular Intensive Care Unit (2000)
Completed specialty training in nursing management of life-threatening conditions for 3-credit critical care class.

Surgical Technician – Burn Treatment Center [weekends/holidays] (1999–2000)
Provided direct patient care; performed dressing changes and wound care. Provided technical assistance and maintenance of equipment and instrumentation for critical care procedures.

Professional Affiliations

American Nurses Association (ANA)
Nurse Practitioners in Women's Health (NPWH)
Association of Women's Health, Obstetrics and Neonatal Nurses (AWHONN)
Iowa Council of Nurse Practitioners
Alpha Lambda Delta [national honor society]

KEY POINTS: Quick summary box at top • Credentials on page 1 • Most relevant experience in separate section on page 1

SAMUEL GLAVIN, PhD

Columbus, OH · sglavin@gmail.com · 614.587.4447

MICROBIOLOGY GROUP LEADERSHIP

Unique complement of research expertise and interpersonal skills. PhD in Microbiology with 4 years of post-doctoral research experience, 2 years of industry experience, and expert knowledge of CLSI methodologies. A quick study of new technology and project requirements. Expert in data interpretation and presentations to widely diverse audiences. Led numerous project teams and developed reputation as an innovative and collaborate leader.

SELECT AREAS OF EXPERTISE

- Antimicrobial susceptibility testing
- Proteomic analysis (2DGE; Luminex platform)
- RNA, protein, and DNA extraction from vitro and in vivo sources
- Expression analysis (Affymetrix and Illumina platform)
- Mammalian cell culture
- PCR and RT-PCR
- Flow cytometry

PROFESSIONAL & RESEARCH EXPERIENCE

REDFIELD HEALTHCARE DIAGNOSTICS, Columbus, OH   2007 – Present
R&D Manager (2010 – Present)
Sr. Microbiologist (2007 – 2010)

- Responsible for Yeast Antimicrobial Agent Susceptibility Test (AST) development, including Feasibility, Development, and Verification testing. Manage 3–4 direct reports.
- Rapidly established exceptional communications with intradepartmental groups, e.g. Marketing, Regulatory Compliance, and Manufacturing.
- Gained invaluable insight to the product development best practices of this industry leader.
- Initiated polices that reduced product manufacture costs 10%.
- Strengthened process improvement standards, e.g., updated Failure Modes Risk Analysis (FMRA).
- Serve as key member of the YAST team to assure completion of product development projects within guidelines for all groups, including Regulatory Affairs, Clinical Affairs, Manufacturing, Statistical Analysis, Global Product Support, Software, and Marketing.

OHIO STATE UNIVERSITY:
Health Care Cancer Center, Columbus, OH   2005 – 2007
Post Doctoral Scholar

- Served as lab manager with 7 reports.
- Applied for and secured funding for DOE and NIH grants.
- Among select projects, performed human in-vivo research using low-dose ionizing radiation. Search results published (Glavin et al 2009, 2008, 2007; Teller et al, 2006).

OHIO STATE UNIVERSITY:
Department of Medical Microbiology and Immunology, Columbus, OH   2001 – 2005
Research Associate

- Researched membrane protein expression of *Nocardia asteroides*. Used 2-dimensional gel electrophoresis, membrane protein extraction, murine polyclonal antibody production, and Western blots.
- Applied for and received grant for M. tuberculosis DNA microarrays, from Pathogen Functional Genomics Resource Center at TIGR (2003).
- Served as teaching associate for Microbiology (255L, 202L) and Bioscience 2A courses.

Continued

Submitted by Mark Bartz

SAMUEL GLAVIN, PHD

Page 2 · sglavin@gmail.com · 614.587.4447

PUBLICATIONS, ABSTRACTS & POSTERS

Research Papers

Glavin SJ, Jacobs DM, Wo J, Smith C, San A, Stern R, Lehrs J, Kelly C, Mels Z. Transient Genome-Wide Transcriptional Response to Low-Dose Ionizing Radiation In-Vivo in Humans. Int J Radiat Oncol Biol Phys. 2009. Jan 1; 70(1):229–234

Glavin SJ, Santana RW, Renalds ML, Roo R, Mels Z. Proteomic Analysis of Low-Dose Arsenic and Irradiation Exposure on Keratinocytes. Proteomics. 2008. March; vol 9, 1925–1938

Glavin SJ, Santana RW, Jones A, Stern RL, Lehmann T, and Mels, Z. Optimized Methodology for Dual Extraction of RNA and Protein from Small Human Skin Biopsies. Journal of International Dermatology Research. 2008. Feb; 127(2):347–353

Abstracts and Posters: collectively 9. Full detail available.

EDUCATION & TRAINING

OHIO STATE UNIVERSITY, Columbus, OH
Post Doctoral Scholar (2005 – 2008)
David Jacobs, PhD, and Zelda Mels, MD
OSU Cancer Center and Department of Public Health Sciences

PhD, Microbiology (2005)
PhD Advisor: Leslie L. Beaman, PhD, Medical Microbiology and Immunology, SCHOOL OF MEDICINE
DEB Advisor: Judith A. Krantz, PhD, Director, OSU Davis Biotechnology Program

OSU Biotechnology programs include: Flow Cytometry (2007); Proteomics: Fundamentals & Technology (2005)

CENTRAL MICHIGAN UNIVERSITY, Mt. Pleasant, MI
Bachelor of Science, Biology – Emphasis Cellular Biology (1999)

TRAINING INCLUDES: Situational Leadership: Effective Leadership Skills from within the Company (2009; based on John C. Tolland book); Time Management; Radiation Research Scholar in Training Workshops (2004, 2005, 2006, 2007; Randall Research Corporation.)

ASSOCIATIONS & SERVICE

Member (current or previous)
AMERICAN ASSOCIATION FOR CANCER RESEARCH (AACR)
AMERICAN SOCIETY FOR MICROBIOLOGY (ASM)
HUMAN PROTEOME ORGANIZATION (HUPO)
RADIATION RESEARCH SOCIETY (RRS)
TOASTMASTERS

Service (OSU)
Student Representative on the Executive Committee for the Designated Emphasis in Biotechnology Program;
Student Representative on the Microbiology Graduate Group Admissions Committee;
Vice President of the Microbiology Graduate Student Association

Service (Other)
Next Wave Representative for the American Association for the of Science Advocates (AASA);
Community Involvement Team Committee for Redfield Healthcare Diagnostics

KEY POINTS: Experience and knowledge on page 1 • Publications and more on page 2 in traditional medical CV style

Christopher S. Lorenzo

3515 Stenton Avenue | Philadelphia, PA 19012 | 215-292-1086 | chrislorenzo@gmail.com

PROFESSIONAL SKILLS SUMMARY

Resourceful, determined, and focused Environmental Scientist. Strong educational background in environmental sciences, chemistry, and ecology complemented by field research and professional work experience in water quality testing. Excellent technical, analytical, teamwork, and interpersonal skills.

Strengths:

Water Quality Testing Techniques & Methods	Research & Data Analysis
Quality Assurance & Control Protocols	Project Planning & Management
Aquatic Biology Field & Lab Instrument Use	Technology & Computer Knowledge

EDUCATION

LYCOMING COLLEGE, Williamsport, PA
Bachelor of Science, Double major in **Ecology** and **Chemistry**, May 2012

- Extensive training in water quality testing techniques and methods and chemical analysis of water samples in freshwater lakes, streams, and rivers.

ACHIEVEMENTS:

- 3.85 GPA, Phi Sigma Biological Honor Society — President
- Presented research findings of Susquehanna River water quality and ecological and habitat data of Eastern Hellbender Salamander at 5th Annual Susquehanna River Symposium in Harrisburg, PA.
- Co-wrote the 2012 College Environmental Audit and presented to College's Board of Trustees.

EXPERIENCE

CLEAN WATER INSTITUTE, Williamsport, PA   2010–2012
Intern (May 2011–April 2012)
Performed water quality sampling and testing on numerous streams, rivers, and lakes in Central Pennsylvania. Analyzed water chemistry on water samples following strict standard methods using both field and laboratory instruments. Tested water quality using benthic macroinvertebrate sampling techniques and identification. Contacted and consulted with landowners to obtain permission for water testing on streams running through their property. Relayed findings and recommendations to landowners.

KEY PROJECTS:

- Partnered with PA Fish and Boat Commission on the Unassessed Waters Project. Collected and compiled samples to determine stream habitat, water quality, water chemistry, and hardness.
- Collaborated with Trout Unlimited organization in various trout studies and water quality tests.
- Performed stream and habitat restorations, reversing years of damage caused by humans.

Research Assistant (May–August 2010)
Selected by biology department faculty to participate in Eastern Hellbender Salamander research project. Conducted ecological and geological surveys of their habitat and performed water quality and chemistry testing. Completed live capture and health assessments on each aquatic salamander and recorded data in database. Gave public talks and demonstrations at local watershed group and coalition events.

HEMLOCK ACRES GAME FARM & HUNTING PRESERVE, Benton, PA   2008–Present
Sporting Clays Guide
Monitor shooters to ensure compliance with regulations and safety practices during competitions.

KEY POINTS: 1-page resume for new grad • College internship and research presented as professional experience

---

Submitted by Anne Landon

JASON KIPTON

216-281-5007 | jkipton@gmail.com
W6098 Number 10 Road • Cleveland Heights, OH 44106

MANUFACTURING ENGINEER • MECHANICAL SUPERVISOR

Manufacturing professional skilled in generating efficient production methods that meet cost, safety, and quality requirements. More than 13 years of experience in various manufacturing environments spanning tool making, machining, maintenance, and supervision. Recognized for a high-energy work ethic, business acumen, company dedication, commitment to quality, and personable interaction with people at all levels of an organization. Excel in leading teams and projects, diffusing conflicts, and fostering a culture of creative problem-solving.

Machining: Journeyman Toolmaker (State of WI Apprenticeship with 8,320 hours), Knee Mills, Machining Centers (vertical, horizontal), Turning Centers, Screw Machines, Grinders (tool, surface, cylindrical), EDM (wire, ram), Manual and CNC Plasma Cutting Machines

CNC Machine Tools: Centroid, Fanuc, Hurco, Mazak, Mitsubishi, Okuma

CAD/CAM: AutoCAD, Autodesk Inventor, Rhino, Virtual Gibbs, Smart Cam, Master Cam, Visual Mill

Quality: Experience with Kaizen, 5S, engineering scales, gauges, micrometers, height stands, comparators, CMM, tensile and hardness testing

Welding: Certified and experienced in GTAW, SMAW, SAW, GMAW, short circuit, spray arc welding

Maintenance: Certified in Plant Engineering Mechanical Maintenance and Electrical Maintenance including troubleshooting, repair, and preventative measures

PROFESSIONAL EXPERIENCE

EDUCATIONAL SABBATICAL   2010–2012
Earned AAS degree in Business and Engineering at Cleveland State University.

DYM INDUSTRIES – Bedford, OH   2005–2010
$200M manufacturer of pistons and piston rings; 950 employees.
Toolmaker
Advanced department's production goals by recommending improvements to increase output, enhance quality, promote safety, and reduce costs. Built and repaired all types of tooling: Jigs, Fixtures, and Single and Dual Cavity Molds. Used manual and CNC-controlled mills (3 and 4 axis), lathes, grinders, EDM (ram), and 2d and 3d programming.
- Completed apprenticeship to achieve Journeyman Toolmaker designation.
- Increased machine uptime, decreased tooling costs, and reduced machine runtime by implementing additional chip evacuation techniques.
- Served as a liaison with other company departments, machine technical staff, and vendors to troubleshoot and address system malfunctions and repairs.

OHIO FOUNDRY – Lima, OH   2002–2005
Leading non-captive iron foundry.
Maintenance
Completed plant repairs and performed preventative mechanical and electrical maintenance on equipment. Engaged in part procurement, machine installation and removal, shoring, rigging, metal fabrication, repair of conveyers (belt, chain, and kinetic), transport systems, dust collection, water systems, induction furnaces, bearings, gearboxes, hydraulics, pneumatics, pumps, generators, cranes, heavy equipment, forklifts, and gas and diesel engines. Selected for Emergency Response Team tackling issues including evacuations and HazMat spills. Participated in Kaizen and 5S programs.
- Reduced plant downtime through expert troubleshooting and swift repair of manufacturing systems.
- Increased line uptime through an aggressive preventative maintenance plan.
- Lowered costs by reverse-engineering machine components for manufacture during uptime.

• Continued •

Submitted by Mary Schumacher

SUPERIOR MACHINES – East Cleveland, OH   1999–2001
Provider of in-house machinery for aerospace, medical, recreational, and consumer product industries.
Machinist • Lead Man
Recruited to quickly ramp up use of new machinery following recent operations expansion. Charged with reducing costs and accelerating production of components for airplane industry. Oversaw production and quality of machined parts from employees on all shifts. Programmed and maintained manual and CNC mills and lathes.
- Introduced new tooling ideas that reduced manufacturing time and costs of components.
- Cut lead times between changeovers.
- Increased machine output capacity through standardization and use of best practices.
- Implemented preventative maintenance program that boosted machine uptime.

FREED INDUSTRIES – Bedford, OH   1997–1999
Manufacturer of world-class pressure vessels and metal fabrications for U.S. and global markets; 325 employees.
Machinist • Welder
Performed hand welding for fabrication of pressure vessels. Operated forklifts, overhead cranes, rollers, shears, brakes, CNC punches, CNC plasma, and torch tables. Subsequently transitioned into machining department to operate manual and CNC-controlled mills and lathes.
- Gained reputation for willingness to perform any role needed on the manufacturing floor.
- Decreased production time on custom tank jobs by using innovative solutions in fitting of assemblies.
- Achieved designation as a certified welder in GMAW, GTAW, SMAW, and SAW welding processes in both stainless and carbon steel in accordance with ASME code.

MADHANY, INC. – Akron, OH   1996–1997
Manufacturer of towing hitches.
Welder • Operator
Hired to support manufacture of receiver and 5th wheel–style hitches. Gained a strong foundation in GMAW and SMAW welding, CNC plasma table, brakes, presses, broaches, swedges, punches, dies, benders, grinders, and saws.

QUALIFICATIONS

EDUCATION
AAS in Engineering & Business, CLEVELAND STATE UNIVERSITY – Cleveland, OH, 2012

OHIO TECHNICAL COLLEGE – Cleveland, OH
Certificate in Maintenance Electricity, 2006
Certificate in Plant Engineering Mechanical Maintenance, 2003
Technical Diploma in Machine Tool Technics (Tool & Die Making), Honor Graduate, 2000
Certificate in Welding, 1998
Student Body Vice President 1998–1999 • Student Body President 1999–2000

SAFETY & TECHNICAL TRAINING
10-hour OSHA General Industry Safety and Health • Emergency First Aid / CPR & AED

OHIO TECHNICAL COLLEGE – Cleveland, OH
16-hour Incident Command • Confined Space: Entrant-Attendant-Supervisor
Confined Space: Rescue & Rope Techniques • Industrial Emergency Response 40-hour Technician
Trained in Fall Protection • Forklift • High Lift • Scissors Lift • Articulated Loader • Fire Protection • Lock out / Tag out •
High Voltage up to 12,470 volts • Fire Extinguisher Training • Crane Inspection & Safety

KEY POINTS: Keyword-rich from expertise list through position descriptions • Time off for education shown on page 1

BERNARD F. BLACK JR.

843-320-1820   526 Oak Lawn Drive • Greenville, SC 29602   bblack@gmail.com

IT HELP DESK SUPERVISOR • TECHNICAL MANAGER

Applying people, problem-solving, and technical skills to help businesses thrive

Customer-focused technology professional and help desk manager with excellent technical qualifications and a reputation for quality, efficiency, and reliability. A+ certified computer technician who blends interpersonal skills with expertise in installation, preventative maintenance, networking, security, and troubleshooting. Calm under pressure.

Platforms:	DOS – Windows – Unix
Applications:	MS Office – Outlook & Outlook Express – Macromedia Dreamweaver MX – TBS (Telecom Business Suite) – Visio – Turnstone Systems – Copper Mountain System
Hardware:	Nortel Systems (Shasta 5000) – Cisco Routers – Wide Area Networks (WANs) – Local Area Networks (LANs) – Netgear routers & firewall – RAS (including Shiva)
Customer Service:	Repair & maintenance of PCs, printers & plotters – Network accounts management – Help desk & call center management & support – Internet & intranet services – DNS configuration

PROFESSIONAL EXPERIENCE

TECH RIGHT   Greenville, SC • 2004–Present
IT services firm serving small and medium-sized clients.
IT Support Manager • Operations Manager

Manage customer accounts and internal operations including IT. Serve as main point of contact for customers for new service and problem resolution. Hire and train all office and field employees.

- Established company's technology infrastructure, including installation, maintenance, and repair of computer systems, peripherals, accessories, networks, routers, and telephone systems. Installed software and created email and voicemail accounts.
- Led design and implementation of call center and computer system.
- Responded to economic downturn by focusing advertising efforts on digital marketing. Redesigned website with promotions and streamlined functionality.
- Developed operational systems, including financial reporting, employee handbook, job descriptions, and policies and procedures manual.

POLO COMMUNICATIONS   Mauldin, SC • 2000–2003
Provider of DSL and T-1 data communications services.
Supervisor, Customer Services Level II Technical Support Team (2001–2003)
Technical Lead, Customer Services Level II Technical Support Team (2000–2001)

Hired full-time after a 5-month contracting assignment. Served as single point of contact for ongoing projects that included customer migrations and backhaul migrations. Subsequently promoted to supervisory position directing Level II support for IIec, enhanced services, IP allocation, and vendor issues. Assigned national and high-profile accounts to technicians. Hired staff and trained in technical knowledge and communication skills.

- Built a high-performing technical support team through individual mentoring and by establishing clear expectations.
- Teamed with vendors to identify root causes and correct customer issues.
- Implemented process improvements to decrease customer telephone hold times.
- Created courses for in-house training.

PAGE 1 OF 2

Submitted by Mary Schumacher

KIKKLAND SYSTEMS (onsite at Polo Communications)   Greenville, SC • 2000
Leading technology staffing and services company.
Level II Technical Support Specialist, Customer Services

Provided telephone support for customers having difficulty accessing the DSL line. Performed PC and network configurations, implemented firewalls, translated port addresses and network addresses, and configured DHCP.

- Delivered excellent customer support for individuals having trouble receiving and sending emails.
- Troubleshot and repaired circuit issues with telecommunications companies and outside vendors.
- Used Turnstone CX100 to perform maintenance and line conditioning tests.
- Configured Shasta and Copper Mountain DSLAMs for new and existing customers.

MITCHELL CORPORATION (on-site at MGB Pharmaceuticals)   Augusta, GA • 1999–2000
Performance improvement company providing training, engineering, and technical services.
Computer Systems Analyst • Level 1 Operator

Maintained and enhanced network systems for MGB's globally accessed NT, Unix, and VMS platforms. Worked on-site within a large data center.

- Ensured business continuity and quality performance of applications by monitoring back-up processes of databases, web-based applications, and system checkouts.
- Provided after-hours help desk support and account management for local and international client users.

REDNISS, INC.   Augusta, GA • 1996–1999
Provider of computer services and support.
Computer Technician • Network Supervisor (1998–1999)
Computer/Network Technician (1996–1998)

Tackled computer and networking problems and delivered rapid results by applying diagnostic and troubleshooting skills for software, system hardware, and printers/plotters.

- Promoted to supervise both scheduled maintenance and emergency repairs of network problems, ensuring quality results for all jobs.
- Earned wide range of hardware certifications to provide hands-on leadership for issue diagnosis and maintenance of computer networks.
- Led support services to the next level by instituting system inventory programs and technical training for new employees.

QUALIFICATIONS

- Industrial Electronics Certification, Savannah Regional Vocational Technical School – Savannah, GA
- Hewlett Packard Certified
- In-house Training: Shasta 5000, Copperview, Netopia routers, Efficient Network routers, Turnstone Crossconnect Switch, TBS, DNS, Service Desk
- A+ Certification

KEY POINTS: Technology summary key for many tech-related jobs • "Qualifications" replaces traditional education listing

RONALD DEWEY

45417 Dolphin Road ♦ Clarkson, UT 84074
Phone: 385.555.1221 ♦ Email: rdewey@gmail.com

PROGRAM / PROJECT MANAGER

Project Management professional with strong track record of matrix-managing cross-functional teams that collaborate to achieve aggressive business goals. Particularly effective at directing technical and non-technical solutions from concept through implementation. Consistently balance needs of the customer, team, and project. Core competencies include:

- ☑ Strategic Planning & Leadership
- ☑ Team Building & Management
- ☑ Lean Six Sigma Methodology & Tools
- ☑ Productivity Improvement
- ☑ Cost Reduction & Avoidance
- ☑ Change Management

Cited by Managers:

"Ron is always asking for additional responsibility and excels in everything he does. He has contributed to multiple areas of the Bank and continues to be a sought-after team member." AC
"Ron has been tremendously successful on all his assignments ... delivered exceptional results." TD

PROFESSIONAL EXPERIENCE

TOTAL BANK, Salt Lake City, UT   2006–Present
A leading financial institution worldwide ♦ $266M revenues, 85M customers

Fast-track promotion through a series of increasingly responsible positions based on strong performance in customer service, team leadership, and process improvement.

Project Analyst (2011–Present)
Business Analyst (2009–2011)
Selected as a champion to promote a continuous improvement culture using **Lean Six Sigma** methodology. Partner with business leaders to identify critical issues. Prioritize and implement projects. Design and monitor pre- and post-performance indicators to analyze progress. Build relationships across business sectors. Create and update concise, comprehensive documentation.

Process & Product Improvements:
- Selected as key member of team that replaced mortgage origination software with no downtime and achieved savings of >**$7.6M** in **5** years.
- Utilized **Agile sprint process** for IT requests from business need to final deployment.
- Participated on team that redesigned web front-end for mortgage customers and sales representatives, leading to a **28%** increase in approvals and **37%** jump in funding.
- Led team that created standardized data collection templates and processes that created inter-departmental consistency.

(continued)

Submitted by Jane Falter

RONALD DEWEY   385.555.1221   rdewey@gmail.com

TOTAL BANK (continued)

Team Building/Leadership:
- Trained and mentored team members on Six Sigma methods and lean principles, including data collection, data measurement, and statistical process control.
- Chosen to rescue project already in progress. Earned respect of stakeholders when input and contributions quickly improved project direction and results.
- Recognized for **leadership abilities** that foster motivation and consistently achieve positive results—while maneuvering conflicting team member demands and schedules.
- Implemented communication channels to retain and promote team member commitment, development, and accountability.

Loan Coordinating Team Representative (2008–2009)
Business Development Associate (2007–2008)
Promoted after only 7 months in previous capacity. Prioritized needs and identified critical projects, collected data, and mapped processes. Participated as a vital team member for large-scale projects.

- Delivered significant increase in approved brokers and applications, resulting in **$875M** submissions in **8 months**.
- Increased utilization of products through client training and communication.
- Selected to train loan originators and loan processors on products and processes.
- Earned **Orange Excellence Award**, 2008 (outstanding sales averaging **$100M** monthly).

Senior Sales Associate and Asset Sales Associate (2006–2007)
Accountable for sales team performance. Mentored 5 associates on techniques and policies.

- Received **Customer Experience Award**, 2007 (presented to 3 of 300 associates nationally).

GAMESTOP, Clarkson, UT   2003–2006
Game and entertainment software retailer
Assistant Manager (2004–2006)
Game Advisor (2003–2004)
Managed inventory and **15** sales associates. Recruited, trained, and developed staff.

- Recognized for exceeding performance goals – 2 quarters, 2005 and 2006.

EDUCATION / AFFILIATIONS

Bachelor of Science in Business Management – University of Phoenix   2011
Certified – Lean Six Sigma Green Belt
Candidate – Lean Six Sigma Black Belt

Member – **American Society for Quality**
Member – **Project Management Institute**

KEY POINTS: Manager kudos highlight Summary section • "Fast-track promotion" box summarizes career with 1 company

SUSAN T. RICHARDSON
(714) 672-7363 ♦ STRichardson99@yahoo.com

The Substitute every Principal wants on Speed Dial.

EXPERIENCED SUBSTITUTE TEACHER
SPANISH ▪ FRENCH ▪ ENGLISH ▪ ESL ▪ SOCIAL SCIENCES ▪ SPECIAL EDUCATION ▪ SCIENCE ▪ MATH

Dynamic, creative teaching professional with more than 5 years of classroom experience. Ready to implement existing lesson plans or bring original, subject-specific, interactive lessons to the classroom. Partner effectively with teachers and staff to facilitate continual learning in the absence of primary teacher. Complimented for ability to quickly gain the attention and participation of students.

CERTIFICATION | LANGUAGES
CBEST—STATE OF CALIFORNIA
FLUENT IN ENGLISH, SPANISH, AND FRENCH

TEACHING EXPERIENCE
DIEGO RIVERA INSTITUTE CHARTER SCHOOL, Los Angeles, CA
Multiple Subject Substitute (July 2010–Present)
* Introduced Spanish to "Promotion in Doubt" students during summer session.
* Completed 6-week assignment teaching Science and Social Studies (Grades 6–8).
* Taught Intermediate Spanish class (Grades 6–8) for one semester.
* Developed cultural diversity activities and lessons to use when lesson plan not available.

PASADENA UNIFIED SCHOOL DISTRICT, Pasadena, CA
Longfellow Middle School, Highland Park Middle School, Lincoln High School
Foreign Language Teacher (2002–2004)
* Taught Spanish 8 (Accelerated & Regents), Mixed-level French 8, and 9th Grade French.
* Achieved close to 100% pass rate for students taking California State Proficiency in a Second Language.

LOS ANGELES UNIFIED SCHOOL DISTRICT, Los Angeles, CA
Foreign Language Teacher (June 2001–June 2002)
* Taught Spanish to General Education, Self-Contained, and Special Education classes at multiple sites.

HOLMES JUNIOR HIGH SCHOOL, Riverside, CA
Long-term Substitute Foreign Language Teacher (September 2000–March 2001)
* Taught Spanish, developed exams, and met with parents (Grades 8–9).

PROFESSIONAL DEVELOPMENT
Workshops—California Charter Center Consortium
Strategies for Dealing with Difficult Students—Los Angeles Unified School District
Enhancing Instruction in Your Foreign Language Classroom Workshop—University of California, Los Angeles

EDUCATION
M.A., Spanish, Antioch College, Los Angeles—2010
B.A., Spanish Literature, University of California, Los Angeles—1999

KEY POINTS: Unique "tagline" and color graphic at top • Strong resume for a substitute who is not a certified teacher

Submitted by Lorraine Beaman

Kate L. Foresman

2689 Canyon Avenue, Riverside, CA 92521
951.506.1039 | kforesman@gmail.com

Middle School Art Teacher

Enthusiastic, creative, and talented art teacher with ability to foster student curiosity, creativity, and self-discipline in a positive learning environment. Collaborative educator with outstanding interpersonal and communication skills complemented by strengths in interactive learning and differentiated instruction.

Education & Credentials

Certification: Art—California and Pennsylvania Permanent K–12
Bachelor of Science in **Art Education**, 2011
Kutztown University, Kutztown, PA

Jewelry Technician Certification, Revere Academy of Jewelry Art, San Francisco, CA, 2011

Employment Experience

John F. Kennedy Middle School, Riverside, CA   September 2011–June 2012
LONG-TERM SUBSTITUTE ART TEACHER
Planned projects and taught art classes for more than 150 students at John F. Kennedy Middle School in grades 6–8. Designed and implemented interactive lesson plans and units and educated on proper methodologies and techniques. Evaluated each student's progress and adjusted lessons accordingly.
- ✓ Initiated first after-school Art Club to provide students additional opportunities to further their creative capabilities and explore new mediums.
- ✓ Selected and matted 120 pieces of student artwork for exhibition at prestigious art gallery show.

J.P. McCaskey High School, Lancaster, PA   January–April 2011
STUDENT TEACHER
Raised student awareness and appreciation of the arts through creative lesson plans and teaching methods. Provided small-group instruction in basic jewelry-making, water colors, acrylics, and etching.

Kate Louise Designs (www.katelouisedesigns.com), Riverside, CA   2009–Present
ENTREPRENEUR / METALSMITH
Started small business to manufacture unique sterling silver and bead jewelry. Created business and marketing plan, prepared budget, and purchased tools. Traveled throughout region and country to display and sell jewelry at juried craft shows and exhibitions.
- ✓ Collaborate with individual customers to design and create custom jewelry.
- ✓ Network with boutique owners, customers, and juried craft shows to promote designs.

Professional Associations

Bald Eagle Art League, Board Member   **Society of American Goldsmiths**, Member
California Guild of Craftsmen, Member   **National Art Education Association**, Member

"I found I could say things with color and shapes that I couldn't say any other way — things I had no words for." —Georgia O'Keeffe

---

KEY POINTS: Eye-catching color graphic • Both teaching and artistic experience • Meaningful quotation

---

Submitted by Anne Landon

CHARLES V. EDWARDS

1949 East Brookhurst Ave., Garden Grove, CA 92840 ✳ 714.741.5994 ✳ charles.edwards@gmail.com

PROFESSIONAL PROFILE

Talented, dedicated musician and teacher bringing to the classroom each day a love of music and a passion to inspire students. Utilize music education to nurture confidence, personal responsibility, and self-motivated learning. Consistently develop student talent and appreciation of music in inner-city and suburban schools. Successfully partner with other teachers to develop multicultural and multidisciplinary educational experiences.

"Mr. Edwards will be a wonderful addition to any school music program."
Michelle Donavan, Director of Bands, Trident High School, Anaheim, CA

TEACHING CERTIFICATIONS

MUSIC EDUCATION K–12
— California: Clear Single Subject Credential—Music
— Nevada: Secondary License—Music Endorsement
— Oregon: Initial Teaching License—High School Music

EXPERIENCE

SCHOOL DISTRICT OF LOS ANGELES, Los Angeles, CA   2009–Present
Class Instrumental Music Teacher
- Plan and teach individual and small-group brass and percussion lessons that nurture talent and develop an appreciation of music in 140+ students in 5 K–8 schools.
- Select and orchestrate age-appropriate, student-engaging musical selections; create lessons that engage students with various learning styles; conduct and coordinate beginning and intermediate band ensembles at each school.
- Provide parents, staff, and students the opportunity to recognize individual improvement and showcase student talent by producing 2 concerts a year at each site.
- Collaborated with orchestra teacher to integrate top brass and percussion students into orchestra and prepare classic Chinese folk tunes for performance at district Chinese New Year Music Celebration.

FIFTH STONE MUSIC SCHOOL, Garden Grove, CA   2009–Present
Private Lesson Instructor
- Take students from beginning to advanced performance levels.
- Develop individualized practice routines designed to self-motivate students.

CESAR CHAVEZ SCHOOL, Los Angeles, CA   2009
KING HIGH SCHOOL, West Covina, CA
Student Teacher
- Transformed class with record of poor behavior into tight group of young musicians.
- Developed and implemented lesson plans that improved student performance in concert band, jazz band, and music appreciation (grades 6–8).
- Achieved student learning outcomes in guitar class, jazz band, percussion ensemble, and symphonic band (grades 9–12).

PROJECT M.U.S.I.C., Los Angeles, CA   2008–2009
Teaching Artist
- Volunteered for program bringing music into economically challenged schools.
- Introduced instruments to 3rd graders through interactive presentations and performance.

Submitted by Lorraine Beaman

CHARLES V. EDWARDS
714.741.5994 ✳ charles.edwards@gmail.com

RIDGECREST HIGH SCHOOL MARCHING BAND, Anaheim, CA   2008
Wind Instrument Assistant/Instructional Staff
 • Coached band members to achieve superior performances while executing
   precision drills.
 • Band reached top ranking in State of California competitions.

TRIDENT JUNIOR HIGH SCHOOL MARCHING BAND, Anaheim, CA   2006–2007
Wind Instrument Assistant/Instructional Staff
 • Encouraged and inspired players to meet rehearsal and practice expectations.
 • Improved marching skills with positive coaching and critiques during drills.
 • Band achieved recognition in Southern California Regional Competition.

INTER-FAITH COMMUNITY CENTER OF LANCASTER, Orange Grove, CA   2006–2007
Music Instructor
 • Created music program for 3- to 12-year-olds. Choreographed talent show
   to showcase each child's talent and develop stage presence. Encouraged
   support for other performers.

PRIVATE INSTRUCTOR, Santa Ana, CA   2005–2007
Clarinet and Saxophone
 • Developed fun, challenging weekly lessons and practice routines to achieve
   improvement of performance skills by beginning, intermediate, and advanced
   students in grades 5–7.

PROFESSIONAL DEVELOPMENT

Performance and Subject Matter Expertise
Performer, Orange County Symphonic Brass Band
Attendee, 2009 Western Division, Music Educators National Conference (MENC)
Member, Music Educators National Conference (MENC)
Member, California Music Educators Association (CMEA)

Classroom Instruction and Management
School District of Los Angeles, Continuous Professional Development
School District of Los Angeles, New Teacher Induction Institute

EDUCATION

Special Education Certification, Antioch University, Los Angeles, CA
Anticipated Completion: August 2012

Bachelor of Music in Music Education, University of California, Los Angeles, CA, 2009
 • Dean's List: 2005–2009; Sigma Alpha Iota Honor Certificate
 • President & Treasurer, Sigma Alpha Iota Women's Music Fraternity
 • Rank Leader, Bruin Marching Band

KEY POINTS: Musical staff design • Focus on engaging and empowering students

CHARITY FITTON

909 East Dear Street • Columbia, MO 65201
573.231.4113 • charityfitton@yahoo.com

EXPERIENCED OFFICE MANAGER

Highly organized and efficient officer manager with exceptionally strong computer skills and superior financial management capabilities. Consistently demonstrate initiative, composure, and multi-tasking ability under the most challenging circumstances.

SKILLS

• High-Volume Customer Service	• Multi-Line Phone Systems	• Adobe Illustrator, FrontPage, InDesign
• Scheduling	• Copier, Printer, Fax Operations	• Microsoft Office Suite
• Event Planning & Logistics	• Wide-Format Printer	• Database Creation & Management

PROFESSIONAL EXPERIENCE

Columbia Regional Transportation Service   2009–Present
Office Manager
Ensure smooth running of office operations. Provide clerical support, including paying bills, scheduling fleet vehicles, documenting incidents, answering multi-line phone, and managing incoming and outgoing mail. Create multiple brochures and fliers to promote programs offered throughout the year. Enter receipts into online system; receive, record, and reconcile payments.

Key Accomplishments:

- Developed an Access database for fleet vehicle requests and reminders. As a result, employees had access to vehicles in a timely manner, vehicles were rotated evenly, and reports on usage were accurate and readily accessible.
- Established an Excel spreadsheet to track personal assistant services for clients, leading to improved accountability and greater control over client resource use.
- Created an Excel spreadsheet for clients who receive funding, documenting the application for, approval of, and disbursement of allotments.

Columbia College Career Center   2005–2009
Administrative Assistant
Managed all office budgets, including supply inventory, student worker payroll, and equipment purchases. Coordinated appointments and program requests for full-time staff from faculty, campus organizations, and students. Compiled complex annual statistics of service usage. Led planning for two career expos every year, coordinating the employers, students, facilities, and equipment to ensure event success.

Key Accomplishments:

- Saved time and increased accuracy by initiating new administrative processes, including an Access database to analyze Center usage and an Excel spreadsheet to view budget information.
- Served on the Columbia College Staff Council as a member of the University & Community Relations Committee; co-initiated the "Head to Toe: Keeping Local Kids Warm" campaign.
- Maintained donation records for United Way campaigns in 2005 and 2006; outstanding record-keeping and follow-through helped University reach 111% of goal in 2006 and 102% of goal in 2007.

EDUCATION

Moberly Area Community College – **Associate of Arts**

KEY POINTS: Detailed skills list • Multiple bullet points documenting initiative, efficiency, and results

Submitted by Lesa Kerlin

Sarah Johnsmerry · *586-331-4212* · *Sajohmer@aol.com*

Executive Administrative Assistant / Executive Secretary
People | Critical Thinking | Results

An energetic professional with more than 10 years of progressive, administrative service and experience building relationships, streamlining processes, managing complex schedules, developing and reviewing business correspondence, overseeing inventory, conducting research, handling expense reports, and supervising employees. Maintain integrity of confidential documents and communications. Appointed to interview candidates for the Assistant Director Position.

Expertise in:

- Interacting with and supporting senior-level leaders in diverse capacities.
- Organizing conferences and planning large-scale events.
- Multi-tasking and prioritizing multiple projects to ensure timely completion.
- Processing intricate travel arrangements and timely reimbursements.
- Delivering dynamic presentations.

TECHNOLOGY SKILLS SUMMARY

Microsoft Office Suite:	Google Calendar	MS Publisher
Word, Excel, Access, Outlook	Meeting Maker	QuickBooks
Word Processing: 80 wpm	PeopleSoft	Adobe Acrobat

PROFESSIONAL EXPERIENCE

Executive Administrative Specialist 2009–Present
University of Michigan, Ann Arbor, MI

Hand-picked by the Director of Academics to serve in current position. Support three senior-level leaders with yearly budget setup, automated donor management system, and oversee stewardship reporting.

- Automated Donor Management System to track donor status, critical contributions, and involvement in university's activities—providing a quick review for leaders.
- Designed a formatted event sheet that outlined required fields, reduced errors, and ensured flawless execution—eliminating director involvement.
- Conducted one-on-one chats with each director to understand their budgetary needs, documented applicable concerns, and ensured timely reimbursements—reducing processing time by 19 days.

Executive Office Administrative Assistant 2007–2009
Wayne State, Detroit, MI

Provided dual administrative support to the Vice Chair of Education and Director of the Residency Program. Supervised three employees on administrative tasks.

- Coordinated, managed, and executed error-free calendar events for two senior-level leaders.
- Championed process to eliminate congestion and ensure parking ease for pediatric and medical staff.
- Singlehandedly designed a strategy to plan and execute medicine conferences.

CONTINUED

Submitted by Renee Green

Sarah Johnsmerry · *586-331-4212*

PROFESSIONAL EXPERIENCE, CONTINUED

Accountant   2007–2008
Urban Partnership and Community Program, Detroit, MI

Recorded entries in QuickBooks, processed accounts receivable, and reconciled bank statements. Supported director by organizing program budgets and financial reports for the executive director, board of directors, and funding agencies. **Key competencies:** *Effective communication, risk taking, critical thinking.*

Residency Assistant   2006–2007
RHSC, Inc., Health Partners Family, Detroit, MI

Resolved concerns between internal residency and external rotation staff. Controlled department expenses for residents, tracked curriculum calendar, and scheduled medicine deliveries. **Key competencies:** *Proficiency in technology, listening, attention to detail, interpersonal skills.*

Administrative Assistant   2005–2006
Chase Bank, Detroit, MI

Processed applications, organized verbal background investigations, requested documents, and shipped files throughout the United States. **Key Competencies:** *Ability to work independently or in a team.*

Customer Service Representative   2003–2005
Spherion Temporary Agency, Detroit, MI

Assisted customers with their orders and resolved any concerns that arose. **Key competencies:** *Problem solving, interpersonal skills, patience, effective communication.*

Education Assistant   2002–2003
Detroit Public School District, Detroit, MI

Instructed students in Microsoft Office, graded assignments, and helped with special educational needs. **Key competencies:** *Critical thinking, patience, attention to detail, effective communication, problem solving.*

Data Communication Intern   2001–2002
University of Phoenix, Detroit, MI

Installed and upgraded software and hardware components for desktops and laptop workstations, performed basic lab maintenance and repairs, and operated help desk to assist clients with computer concerns. **Key competencies:** *Proficiency in technology, problem solving, time management, attention to detail.*

EDUCATION & PROFESSIONAL DEVELOPMENT
- BS, Management Information Systems, University of Phoenix, Detroit, MI, 2010 • GPA 3.5
- Talent Development Workshop, Wayne State, Detroit, MI, 2011
- Certificate in Leadership Development, Wayne State, Detroit, MI 2010

KEY POINTS: Bullets highlighting initiative and contributions • "Key Competencies" for each job description on page 2

 JESSICA COLES

2555 Groveland Circle ▪ Dover, DE 19905 ▪ jessicacoles2555@email.com ▪ 302-555-7898

OFFICE MANAGEMENT / EXECUTIVE SUPPORT

Create and support administrative processes that integrate technology, enhance workflow, and control expenses, optimizing office operations and customer service.

Meeting & Webinar Planning ▪ Workflow Management ▪ New Branch Startups ▪ Project Management
Scheduling & Calendar Maintenance ▪ Expense Management ▪ Staff Training & Development ▪ Customer Relations

TECHNICAL PROFILE: MS Word ▪ Excel ▪ PowerPoint ▪ Outlook ▪ Publisher
Dreamweaver ▪ QuickBooks

PROFESSIONAL EXPERIENCE

NEWTON LAND DEVELOPMENT, INC., Dover, DE   2006–present
Premier commercial developer specializing in riverfront revitalization projects throughout Delaware.

OFFICE MANAGER
Recruited to coordinate and manage startup of 5,000-square-foot branch office. Selected interior design layouts, scheduled phone and computer installations, and set up all administrative processes to comply with corporate guidelines. Hired and trained 4 customer service specialists and 2 administrative assistants, managing payroll and healthcare benefits. Oversee all administrative details for branch director and 3 consultants. Prepare contracts, organize meetings and travel, and maintain master calendars and project timelines.

- Reduced interrupted workflow caused by employee absences and vacations by instituting a staff partner system and cross-functional training.
- Identified and implemented paperless systems that were adopted by corporate. Decreased annual paper expense 25% and technically overhauled the organization of files and resource materials, providing employees easy access to branch data and company-wide information.
- Maintained 100% staff retention rate since 2007.
- Presented with letters of commendation by 2 key clients for service excellence and for addressing a challenging situation with favorable outcomes.

TIPTON TRANSPORTATION, INC., Atlanta, GA   2001–2005
Privately owned trucking company providing national freight services since 1980.

ADMINISTRATIVE TEAM LEADER (2003–2005)
Promoted to supervise 6 administrative clerks in the traffic analysis department. Created detailed spreadsheets, charts, and reports to monitor revenues, shipments, and fuel surcharges. Set up pricing schedules and automatic billing for new and existing clients.

- Planned company-wide transition of new technical information system. Collaborated with the IT department in creating a reference manual and formal training program for 3 departments.
- Overhauled administrative processes to enhance productivity and customer service.
  - Cut employee overtime 15%.
  - Established in-house document scanning to reduce storage costs and retrieval time.
  - Improved clerk accountability by instituting tracking system to monitor and manage performance.

GENERAL ASSISTANT (2001–2002)
Supported the executive administrator in scheduling appointments, developing sales presentations, and generating daily financial reports for company president.

EDUCATION

TYLER SCHOOL OF BUSINESS, Atlanta, GA   **Certification–Accounting Technologies** (2005)
                                               Certification–Business Systems (2002)

KEY POINTS: Eye-catching design • Quick-skim summary and skills list • Strong bullets with specific achievements

Submitted by Anne Kern

SAMANTHA L. PORTER

1600 Barnett Road, Bronxville, NY 10708
914.665.5555   sporter@gmail.com

PARALEGAL

Sharp, experienced paralegal with outstanding record of results. Reputation as highly responsive and effective "go-to" person for major clients, often handling challenging and complex situations. Valuable combination of big-picture perspective and ability to manage all details. Quickly learn new content. Independently deliver beyond expectations.

**Legal Knowledge • Research • Writing/Drafting • Client Relationship Building
Project Management • Accounting • Communication • Negotiation**

EXPERIENCE

Darren & Howard, LLP, New Rochelle, NY
PARALEGAL II, 2003–Present
PARALEGAL I, 1997–2003

Work with and report directly to well-known firm partner, handling and prioritizing diverse responsibilities for ~20 clients simultaneously (representing ~$10,000 in monthly billings). Draft pleadings and prepare, process, organize, and track all documents for litigation. Research issues and cases and conduct fact-checking. Efficiently manage all work within tight timelines.

- Serve as key point of client contact for all of partner's cases; established and sustained relationships with all major clients and with contacts in Attorney General's office.
- Consistently tapped to handle special projects and assignments, often requiring high levels of confidentiality, diplomacy, and client responsiveness.
- Coordinated successful major arbitration (won on all 5 points), including preparing documentation, arranging hearings, and handling all process steps.
- Planned and managed key symposia (150+ attendees) for NY Bar Association, including all arrangements and speakers; generated major visibility and goodwill for firm and partner.
- Steered highly complex, 1.5-year application process for client. Prepared applications, supporting documents, and ongoing responses to state agency questions.
- Managed and sold 3 of client's properties in down market.
- Led multiple pro bono assignments to successful conclusion for clients.

EDUCATION

PARALEGAL CERTIFICATE, Westchester College—graduated 4th in class
HOMESTEAD UNIVERSITY—2.5 years completed toward BA in English and Psychology

KEY POINTS: Concise 1-page resume describing just 1 professional job • Detailed bullet points

Submitted by Cathy Alfandre

GRACE HEBERT, SPHR

4793 Peachtree Drive ◊ Atlanta, GA 30303
Cell: 404.856.5765 ◊ gracehebert@sbcglobal.net

HUMAN RESOURCES DIRECTOR

High-energy leader who builds trust at all levels and possesses outstanding ability to assess and mitigate risk to the organization. Proven problem solver with innate skills in influencing leaders to consider alternative solutions to pressing challenges. Track record of developing a culture of learning at all levels of the organization. Extensive experience in both union and non-union environments in the service and manufacturing industries.

PROFESSIONAL EXPERIENCE

National Foodservice, Inc.   2003–Present
Second-largest food distributor in the U.S., with 25,000 employees.

Regional Human Resources Business Partner, Southeastern U.S. (2011–Present)
Collaborate with local HR teams on recruiting, employee relations, and policy development/enforcement for 1,800+ employees. Work with senior executives on leadership development and strategic planning.

Executive Coaching:
- →Conducted a full talent assessment of all leaders within first 90 days; also collaborated with leaders to develop training, coaching, and experience-building plans for high-potential employees.
- →Coached and provided tools to a VP regarding a new director who was not meeting expectations.
- →Worked through potential ADA issue so that employee was able to reach acceptable performance levels.
- →Guided a VP in reorganizing his operations department to upgrade the talent of the supervisors.

HR Leadership:
- →Played a key role in creating the Human Resources Business Partner Group, which transformed the HR structure from decentralized and transaction-focused to shared services.

Divisional Director of Human Resources (2007–2011)
Promoted to one of the largest facilities in the company, with 600+ employees including 350+ unionized warehouse and transportation employees, 175+ outside sales force, and administrative support personnel. Maintained relationships with five unions. Selected to be a regional diversity trainer.

Company-Wide Leadership:
- →Launched an affinity group, Women in Foodservice – GA, that helped retain women in the company and developed them personally and professionally. Developed a mission statement and purpose, gained the full support of the leadership team, generated interest in participating, and managed the group.
- →Launched a Go Green Team and attained Green Certification for the company. Recruited team members and led a cross-department group on a variety of projects.
- →Recipient of company values award two consecutive years.

HR Leadership:
- →Implemented a new leave policy, changing a long-standing practice to manage absences more effectively and remove the burden of tracking from managers.
- →Reduced worker compensation reserves by $1.5M in one year, resulting in a financial pick-up of $350K, through a combination of safety initiatives and more rapid claims resolution.
- →Revamped recruiting process from a paper focus to a focus on strategic partnerships.
- →Partnered with sales VP to change his approach to the recruiting process to source a more qualified and diverse pool of new hires, resulting in increased sales and improved market share.
- →Passed OFCCP audit and obtained a summary ruling on FMLA case.

Union Relations:
- →Negotiated to achieve long-term wins including breaking and creating practices during non-negotiation years to set up for the next negotiation year.
- →Reduced number of clerical titles and classifications and blurred delineation of tasks despite union resistance. Achieved greater efficiency, opportunities for cross training, and workforce reduction.

Continued

Submitted by Lesa Kerlin

District Human Resources Manager (2003–2007)
Recruited for #2 role in 350+-employee location with strong union background. Oversaw non-union meat and produce processing/manufacturing facility.

➢→ Recruited an average of 10 warehouse hires monthly until turnover decreased. Collaborated with operations management to improve training program through feedback from new hires.
➢→ Implemented an innovative return-to-work program for injured employees who would otherwise be de-motivated by performing light-duty tasks. Employee work time was donated to a local non-profit to assist with developmentally disabled adults.

Cannon Mills Cabinets   1999–2003
Family-owned kitchen cabinet manufacturer, supplying home improvement centers such as Lowe's.

Corporate Human Resources Director, Atlanta, GA
As HR leader for 500-associate operations in three states, managed entire spectrum of HR, including policy development, benefits negotiations, employee relations, and recruitment. Seven direct reports.

➢→ Won a formal union campaign, which allowed the newest and largest facility to operate non-union.
➢→ Developed and introduced a compensation and promotion program for manufacturing-line positions based on market research data. Increased the company's ability to recruit and retain top talent.
➢→ Initiated and managed a training-grant program that included management development and personal skills for hourly workers.
➢→ Promoted from **HR Associate** to **HR Manager** to **Director** in four years.

EDUCATION_____

University of Minnesota – Minneapolis   1996
Bachelor of Science in Management & Finance

PROFESSIONAL DEVELOPMENT_____

Senior Professional in Human Resources (SPHR)
Taught SPHR/PHR prep course at Georgia State University (2006)

Certified Labor Relations Professional (CLRP)

Development Dimensions International Certified Trainer

PROFESSIONAL ORGANIZATIONS_____

Society for Human Resource Management (SHRM)

Women's Foodservice Forum

COMPUTER SKILLS_____

Microsoft Office Suite ◊ Excel (including pivot tables, v-lookup) ◊ PeopleSoft ◊ Taleo

KEY POINTS: Concise summary • Subheadings to break up lists and highlight areas of expertise •Colored rules and box

Laura Vogel

941-421-4120   2838 Mayflower * North Port, FL 34286   laura70@gmail.com

Sales Professional

*Self-Motivated * Personable * Excellent Listener * Relationship Builder * Strong Work Ethic*

More than 20 years of experience driving revenue growth and profitability in product and service industries. Demonstrated skills in territory development and management, high-level presentations, and new business development. Proficiency and persistence in all stages of the sales cycle combined with a strong closing ratio. Proven success in customer needs assessment and relationship building.

Skilled in MS Office Suite (Word, Excel, Outlook), accounting software, web-based applications

Professional Experience

Outside Sales Professional   2010 to Present
Quality Water Services, North Port, FL

Travel throughout Port Charlotte and surrounding area to sell and/or rent water softener systems and reverse osmosis machines to residential and commercial customers through cold-call sales and consultative selling techniques. Manage territory, customer sales, estimates, purchase orders, contracts, relationships, and customer service.

- Doubled size of sales territory in less than 2 years, adding at least 6 new accounts weekly.

Independent Agent (Part-time)   2009 to Present
Colonial Life & Accident, North Port, FL

Contracted through agency to travel throughout Florida to sell supplemental employee benefits to businesses — short-term disability, accident, cancer, medical bridge life insurance, term/whole life, and university life insurance.

- Delivered effective presentations to business owners and key personnel.
- Received the T390 Award for opening 10 new accounts in excess of $60,000 in annual premiums within the first 3 months of employment.

Financial Advisor   2004 to 2009
Edward D. Jones & Company, North Port, FL

Set up and managed satellite office to service existing and new clients on financial products that included CDs, mutual funds, stocks, and bonds.

- Developed marketing strategies to enhance a strong customer base through print media advertising, cold-calling, and referrals.
- Earned Newcomer Award for fastest growth in the state in first 6 months in business.

Prior: Staff Accountant, *Parsons, Thompson, Shimmer & Johnson*, Orlando, FL, 2002 to 2004; Route Driver, *Frito-Lay*, Gillette, WY, 2000 to 2002.

Education

BA in Business Administration & Accounting, Gillette College, Gillette, WY, 2002

KEY POINTS: Under headline, listing of key traits that point to success in sales • Concise job descriptions and specific achievements

Submitted by Roxie Herrman

PAOLO GARCIA

212-55 212Street • Queens Village, NY 11428 • H: 718-577-6595 • C: 917-362-6979 • paologarcia@gmail.com

B2B / B2C / B2G BUSINESS DEVELOPMENT & SALES PROFESSIONAL

- SALES — Success capturing new market share, accelerating revenues, and building customer loyalty.
- OPERATIONS — Ability to streamline protocols and workflow to improve account management processes.
- LEADERSHIP — Adeptness in in-sourcing, managing, and motivating teams of top sales performers.
- EXPERTISE

Corporate & Government RFQs	Sales Tracking & Reporting
Business Process Optimization	Business/Pipeline Development
Account Management	Contract Negotiations

Fluent in Spanish, French, and Italian

PROFESSIONAL EXPERIENCE

SALES MANAGER, CORPORATE & GOVERNMENT SALES, INDUSTRY SURPLUS, INC., NEW YORK, NY   2007 TO 2012

Oversee Northeast and Midwest territory for leading provider of private-label and brand-name industrial equipment and supplies. Revenues: $100M; Staff: 26 account managers for corporate, government, and reseller accounts.

- Exceeded sales goals by 30%+ for 3 consecutive years while decreasing budget. Increased revenues 30% to 40% annually despite a challenging and volatile economy.
- In just 2 years, grew government account penetration 100% by expanding pipeline of federal contracts and bidding on local government agency contracts.
- Accelerated bid opportunities significantly by registering company with various state procurement departments and sourcing dozens of additional databases and websites for capturing new business opportunities.
- Streamlined operations and improved account management processes by redistributing accounts/territories.
- Implemented company's first monthly reviews for entire staff; set performance goals, quotas, and objectives and reviewed performance against those goals to manage expectations and motivate staff.

SALES MANAGER & CONTRACTS MANAGER, CONSOLIDATED EQUIPMENT CORP., NEW YORK, NY   2005 TO 2007

Managed up to $4M in revenue and staff of sales professionals, engineers, and mechanics.

- Increased account penetration 40% by researching bid opportunities on government websites.
- Captured $100K in new revenue in 2 years by leveraging bid opportunities with Federal Bid Reversal auctions.

FINANCIAL ADVISOR, SMITH INVESTMENTS, NEW YORK, NY   1996 TO 2005

Managed $17.5M in assets and 145 portfolios for high-net-worth individuals. Sourced clients through referrals, networking, cold calling, and investment seminars.

- Built client base from zero to 145 in 3 years, grew investor portfolio 14% annually for 7 years, and retained more than 90% of client base during tenure.
- Led investment seminars to garner $500K in new business; generated 75% of sales from referral business.

STORE MANAGER, MILLER HOUSEWARES, NEW YORK, NY   1992 TO 1996

Oversaw a 1,500-square-foot, $6M high-end housewares store. Managed staff of 12.

EDUCATION

Bachelor of Arts, Business Administration, SUNY Buffalo, Buffalo, NY

KEY POINTS: One- and two-line paragraphs and bullets • Emphasis on numbers and percentages

Submitted by Barbara Safani

JOHN SMITH

jsmith@aol.com ◆ (916) 555-1212

SENIOR ACCOUNT EXECUTIVE

BUSINESS DEVELOPMENT – CLIENT MANAGEMENT – SERVICE DELIVERY
EXPANDING MARKETS – INCREASING PROFITS – RETAINING CLIENTS

Creating business opportunities in undiscovered markets

Dynamic corporate contributor with a record of delivering year-over-year profit increases in a challenging economy. Natural networker who leverages extensive regional and national connections to gain access to key decision makers. Trusted advisor to industry-leading corporate executives on the development and launch of services and products.

A desire to excel that fuels self-directed study and continued development of expertise in **marketing**, **consulting**, and **organizational change**.

STRENGTHS

✓ Consultative Sales
✓ Revenue & Profit Growth
✓ Market Share Increases

✓ Team Leadership
✓ Trust-Based Partnerships
✓ Loyal Client Relationships

PROFESSIONAL EXPERIENCE

J&J, Manteca, CA

1998–Present
1993–1996

Recruited by one of the original owners of J&J to lead an innovative multi-company regional marketing project. Returned to accept a service delivery position and then promoted to management position. Key contributor to seamless transition of business to International Human Resource Solutions.

Recently promoted to manage all Northern California accounts and supervise daily sales for Manteca and Fresno offices.

Account Manager/Business Development (2001–Present)
Sell complex organizational staffing solutions, including Top-Performance Coaching, Succession Planning, Team Building, Change Management, and Coaching Practices for Leaders. Deliver company-leading sales, revenue, and margins.

- Recorded regional profit of $862K on revenue of $1.4M in 2011, surpassing all other offices serving regions with the same number of employers.
- Outperformed competitors to secure #1 provider ranking in region.
- Built office's regional reputation as the leader in human resource management through executive-focused events and presentations.
- Cultivated Central California book of business that includes eight of the ten largest employers headquartered in the Greater Fresno Metropolitan area.
- **Recipient "Best Individual Contributor in J&J Northwest Region" award.**

PAGE 1 OF 2

Submitted by Lorraine Beaman

Adjunct Consultant/Trainer (1998–2001)
Delivered career transition products, training, and consulting services.
- Coached supervisors and executives on ethical methods for terminating employees and managing and motivating remaining workforce.
- Credited with giving recently terminated clients the confidence and skills they needed to conduct a job search; rated as one of J&J's top trainers.
- Secured continued business with on-time delivery of excellent services and consistent follow-up.

Director, First Stop Career Center (1993–1996)
Simultaneously marketed and managed sales of two innovative business concepts developed by Steve Jones, President of J&J, and the executive team of First Stop, a regional outplacement agency.
- Secured regional recognition of J&J within six months and met all sales goals.
- Transitioned First Stop Career Center to a full service J&J office.

UNITED AGRICULTURE, Manteca, CA   1996–1998
Manager, Corporate Training and Development
Designed and delivered training in response to departmental requirements. Managed a team of five Training Specialists and supervised a staff of 35.
- Established processes and operational procedures for department.
- Set up onsite GED and college programs for employees.
- Created and launched career management program that fostered recruitment and retention.

PROFESSIONAL MEMBERSHIPS

SHRM (Society of Human Resources Management)
Manteca Area Human Resources Association – Board Member (2005)
Manteca Organizational Development Network

CERTIFICATIONS

ZENGER-MILLER
Certified Presenter

J&J
Executive Leadership – Management Notification – Career Decision Making – Resiliency

LANGUAGES

Fluent in English and Portuguese
Conversant in Spanish

KEY POINTS: Headline and subheadings that quickly establish "who" candidate is • Numbers and results in bullets

CRAIG RICHMOND

231 Pacific Avenue, Milpitas, CA 95035 • 408.445.1111 • crichmond@yahoo.com
http://www.linkedin.com/in/craigrichmond

TECHNOLOGY SALES & BUSINESS DEVELOPMENT LEADER

**Account Growth · Strategic Partnerships · Community Building
Operations · Project Management · Team Leadership**

Tenacious business builder who grows revenues and customer relationships. Recent accomplishments include $1+ million contracts with MTech and Acme. Innate ability to grasp customer needs and craft critical, integrated solutions. Key experience in forging partnerships and developing communities.

Professional Activity

Blog: highpower.blogspot.com • Twitter: HighPower

Actively participate in industry events: Sifma, PAW, OSCON, JSM

Organize and attend monthly nationwide meetups of groups such as
ASA, Predictive Analytics, Machine Learning, Hadoop, Data Visualization

Experience

HIGH POWER COMPUTING, INC., Milpitas, CA   **2010–Present**
Startup provider of high-performance computing and analytics consulting for large-scale deployments.
Director, Sales & Business Development
Drive business and community development, customer relationships, and pursuit of venture capital investments for new high-tech enterprise. Formed and manage flexible pool of talent to support customer projects.

➢→**Secured 3 ongoing contracts with Acme** (invoicing $1+ million so far); sustained and grew relationship through reorganizations and transition to new platforms.

➢→**Landed major new health care customer**—Major Hospital.

➢→**Developed key partnerships with MTech, ZSys, and MegaPC** to support their software implementations; deliver cloud implementations of HPC computing and analytics.

➢→**Rebuilt Greater LA user group and Predictive Analytics group in ~6 months,** converting them from inactive to vibrant groups with 500+ members each.

TRANSFORMATION SYSTEMS, INC., Santa Clara, CA   **2009–2010**
Provider of commercial support and capability enhancement (proprietary packages and consulting) for leading open source analytics software.
Senior Sales Executive
Led rapid sales growth that positioned start-up company for successful sale.

➢→**Instrumental in growing business from scratch to $30 million valuation** in 2 years.

➢→**Established key partnerships** with MTech, ABCyber, BigNameTech, ZSoft, Megaware, Big Pharma, and Acme.

➢→**Converted 2 partners (MTech, Acme) to customers;** deals valued at $1+ million.

Continued

Submitted by Cathy Alfandre

CRAIG RICHMOND · 408.445.1111 · crichmond@yahoo.com   Page 2

TRANSFORMATION SYSTEMS, INC., continued
> → **Served as Account Manager for Acme, representing 40% of revenues;** ultimately won enterprise-wide license (supplanting 27 products previously supported there).
> → **Helped create and sponsor first users group** and supported emerging groups (67 groups today with thousands of members worldwide).
> → Managed SEO and Internet ad campaign, and achieved status as 1 of top 10 analytics software sites.

SPECIAL CIRCUITS, INC., Milpitas, CA   **2004–2009**
High-end printed circuit board manufacturer, supplying leading automakers and cell phone industry;
$125 million–$130 million in annual sales and 1,200 employees at highest point.
Director of Sales
Provided steady leadership of the sales organization during periods of rapid growth and major decline in #1 customer base (auto industry).
> → **Secured 2 MajorAuto projects—$40+ million in business**—based on request from plants; rewarded for continuously meeting customers' needs in terms of delivery, quality, and flexibility.
> → **Grew sales from $1.8 million to $20 million** in annual revenues in less than 5 years.

Education

Cornell University—BS in Operations Research and Industrial Engineering

KEY POINTS: "Professional Activity" section highlights industry and social media activity • Bold type emphasizes results

Mark Deliantes
20 Dale Road, Lake Success, NY 11042 ▪ 516-799-6201 ▪ mdeliantes@gmail.com

District Sales Manager ~ *retail* ▪ *high traffic* ▪ *high volume* ▪ *multi-site environments*

Core Competencies	Value Offered
◆ Retail Sales & Operations ◆ Product Marketing/Sales ◆ Net Operating Income (NOI) ◆ Customer Service ◆ Talent Sourcing & Recruiting ◆ Performance Management ◆ Succession Planning	◆ Year-over-year success managing retail sales operations and exceeding all targets for net operating income, profit margin, and commissions. ◆ Consistently ranked as a company-wide top performer, even under volatile economic and industry conditions. ◆ Extensive experience hiring, managing, and developing sales and support professionals in multiple offices across a geographic territory. ◆ Ability to streamline operations to optimize staff and resources and cut costs without compromising product standards or customer service.

Professional Experience

LINCOLN OFFICE SUPPLIES, New York, NY 1990 to 2012
Held several managerial positions with progressive responsibility for this leading office supply chain with 200 stores.

DISTRICT SALES MANAGER, NEW YORK, 2010 to 2012
Promoted to the most prestigious and most challenging district in the company based on past performance.

◆ Trimmed average store headcount by 17% in 2 years without sacrificing quality. Increased profits by cross-training staff, preparing succession plans, and replacing poor performers.

DISTRICT SALES MANAGER, NEW ENGLAND, 1998 to 2010
At peak, managed $83.3M in business, 125 employees, and 20 stores in New York, Connecticut, and Massachusetts. Attained profit margin of 12.22% and $10.2M in commissions.

◆ Achieved a 3.5% revenue increase between 2008 and 2009 when all 11 other district managers achieved zero gains.

◆ First district sales manager in company's history to receive a performance bonus.

◆ One of only 2 district managers out of 12 to achieve revenue gains in 2001 despite industry volatility.

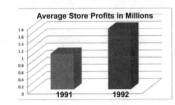

Head Count (chart: 2007, 2009)

#1 in revenue gains, 2006
One of top revenue performers, 2009
Sole district manager to ever achieve bonus
Youngest manager in company's history

MANAGER, 1992 to 1998

◆ Selected by senior management to oversee one of the company's ten largest stores.

◆ Improved store average profits by 70% and propelled store ranking to #3 in the company in just 2 years.

MANAGER, 1991 to 1992

◆ Grew business by 50% within first year in a management role.

Average Store Profits in Millions (chart: 1991, 1992)

SALES ASSOCIATE, 1990 to 1991

◆ Recruited for the company's fast-track program in the #1 most profitable and highest volume store in the company.

Education

B.A., English, University of Vermont, Burlington, VT, 1988

KEY POINTS: "Value offered" spelled out in summary • Key results showcased in eye-catching graphs and shaded box

Submitted by Barbara Safani

HOWARD KLIPPENGER

843 Juniper Drive ▸▸ San Francisco, CA 94109 ▸▸ 415.609.2611 ▸▸ hklip@email.com

TECHNOLOGY SALES LEADER

Top sales performer with 15 years of award-winning experience selling technology solutions to Fortune 100 accounts. Overachiever who inspires loyalty, record sales, and operational excellence.

Earned 2 Microsoft Golden Circle and 2 Leadership Awards for exceptional sales management. Team performance includes 107% to 279% achievement against plan in 1997 to 2005 and up to triple-digit performance against plan from 2006 to 2012:

2006	2007	2008	2009	2010	2011	2012
235%	247%	168%	149%	23%	12%	38%

SALES LEADERSHIP COMPETENCIES

B2B Sales Management	Cloud Computing	Software-as-a-Service
Integrated Service Management	Business Process Management	Pipeline Maximization
Strategic Sales Planning	Leadership Development	Sales Training

SALES LEADERSHIP EXPERIENCE

Microsoft Corporation, San Francisco, CA   1996–Present
Director – Group Sales [2010–Present]
Lead group sales for small- to medium-sized businesses in North America with $52 million in revenue. Captured 42% software growth—34% greater than average.

▸ Pushed 2010 revenues 29% to $479 million, attaining 104% of plan with 29% YOY growth. Led software results for General Business Unit for 2 years in a row.
▸ Increased direct sales close rates to 31.6% and business partner close rates to 26.7% while growing partner pipeline 38%.
▸ Initiated sales best practices—pipeline quality, No Lead Left Behind, and deal clinics—that were later adopted division-wide. Reduced aged pipeline 47%.
▸ Propelled 24% jump in year-over-year user conference attendance through aggressive management of 764 leads from > 600 global companies. Created $371 million in opportunities by driving 1,463 global customers to this high-profile event.

Software Business Executive | Mid-Atlantic Region [2006–2010]
Ensured Mid-Atlantic region success with oversight of sales, pre-sales technical, and marketing for 5 prestigious brands. Led negotiations on large deals and competitive wins, including Labcorp, Lowes, Advance America, and SEI.

▸ Produced 3 consecutive years of YOY sales growth, achieving up to 10% increase in a declining market.
▸ Bolstered gross profits, discounting 39% less than other NA business units and 15% less than peers.
▸ Generated $250 million in new orders through introduction of *Forging your Destiny* program via 2 self-funded sales contests. Program boosted revenue conversion.

Sales Executive [2004–2006]
Aligned solutions with market, sector, channel, client, and services needs within the largest region in the world. Oversaw 100 indirect personnel. Tapped for executive succession planning program and the Delta Community, a group of Top 100 global leaders.

▸ Achieved 235% and 147% of quotas for 2 consecutive years—the highest production of software brands worldwide—and recognized with the *Golden Global Circle Award*.

Continued

Submitted by Cheryl Simpson

EARLY CAREER PROFILE

TEC SYSTEMS ▸▸ **Northeastern District Manager | Senior Account Manager**
BROWARD TECHNOLOGY ▸▸ **Sales Representative**
DELL ▸▸ **Sales Representative**

Rose through the volunteer firefighter ranks with the State of New Jersey, serving in 7 progressively responsible leadership roles.

EDUCATION, CERTIFICATION & PROFESSIONAL DEVELOPMENT

BOSTON COLLEGE ▸▸ **BS with Double Majors in Marketing & Management**

Software Top Gun Certification ▪ Motivation: Enhancing Employee Performance ▪ Building 1000 High Performance Teams ▪ K & R Negotiations ▪ Leading a Winning Sales Team ▪ Negotiation Skills ▪ Signature Selling Methodology

Complete professional development list available upon request

KEY POINTS: Sharp design in black, red, and gray • Table that illustrates consistently strong sales performance

KARA L. BARNES

80 SMITH PLACE ▪ THOUSAND OAKS, CA 91319 ▪ 213-468-1288 ▪ KARA.L.BARNES@YAHOO.COM

PRODUCT MARKETING PROFESSIONAL with experience analyzing/managing customer experience, communicating sensitive messaging, and developing programs to accelerate customer base, retention, and loyalty. Expertise in:

- New Product Communications
- Customer Experience/On-Boarding
- Product/Customer Service Scripting
- Regulatory Messaging
- Quality Assurance Management
- Direct Mail Marketing Campaigns
- Automated Customer Messaging
- Website/Landing Page Messaging
- Social Media Marketing
- Focus Groups/Trials/Survey
- Market Research/Analysis
- Affinity Marketing Programs

PROFESSIONAL EXPERIENCE

CABLE COMMUNICATIONS, Los Angeles, CA   2005 TO PRESENT
CUSTOMER EXPERIENCE MARKETING SPECIALIST, 2009 TO PRESENT
Program-manage customer experience/CRM initiatives and oversee work of external marketing agencies.

- **MARKET SHARE GROWTH:** Realized $100M revenue increase and $22M content cost savings by creating marketing strategy and messaging to introduce a sensitive company-mandated Cable Repackaging program.
- **PRODUCT MESSAGING:** Crafted messaging detailing on-boarding and service changes and successfully delivered 100% of programs under churn forecast and without increasing customer inquiry call volume.
- **MARKETING COLLATERAL:** Developed and executed product collateral and customer awareness campaigns and tracked messaging campaign ROI.
- **PRODUCT MANAGEMENT:** Created and managed new customer online portal and product education site.
- **MARKETING EFFICIENCIES:** Trimmed $2.5M from operational costs by negotiating with regulators to allow company to transition from print-centric service messaging to electronic messaging.
- **CUSTOMER COMMUNICATIONS:** Introduced a customer service "playbook" that systematized protocols for routine customer inquiries and processes, reduced redundancies, and expedited customer response time.

> **DECREASED:**
> CUSTOMER CHURN
> OPERATING EXPENSES
> CONTENT COSTS
> **INCREASED:**
> PROFITS/MARKET SHARE
> CUSTOMER AWARENESS/CONFIDENCE
> **IMPROVED:**
> CUSTOMER ON-BOARDING
> COMMUNICATIONS PROCESSES
> PRODUCT LINE PROFITABILITY

MARKET RESEARCH SPECIALIST, 2007 TO 2009
Managed market research trial programs and focus groups; developed insight surveys and analyzed results.

- **PRODUCT SCRIPTING:** Created customer service product scripting and acted as product subject matter expert for customer experience team. Advised on scripting, product fulfillment, and customer inquiry escalation procedures.
- **PRODUCT TRIALS:** Restructured product trials program, instituting standard operating procedures that were quickly adopted as best practices company-wide.

MARKETING DEVELOPMENT ROTATION PROGRAM, 2005 TO 2007

> RECRUITED DIRECTLY FROM COLLEGE FOR ONE OF 12 SPOTS IN THIS HIGHLY COMPETITIVE MARKETING TRAINING PROGRAM.

Worked on competitive analysis, market strategy, and sales support projects.

- **PRODUCT LAUNCH:** Team lead/SME for *TV on Demand* product launch.
- **AFFINITY MARKETING:** Project-managed nonprofit affinity marketing program that delivered $10M in payments to charities in first year.
- **SALES TRAINING:** Developed and implemented training materials for 300+ sales representatives that improved monthly sales and service metrics 3%–5%.

EDUCATION

B.S., MARKETING, University of California, Los Angeles, CA, 2005

KEY POINTS: Bold, dark blue boxes that call notable accomplishments • Keyword introductions to each bullet point

Submitted by Barbara Safani

Kate Michaels
MARKETING DIRECTOR

100 Parkway Road, 4E ♦ Los Angeles, CA 90001
213.848.3346
katemichaels@yahoo.com
www.linkedin.com/in/katemichaels

Broad and deep integrated marketing expertise, using unparalleled creative ability to build brand awareness, generate measurable increases in market share, drive sales, and catapult profitability. Outstanding market research skills, uncovering market voids, gathering competitive intelligence, developing customized programs, and assessing ROI. Fearless in tackling the most challenging projects, with consistently successful outcomes.

Proven track record of coordinating highly successful cross-functional teams for product launches, collaborating with designers and outside vendors to create synergy, excitement, and superior results.

PROFESSIONAL EXPERIENCE

Smith-Jones Business Services (A Canon Group), Los Angeles, CA   2008–Present
A global document and information management services company with more than 1,250 client sites worldwide, 7,000 employees, and revenues of $280M.

Product Marketing Manager—Create scanning and imaging solutions by conducting research and analyzing data to uncover market voids; determine market projections and market-share potential. Establish pricing; develop product-launch sales kits and deliver national training for 100-person sales team. Define products and write technical requirements and specifications.

Coordinate cross-functional teams to drive products to market, communicate value propositions, produce targeted collateral, and provide support throughout the development lifecycle. Manage staff of two.

Marketing:
- Produced industry "Playbooks" to serve as broad strategy and reference guides for selling to the company's core segments. Outlined the trends, business drivers, value proposition, and selling techniques for each primary solution offering.
- Wrote two winning **"Outsourcing Excellence Awards"** applications (out of 250 applicants).
- Played a key role in creating content, layout, and design for website re-launch.
- Started a LinkedIn group that allows employees to gather information; wrote discussions, managed the group, and recruited industry professionals to share their expertise.
- Presented at Association for Information and Image Management (AIIM) industry trade show.

Product Development:
- Developed new service offerings in scanning and imaging that have generated **in excess of $4M** in annual revenue and produced **25 qualified leads** for other solutions offerings.
- Brought to market and launched an electronic mail distribution solution that was purchased by a client, resulting in a **$1.5M cost savings** in the first year alone.

The Sales Group, Los Angeles, CA   1998–2008
A full-service, turnkey marketing agency that provides performance improvement programs to mid-size to Fortune 500 clients, including Coca-Cola, Samsung, and Trump National. Revenues of $10M.

Marketing Manager—Created marketing collateral, including brochures, direct mail campaigns, and ads, to deliver custom programs to clients. Conducted market analysis to understand competitive dynamics and trends and establish baselines around customer experience, positioning, and expectations. Determined which trade shows to attend, designed booth, and followed up with leads after the event. Provided ROI analysis for each program by presenting clients with cost-to-sales analysis. Identified new market opportunities. Managed team of three.

♦ Continued ♦

Submitted by Lesa Kerlin

The Sales Group Marketing Manager, *continued*

Marketing:
- Enticed senior executives to attend Duracell's "Power Council"—a summit on the features and benefits of Duracell batteries—through direct mail and telemarketing. Achieved a **106% increase** in attendance over the previous year. Managed all aspects of event logistics.
- Developed and marketed incentive programs by determining clients' goals and creating programs that would result in a compelling ROI. One program resulted in 32 new dealers to cover the client's product line and **increased sales by 26%;** another program resulted in an **18% sales gain** in a flat industry.
- Coordinated bi-annual seminars and corporate events to highlight incentive services. Managed site selection and all on-site logistics, budget management, and collateral development.

Cost Savings and Revenue Generation:
- Shifted the firm's outsourcing strategy, resulting in **$600K savings** annually.
- Created lead-generation initiatives that resulted in **$3M+** in annual revenue (30% of company's growth).

Nationwide Concepts, Inc., Los Angeles, CA   1996–1998
Integrated marketing services company focusing on tours, concerts, festivals, and in-store marketing events for clients such as Nabisco, Walmart, and Procter & Gamble. More than 80 employees; $78M in revenue.

Western Regional Marketing Director
Assistant Regional Marketing Director
Spearheaded in-store event promotions for national brands, including securing and training employees and negotiating with vendors. Collaborated with local area managers to create seamless planning, execution, and communication throughout the development and implementation stages. Tracked and reported on product movement on a store-by-store basis.

In-Store Promotions:
- Negotiated a lowered national labor rate on contracted employees, **saving the firm $200K** annually.
- Became a certified national trainer and product expert for DirecTV. Hired and thoroughly trained the best-fit candidates for in-store promotions.

Mass Cinema Theatres, Boston, MA   1995–1996
National chain of theatres owned by Pepsi.

Marketing Associate
Played key role in a public relations initiative to conduct presidential straw votes at all Mass Cinema Theatres. Developed point-of-purchase collateral and collected and analyzed results. Also conducted market research on customer preferences concerning branded consumer point-of-purchase material.

EDUCATION & TRAINING

University of California, Los Angeles   1995
Bachelor of Arts, Communications (Cum Laude)

ExecComm
Executive Presentations Skills Training

Six Sigma Certified

KEY POINTS: Boxed endorsement creates immediate interest • Keyword headings break up long bullet lists

---

KARLA SILVEIRA

40 West Street | Los Angeles, CA 90001
818.455.1001 | ksilveira@gmail.com

MARKETING LEADER
STRATEGY | BRAND MANAGEMENT | INNOVATION

Proven brand and business builder, from strategy through execution. Valued for creative leadership on complex, critical, and high-visibility projects. Translate consumer insight and competitive analysis to drive breakthrough marketing campaigns using traditional and emerging media. Manage, align, and motivate teams to deliver. Build relationships with customers, partners, and cross-functional colleagues.

**Product Launch | Strategic Partnerships | Digital Marketing | Multicultural Marketing
People Management | Agency Management | Relationship Building | Communication**

EXPERIENCE

BIG CONSUMER BRAND, INC. 2002–Present
NORTH AMERICA DIVISION, Los Angeles, CA
Director of Marketing, Brand1 – Consumer Engagement (9/11–Present)
Senior Brand Manager, Brand1 – System & Shopper Engagement (9/10–9/11)
Returned to brand role to drive new product launch and brand transformation. Subsequently promoted to lead $1.4 billion brand, including all traditional and digital consumer engagement, long-term strategy and annual operating plans, metrics/analytics, agency management, and customer relationships. Manage multimillion-dollar marketing budget and team of 3 direct reports.

- Reversed long-term business declines and restored growth within 4 months of brand repositioning.
- Directed multi-faceted campaign, including print, TV, radio, and social media; outperformed company benchmarks in ad testing and drove 4-fold increase in Facebook fans in 4 months.
- Delivered robust account-specific activation plans with Target and Walmart; both businesses are up double digits since launch, and Walmart has returned product to core displays.
- Initiated cutting-edge Hispanic marketing plan that included advertising, PR, and retail activation.
- Secured participation of 90+ partners through compelling business case presentations, communications, relationship building, and breakthrough launch planning.
- Selected for 10-person global team charged with developing complex global 2012 strategy.

FOODSERVICE DIVISION, Los Angeles, CA
Senior Innovation Manager (4/09–9/10)
Innovation Manager (1/08–4/09)
Selected by former manager for channel marketing opportunity: driving innovation for Big's largest foodservice customer, from ideation to commercialization. Developed and sustained key customer relationship. Later tapped to contribute to broader corporate innovation strategy.

- Exceeded volume plan by 25% and profit plan by 112%.
- Expanded role to serve as Marketing lead (only senior manager on director-level team) on major, cross-portfolio 5-year innovation and growth strategy; work continues to influence innovation agenda.
- Secured R&D resources; overcame significant complexities to deliver differentiated and consumer-validated proposition, while achieving cost parity to leading competitors.

Continued

Submitted by Cathy Alfandre

BIG DRINK DIVISION, INC., Houston, TX
Brand Manager, BigJuice (2/07–1/08)
Assistant Brand Manager, BigJuicePremium (1/06–2/07)
Launched 2 new product lines over 2 years. Managed all advertising and marketing partnerships. In Brand Manager role, steered multimillion-dollar marketing budget and held full P&L responsibility. Developed and led execution of annual operating plan.

- Championed consumer immersion project that transformed nebulous goals into specific strategy, with clear target market and super-premium product positioning.
- Crafted innovative marketing, media, and product pipeline plans to drive new strategy; achieved rapid results, including positive halo effect of new line on overall brand, new brand presence in produce section, and sales volume levels equal to top competitor.
- Led cross-functional project team that commercialized new product ahead of schedule; earned Growth Leader Award.
- Managed strategic partnership with ABCPartner; alliance quickly became key growth driver.
- Drove comprehensive analysis of Big Drink portfolio, including profitability and strategic fit, that led to 9% SKU reduction.

MEGA BEVERAGE DIVISION, Houston, TX
Assistant Marketing Manager, Mega Equity & Communications (2/05–1/06)
Assistant Marketing Manager, Mega New Products (12/03–2/05)
Marketing Associate (8/02–12/03)
Over 3+ years, steered series of critical, high-visibility initiatives, including new product launch, product and package innovations, and national promotions. Collaborated directly with company President and Chief Marketing Officer.

- Tapped to manage all aspects of 2 largest and most comprehensive national promotions for Mega; commercialized exclusive promotional flavor and second hit flavor in following year, greatly exceeding sales expectations.
- Directed launch of first formula innovation in 35 years on highly aggressive timeline (3 months); jumpstarted languishing initiative, overcame hurdles, and successfully preceded competitive entrant.
- Delivered new package innovations with significantly improved functionality and consumer liking; purchase interest increased 25% and preference over previous bottle was 92%.
- Managed $7 million in launch year marketing tactics, including massive 9-market sampling blitz, in-store programming, and promotions; proactively identified opportunities to improve program efficiency, saving $550,000.
- Received Mega award for outstanding performance in 3 consecutive years.

EDUCATION

NORTHWESTERN UNIVERSITY, Evanston, IL
Bachelor of Science in Economics; Concentrations in Marketing and Management

---

KEY POINTS: Format emphasizes steady promotions throughout career • Bullets are concise and keyword-rich

MATTHEW T. GEORGE

18 Appleton Avenue • Longmont, CO 80503 • 303.123.4567 • mattgeorge18@gmail.com

LOGISTICS MANAGER
Retail / Wholesale

Performance-driven, multitasked Logistics and Import professional providing hands-on leadership for global material movement and management. Expert in analyzing alternatives and implementing strategies and processes to achieve results. Outstanding manager with communication and collaborative skills that get the job done.

Accomplishments and experience in the areas of:

— Import Shipping & Receiving
— Production Operations
— Logistics & Traffic Management
— International Negotiations
— Quality Control Monitoring

— Delivery Scheduling & Expediting
— Customer Relationship Management
— Government Regulations
— Licensee Management
— Resource Allocation

> "Matthew is an extremely experienced professional who has excellent leadership qualities. A person of substance who possesses the highest character and integrity … has shown dedication, drive, and respect for others." CFO

PROFESSIONAL EXPERIENCE

ABC GROUP, INC., Denver, CO   1993–2012
(International retailer for women's & men's apparel, cosmetics, textiles, and accessories; 2500 stores, $342.5M revenues)

Director of Imports & Traffic, USA Division (2005–2012)
Import Manager (1993–2005)

Directed all production aspects in Far East and Europe. Interacted with suppliers, licensees, customs brokers, and traffic managers to ensure smooth movement of product and ingredients. Determined manufacturing and shipping priorities, adhering to aggressive deadlines. Negotiated transportation rates to lower freight costs. Accountable for costing merchandise to increase profit margins. Led staff of 5.

- Served as crucial U.S. Customs legal advisor for company.
- Established shipping controls between countries, reducing time between delivery dates while increasing revenues.
- Resolved major supplier error for key customer in < 24 hours, saving company $35K.
- Recognized as outstanding mentor, coach, and developer of people.

ABBOTT INTERNATIONAL, LTD, Los Angeles, CA   1990–1993
(Importer of men's apparel)

Import Manager

Provided overseas agents and suppliers with production requirements. Tracked orders from placement to final delivery, including drop shipments to client's distribution centers.

EDUCATION & CERTIFICATION

Business Careers Institute — Hampstead, NY
Certification — **U.S. Customs Trade Partnership Against Terrorism**

KEY POINTS: Detailed keyword list will match most job postings • Quote from executive shows third-party endorsement

Submitted by Jane Falter

DAVID WORRELL

1798 Jamison Court, Cleveland, OH 44663
(216) 598-8117 ▪ dworrell@hotmail.com

DIRECTOR OF OPERATIONS / LEAN SIX SIGMA MASTER BLACK BELT

Proactive, performance-driven Operations Professional with 15+ years of progressive experience in leadership and problem-solving for industrial manufacturing operations. Keen understanding of business priorities and genuine commitment to managing operations and projects flawlessly while contributing to revenue-producing activities.

Cross-functional communicator who easily interfaces with high-profile staff, vendors, and clients. Recognized for consistent success in developing the processes and procedures to streamline operations, increase revenues, and enhance profit performance. Able to see the big picture while staying on top of all the details.

Areas of Expertise

Business Analysis
Process Improvement
Executive Leadership
Change Management
Policy Development
Team Leadership
Strategic Planning
Training/Development
Expense Control
Needs Assessment

PROFESSIONAL EXPERIENCE

DCJO Service Company, Cleveland, OH (Wholly owned subsidiary of Praxair, Inc.)   2007–Present
Specializing in cryogenic trailer, mobile high-pressure and stationary tube rehabilitation including repair and testing.

NATIONAL OPERATIONS MANAGER, Cleveland, OH (2010–Present): Provide team leadership in high-level operational work, ensuring quality, productivity, and efficiency throughout all DCJO facilities. Lead in a collaborative, inclusive style, excelling at timely proactive communications with Plant Managers, Finance Managers, Regulatory Affairs Manager, Facilities Engineers, and other senior leaders. Hold full accountability for driving continuous productivity initiatives across all facilities.

- Fostered a culture of "Safety First," resulting in zero lost work days and zero recordable incidents since 2010.
- Conceived, drafted, and executed plan to rebuild core competencies by leveraging bench strength.
- Spearheaded pioneering efforts to improve customer satisfaction and retention ratings. Created critical KPIs to track and improve on-time delivery, customer issues, and safety statistics.

CONTINUOUS IMPROVEMENT MANAGER–LEAN, Columbus, OH (2008–2010): As Certified Lean Six Sigma Master Black Belt, served as Continuous Improvement Manager responsible for selecting, tracking, assigning, and overseeing productivity initiatives in Procurement, Just Do It (JDI), and Lean Six Sigma.

Mentored new Green Belts and provided guidance to optimize project completion. Devised and executed a plan to train key personnel across the organization covering Lean methodologies.

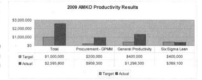

- Personally contributed efforts that led to an excess of $2.5M in productivity savings in 2009.
- Assumed responsibility as Interim Engineering Manager from January to October 2009 and managed a skilled team of 8 engineers, focusing primarily on advancing departmental goals.
- Led Quality Teams at each DCJO facility to eliminate obstacles to quality control and improve overall performance of operations, products, and components.

PLANT MANAGER, Columbus, OH (2008–2009): Managed all operational aspects of the plant and Field Services activities, including Production, Maintenance, Production Scheduling, Warehouse, Plant Support, Process Engineering, Safety, and Quality. Orchestrated plant activities with departmental managers and supervisors to ensure total manufacturing objectives were accomplished in a safe, ethical, and environmentally sound manner.

Continued

Submitted by Wanda Kiser

DAVID WORRELL   Mobile: (216) 598-8117 ▪ E-mail: dworrell@hotmail.com   *Page Two*

PLANT MANAGER *(Continued)*

- Directed the team that won "Overall Best Ratings for On-Time Delivery" among all DCJO facilities, scoring 84%.
- Successfully satisfied all requirements for Six Sigma Green Belt Certification Training.
- Profitably transformed an under-utilized cast into a group of high-potential, future leaders of the company.

Seven Rivers Inc., Cincinnati, OH   2005–2007
Production facility for draw rock shield used in the mining industry and for reconditioning of bulk industrial containers.

DIRECTOR OF OPERATIONS/Leland Manufacturing Division: Directed all aspects of strategic planning and execution to enhance profitability, productivity, and efficiency throughout the division. Ensured compliance and surpassed all regulatory standards with regards to the EPA and OSHA. Coached, mentored, and directed the production manager, traffic manager, and supervisors of press operations.

- Spearheaded an aggressive process-reengineering program that improved productivity, reduced costs, and maximized outputs and profits, increasing output 24%.
- Leveraged proactive management techniques to decrease downtime and improve safety by implementing preventive maintenance for heavy equipment.

Vision Packaging, Columbus, OH   1992–2005
A 150,000-square-foot production facility specializing in corrugated packaging and volume packing.

OPERATIONS MANAGER (2001–2005)
HUMAN RESOURCES MANAGER (1996–2000)
PRODUCTION SUPERVISOR (1992–1996): Earned continuous promotions based on demonstrated leadership and consistently outstanding performance. As Operations Manager, recommended changes when necessary and played a major role in implementation of new processes. Directed labeling, shipping/receiving, and maintenance operations and provided leadership to 6 production supervisors responsible for laborers on 4 assembly lines.

- Devised winning sales presentations utilizing multimedia demonstration techniques.
- Built positive customer relationships, resulting in increased customer satisfaction and customer referrals.
- Architected first-ever Safety Training and Management Program that reduced operations costs, resulting in years of injury-free operations and decreased Workers' Compensation costs.
- Designed a modified production schedule to include an extended 4-day, 10-hour shift. Mapped employees to roles that optimized performance and job satisfaction.

EDUCATION & CERTIFICATION

BSBA, Human Resources & Psychology, 2000
OHIO STATE UNIVERSITY, Columbus, OH

Certified Lean Six Sigma Master Black Belt
KENT STATE UNIVERSITY, Kent, OH

PROFESSIONAL AFFILIATIONS

Compressed Gas Association (CGA)
American Management Association (AMA)

KEY POINTS: Sharp design that highlights expertise (shaded box) and performance (colored graph) • Strong, specific bullets

Meredith K. Holland

2345 NW 151st Street, Vancouver, WA 98685
mholland@gmail.com • 360-294-2570
http://www.linkedin.com/in/meredithholland

SUMMARY

Economic Analyst with MA in Applied Economics and real-world research, analysis, and consulting experience—an effective combination of theoretical and practical knowledge and a solid understanding of how economic principles and policies affect business, social, and political programs.

Key strengths include communication skills, leadership, and the ability to complete projects and deliver results in both individual and team assignments. Proficient in business and statistical software, including MS Excel, SAS, SPSS, and Statistix.

EDUCATION

Master of Arts, Applied Economics   2011
UNIVERSITY OF WASHINGTON, Seattle, WA

- GPA: 3.7 / 4.0.
- University Graduate Scholarship and Assistantship.
- Relevant Coursework: Econometrics, Microeconomics, Macroeconomics, Regional Economics, Cost-Benefit Analysis, International Trade, Quantitative Analysis.

Bachelor of Arts, Economics   2009
SEATTLE PACIFIC UNIVERSITY, Seattle, WA

- GPA: 3.2 / 4.0.
- Selected by faculty committee to participate in SPU study-abroad program; spent four months in London attending Regents College and traveling extensively throughout Europe.
- Resident Advisor, Longworth Hall, 2008–2009.
- Varsity soccer player, 4 years.
- Volunteer Service Award, Washington Special Olympics, 2007.

RELEVANT EXPERIENCE

Co-founder and Principal Investigator, APPLIED ECONOMICS RESEARCH GROUP,
University of Washington Department of Economics   2009–2011

Played a key role in launching consulting practice providing economic analysis for local businesses and institutions. Group grew from initial 4 founders in 2000 to 10–15 investigators.

Developed consulting proposals and led teams in research, analysis, and report preparation; delivered presentations to client Board of Directors or management team.

- Completed economic analysis for major national retailer exploring entry into the Seattle market.
- Performed employment analysis for regional economic-development organization studying immigrant labor issues.
- Established scholarship fund to channel consulting proceeds to graduate economics students.

Page 1 of 2

Submitted by Louise Kursmark

Meredith K. Holland
mholland@gmail.com • 360-294-2570

RELEVANT EXPERIENCE, continued

Research Assistant, DEPARTMENT OF ECONOMICS, University of Washington   2009–2011

Performed research for professor who is an expert consultant and published writer on economic ramifications of tax schemes and financial policies. Read and summarized relevant articles; assisted in paper preparation (credited on four published papers); brainstormed to develop new research topics.

Teaching Assistant, DEPARTMENT OF ECONOMICS, University of Washington   2009–2011

Assisted three professors in managing their course load; taught, guided, and advised economics students in undergraduate Macroeconomics and Microeconomics courses. Held regular weekly office hours for students needing assistance.

Graduate Team Project, REGIONAL SHIFT-SHARE ANALYSIS   2010

Performed shift-share analysis of several Metropolitan Statistical Areas. Located economic data sources and performed quantitative analysis to determine industry mix, location quotients, and regional share index. Prepared comprehensive report and economic recommendations. Analysis currently used as reference material by an economic consultant.

ADDITIONAL WORK EXPERIENCE

Collections Representative, DEBT MANAGEMENT SERVICES, Portland, OR   Summers 2009–2011

Negotiated payment plans with credit card debtors; #1 in collections among 80 in office.

League Coordinator, SEATTLE RECREATION CENTER, Seattle, WA   2006–2009

Scheduled and oversaw games, tournaments, and referees for multiple sports programs in fall, winter, and spring leagues.

Available for relocation.

KEY POINTS: Education up front—suitable for a new grad • Detailed descriptions of college projects and activities

DERRICK HOWARD

(513) 982-7701 | howard_d@gmail.com

128 Cleveland St., Cincinnati, OH 45201

FINANCIAL PLANNING & ANALYSIS MANAGER

Decisive Financial Analyst skilled at hedging risk, dispersing exposure, and identifying major gaps in profitability forecasts, communication infrastructure, information sharing, and business processes. Negotiator and persuasive presenter who listens well and breaks down barriers to achieve a positive and fair outcome. Expert in driving innovation in process redesign and creating/implementing organizational solutions that positively affect the bottom line.

Demonstrated Core Competencies

⇒ Process Improvement	⇒ Treasury Management	⇒ Financial Modeling
⇒ Program Management	⇒ Internal Controls	⇒ Business Development
⇒ Financial Planning & Analysis	⇒ Strategic Planning	⇒ Standard Costing/Pricing
⇒ Talent Management & Recruitment	⇒ Mergers & Acquisitions	⇒ Financial Sales & Marketing

PROFESSIONAL EXPERIENCE & ACCOMPLISHMENTS

PROCTER & GAMBLE (NYSE: PG), Cincinnati, OH   2006–Present
Global leader in consumer products in the areas of pharmaceuticals, cleaning supplies, personal care, and pet supplies.

Finance Manager, Global Business Development (2011–Present)

Work closely with Worldwide VP of Business Development (BD) to identify and act on business expansion opportunities. Manage $21M annual budget.

- Partnered with senior leadership to expand worldwide BD personnel by 52% (from 19 to 29 heads) and increased expense budget from $13.5M to $21M (56%), paving the way for the expanded team to deliver on its commitment to launch 2 new growth platforms in 2012.

- Tapped to head the Ethicon Endosurgery Hire Team and to serve as lead MBA recruiter. Exemplified corporate diversity commitment, driving efforts to identify new analysts and managers outside normal recruiting efforts. Earned Leadership Award from senior management and the Diversity Office.

Financial Analyst, Worldwide Operations Consolidations (2009–2011)

Selected to manage and drive financial performance of the largest expense line, totaling $394M with less than 2% variance. Developed and analyzed end-to-end financial and operational plans to launch Chinese manufacturing and distribution operations relative to costs in existing locations in North America.

- Spearheaded a special financial analysis project, evaluating the viability of establishing manufacturing and distribution in China, resulting in findings favoring the present manufacturing strategy as more cost effective. Strategic analysis included the following steps and benefits:
  ○ Compared cost of current manufacturing model based in Mexico and the United States.
  ○ Assessed labor, tax, and overhead distribution and value-added tax costs.
  ○ Evaluated strategic ramifications of launching Chinese manufacturing operations, including China Free Trade Zones, and analysis of both internal and external supplier capabilities to create a presence in China.
  ○ Developed an analysis providing critical input for establishing a Chinese supplier base. Analysis has since been used by the company to evaluate licensing and acquisition deals in China.

- Captured more than $16M in cost reductions as a key contributor on the Continuous Process Improvement Team, which was formed to implement techniques to strengthen focus on cost avoidance and profit growth.

Continued

Submitted by Wanda Kiser

DERRICK HOWARD

(513) 982-7701 | howard_d@gmail.com

Page 2

PROCTER & GAMBLE, continued

Brand Analyst, Product & Procedure Marketing (2007–2009)

Played an integral role in directing all facets of bariatric business strategy. Conceived and created the financial model and drove sales, NPV, and IRR. Held accountable for performance against immediate and long-range corporate objectives. Managed $3.8M expense budget (within 1% of forecast), $5.5M capital budget, and $19M marketing budget.

- Created and rolled out new financial model projecting profitable sales of $126M and annual growth of 49%.
- Collaborated with Marketing and IM leadership to build an internal consulting organization to drive procedure growth across the Obesity franchise, resulting in 40 consultant engagements with practices and hospitals averaging 25% procedure growth per engagement.

Financial Analyst Intern (2006–2007)

Chosen through a highly selective process for the company's prestigious Management Training program.

- Conceptualized and executed a process to identify intellectual property suitable for donations to non-profits.
- Employed proactive management techniques, utilizing Six Sigma methodologies to enhance the company's intellectual property management system.

PREVIOUS PROFESSIONAL CAREER

- **Manufacturing Engineer, Final Assembly Engineering:** FORD MOTOR COMPANY, Dearborn, MI
- **First Line Production Supervisor, Final Assembly:** GENERAL MOTORS CORPORATION, Doraville, GA

EDUCATION & PROFESSIONAL TRAINING

Master of Business Administration, OHIO UNIVERSITY, Athens, OH, 2006
Bachelor of Science, MERCER UNIVERSITY, Macon, GA, 2001

Certified Six Sigma Green Belt
Johnson & Johnson Management Fundamentals Program
MBA Leadership Development Program

HONORS & AWARDS

Consortium of Graduate Study in Management Fellow, Ohio University
Vice President of Internal Relations, MBA Association, Kelley School of Business, Ohio University
Papa Joe Leadership Award
Justice and Chairman, Mercer University Judicial System
INROADS Atlanta Scholar Internship Program, Mercer University

---

KEY POINTS: Detailed list of keyword competencies • Format showcasing progressive career with a top company

Randy Michael, CPA

19550 SE 37th Ct, Orlando, FL 32801

(407) 208-9050

Randy68@sbcglogal.net

SENIOR FINANCE EXECUTIVE
CFO • VP FINANCE

Dynamic 20-year career in financial management, operations management, and continuous improvement leadership across all core business functions and operations from Finance and Technology to HR and Manufacturing. Strong leadership, communications, interpersonal relations, organizational development, and negotiation skills and a reputation for honesty and integrity. Contributed to significant revenue gains, cost reductions, and profit improvements. Expertise and achievements include:

- Financial Analysis & Management
- Revenue Growth & Profitability
- Team Building & Team Leadership
- Process Redesign & Change Management
- Operations/Multi-Unit Management

- Budgeting & Cash Flow Optimization
- Information Systems & Technologies
- Cost Reduction & Avoidance
- Human Resource Administration
- Tax Management & Regulatory Compliance

Professional Experience

SMITHSON CORPORATION — Orlando, FL
Consultant — 2010 to 2012

Smithson Corporation is a Fortune 500 company that acquired the assets of Fleetwood Aerospace's Cabin Companies. Retained as internal consultant to provide broad-based support to transition the Smithson businesses into the Fleetwood Aerospace organization.

FLEETWOOD AEROSPACE, INC. — Orlando, FL
Leading manufacturer of interiors for the private jet market — 2001 to 2010

Vice President, Corporate Controller – 2007 to 2010
Full responsibility for the strategic planning and leadership of complete finance function for corporation with $330+ million in revenues, 6 subsidiaries, and 2,200 employees nationwide.
- Promoted into position to oversee 92 direct and indirect reports, $250 million budget, daily business operations, financial affairs, annual audits, and human resources.
- Saved company $3 million annually by consolidating accounting and IT functions for 8 businesses into a shared service, eliminating 23 positions and duplicate costs.
- Led the company through a loan amendment process that transitioned $340 million in loans from technical default to viable status.
- Successfully led company through strategic cost-cutting measures and maintained a positive cash flow through a highly volatile private jet market.
- Provided executive-level financial leadership and analysis for Smithson private equity managers and business brokers, resulting in a successful business buy-out in 2010.

Page 1 of 2

Submitted by Roxie Herrman

FLEETWOOD AEROSPACE, INC. (Continued)

Vice President Finance – 2003 to 2007
Promoted into position to oversee the financial controllers for 10 subsidiaries in the Cabin Management Group, representing $250 million annual revenue, $220 million budget, and 1,400 employees. Accountable for corporate reporting, cash flow management, customer relationships, and commercial contract negotiations.
- Spearheaded the management and cost restructuring of 2 operating companies that resulted in a significant increase in EBITDA and cash flow.
- Turned around under-performing companies into profitable units.
- Worked directly with major customer to review cost versus contract and convinced company to increase price paid to Fleetwood $5 million to $50 million.

Director of Finance & Administration – 2001 to 2003
Recruited to manage finance for Precision Pattern, a subsidiary with $60 million annual revenue, $40 million budget, and 15 employees. Accountable for financial management, financial reporting, employee supervision, human resources, information technology, and purchasing.

KREONITE, INC.   **Orlando, FL / US & UK Subs**
Maker of photographic, graphic arts, and medical X-ray processing equipment   1985 to 2001

President –1998 to 2001
Executive Vice President/COO – 1997 to 1998
Vice President, Finance and Administration – 1994 to 1997
Controller – 1987 to 1994
Assistant Controller – 1985 to 1987

Fast-track promotion through a series of increasingly responsible executive positions for a 250-employee, $15 million, high-growth, global manufacturer and distributor. Held complete strategic planning, leadership, and management responsibility for operations, finance, HR, sales, engineering, and manufacturing.

Education

University of Central Florida   Orlando, FL
Bachelor of Business Administration; Major: Accounting

KEY POINTS: Straightforward, "nothing fancy" format • Emphasis on career progression and detailed results

Corinne Sanderson

Permanent Address
119 Old Stone Trail
Guilford, CT 06437

203-248-0973
csanderson@bu.edu

School Address
139 Bay State Road
Boston, MA 02115

Goal	## Internship: Summer 2012 **Public Relations / Marketing / Media Production**

Skills

Media Production: Two hands-on summer internships with a multimedia producer of major corporate programs and events.

Presentation and Communication: Comfortable speaking before groups and in business settings. Model, spokesperson, guide, and peer advisor. Strong writing and editing skills.

Leadership: Repeatedly took on leadership roles in school and community activities. Demonstrated initiative, drive, and ability to manage multiple priorities.

People Skills: At my best when interacting with others and working in a team environment.

Education

Boston University, Boston, MA
BS Communications — anticipated 2013
Concentrations: Public Relations / Film & Television

Leadership

Admissions Representative: Chosen through competitive interview process to work with Admissions Office and represent Boston University to prospective students.
- Greet and assist visitors and prospective students as front-desk representative.
- Lead tours for visiting high school students and returning alumni.
- Served on Recruitment Team; interviewed potential admissions representatives.
- Conducted recruitment events at Cheshire Academy, Connecticut, 2010.

Alumni Bridge: Recommended by faculty member and approved through alumni interview process.
- Volunteer at special alumni events such as new student receptions, athletic events (home and away), and Reunion Weekend.
- Chosen for Recruitment Team; interviewed prospective members.
- Nominated and elected to Executive Board position — VP of Publicity, 2011

Membership Public Relations Student Society of America (PRSSA)

Volunteer Special Olympics Volunteer, 2008, 2009, 2011

Experience

Media Production Internship

Production Assistant, Shoreline Productions, Madison, CT, Summers 2009, 2010
Participated in every aspect of producing corporate media programs for major events. In fast-paced, demanding work environment, performed tasks from PowerPoint programming and tape dubbing to running errands, serving as production crew, and modeling for corporate promotions. Also assisted with office administrative duties.
- **Major projects:** Major corporate convention for $1 billion Mega Products Company (2009 and 2010) and corporate event for Good Stuff, Inc., a $100 million direct-sales company (2010).
- **Media production duties:** Creating and editing PowerPoint presentations; programming TVL; scanning; researching footage; dubbing tapes; propping sets; operating TelePrompTer; assisting with production footage.
- **Requested to return** for third summer internship.

Continued

Submitted by Louise Kursmark

Corinne Sanderson
Page 2   csanderson@bu.edu   203-248-0973

Experience	(continued)
Modeling	**Model,** East Coast Talent, West Haven, CT, 2007–Present
Sales	**Sales Associate,** Ann Taylor, Boston, MA, 2011–Present
	Sales Associate, The Gap, Meriden, CT, 2008–2010

High School

Cheshire Academy, Cheshire, CT
Graduated with Distinctive Honors, 2009

Academic Honors	National Honor Society, inducted 2008
	French Honor Society, President
	Second Place, French, Connecticut Scholastic Achievement Test (team competition)
	Center for the Advancement of Academically Talented Youth / The Johns Hopkins University — Chosen in junior high school based on academic achievement and promise; participated for 6 years.
	Founders Award in History
	Faculty Award in Languages (French)
Leadership	Elected to Student Council, 2 years
	Prom Committee, 3 years; Co-chair, senior year
	Yearbook Editor, senior year
	Peer Counselor
Volunteer	**School-based:** Educational Assistance Program (classroom aide for local elementary school); annual Book Drive for schools in underprivileged neighborhoods; Famine Relief fund-raising initiative
	Community: American Heart Association, Madison Hill Nursing Home, Shoreline Association for Retarded and Handicapped (SARAH)
	Special Project: SARAH Ambassador: Delivered presentations at more than a dozen area schools to promote participation in programs benefiting SARAH and the people it serves.
	• Influenced the launching of SARAH chapters at 7 schools.
	• Named "Ambassador of the Year" (among 20 Ambassadors) for outstanding achievement in community service.
Athletics / Modeling / Travel	Varsity soccer player — 4 years
	Dance — jazz, tap, ballet, pointe
	Midwestern Talent Expo — Model (placed in all 3 categories entered)
	Travel abroad — Australia, most of Europe, Ghana

KEY POINTS: Long for a college student—to include many relevant activities • Different font makes bold type stand out

CARLA BIGIO

cbigio@gmail.com | 760-393-1054
91 El Cajon Drive • Oceanside, CA 92049

EDITOR
**Combining fresh ideas, management skills, and powerful writing
to build brands, attract readers, and drive revenue gains**

Talented writer and editor with commitment to excellence in all aspects of the publishing industry. Engaging and energetic personality with ability to solve problems and inspire action from teams to meet all goals and deadlines. Strong editing and time management skills coupled with an endless desire to learn.

PROFESSIONAL EXPERIENCE

SAN DIEGO FAMILY — San Diego, CA   2007–Present
Consumer magazine for southern California–area families.
Publishing Assistant
Drive publishing process for established publication as both an independent contributor and team leader. Prioritize and conduct research, synthesize large amounts of information, and write articles and column. Partner with advertising sales team to increase revenue. Edit and proofread ad and editorial content. Serve as primary point of contact for clients and readers.

- Launched and wrote magazine's first monthly column in its 20-year history, resulting in growing readership derived from compelling content and celebrity interviews.
- Received acclaim for column, resulting in expansion to 2 related magazines: *San Francisco Family* and *Los Angeles Family.*
- Nominated for 2010 Family Publications of America award.
- Orchestrated 2 major brand-building events annually, featuring 80+ advertising clients and 2,000+ attendees.

THE DAILY AZTEC — San Diego, CA   2006–2007
Publication of San Diego State University.
News Editor
Selected as news editor, quickly enlarged role to provide articles for several other sections of the paper: Op/Ed and Arts & Entertainment. Provided proofreading, copyediting, and graphic design.

- Gained a strong foundation in multiple aspects of newspaper publishing.
- Made the difficult decision to dismiss 2 assistant editors for performance reasons, and stepped up to take on their responsibilities simultaneously with news editor position until the assistant roles were filled.

CHULA VISTA MONITOR — Chula Vista, CA   2007
Leading source of news for Long Beach.
Copy Desk Intern
Performed copyediting for news and wire stories. Wrote headlines, decks, and cutlines.

EDUCATION

Bachelor's Degree in Journalism, 2007
SAN DIEGO STATE UNIVERSITY — San Diego, CA

KEY POINTS: Great tagline differentiates this candidate • Awards and recognition highlighted in bullet points

Submitted by Mary Schumacher

SAMANTHA WILLIAMS

858-774-1219   2943 Los Gatos Road #6B • San Diego, CA 92115   swilliams@gmail.com

CUSTOMER SERVICE & ADMINISTRATIVE MANAGEMENT
Hospitality · Tourism · Nonprofit Associations

Improving Organizational Performance through Heightened Customer Satisfaction, Strategic Vendor Partnerships, and Employee Training and Morale Building

Record of initiative, problem-solving, and results during 16 years of progressively challenging roles with a major hospitality organization and leadership positions with nonprofit associations. Reputation for resolving problems on first contact and improving operations through diligence and determination.

Performance Highlights:
- **Marriott Bayside:** Accepted Concierge position with no prior knowledge or training. Built thriving service and established new cooperative vendor partnerships that benefitted hotel, associates, and guests.
- **Bay Area Concierge Association:** Doubled membership during terms as Board Member and President.
- **Women in Tourism:** Played an active role in launching and running professional association.

Core Competencies:

▪ Start-up & Turnaround Situations	▪ Complaint & Grievance Resolution
▪ Retraining & Change Initiatives	▪ Networking & Relationship Building
▪ Staff Oversight & Administration	▪ Event Planning & Management
▪ Performance Metrics Monitoring	▪ Corporate Image Representation

PROFESSIONAL EXPERIENCE

MARRIOTT BAYSIDE HOTEL *(Operated by Shipley & Simmons)*, San Diego, CA   1996–2012
Waterfront tourist hotel/vacation resort with 220 luxury suites and 7,500 square feet of meeting space

Director of Guest Services & Chief Concierge (2011–2012)

Hand-picked for newly created role with challenge to drive up faltering guest service scores—at an all-time low for the property. Additionally, held oversight responsibility for concierges, bell staff, trolley driver, and front desk (periodically) and managed all aspects of college intern program.
- Monitored performance scores and shared results with staff to increase awareness and identify opportunities for improvement.
- Chaired comment card committee, addressing and rectifying each guest's complaints and concerns.
- Personally responded to all escalated issues and guest written complaints. Monitored guest comments at online hospitality sites such as TripAdvisor.com and composed responses to increase positive feedback.
- Focused entire team on resolving customer problems on first contact.

Results: Boosted guest satisfaction scores from lowest 10% of Marriott properties to top 37%, moving up 184 places in worldwide ranking.

Lead Concierge (1998–2010)

Promoted to Concierge role after demonstrating exceptional ability to plan and orchestrate a key event (New Year's Eve party) that was floundering due to lack of leadership. Directed front-of-the-house activities with free rein to create new activities for guests. Supervised 2 concierges and served as assistant sales manager.
- Initiated practice of building synergetic relationships with area restaurants and tourist attractions.
- Selected to serve on conversion team for rebranding to the Marriott logo. Independently learned and then retrained all staff on new computer system and Marriott policies/procedures.

Results: Built Concierge service into trusted service provider to guests, valued partner to area attractions, and significant revenue driver to hotel. Became region's #1 reseller of San Diego Zoo tickets.

Continued

Submitted by Louise Kursmark

MARRIOTT BAYSIDE (continued)

Front Desk Shift Leader & Sales Assistant (1996–1998)

Provided guests with efficient and friendly service during check-in/check-out. Handled a multitude of details and tasks at once, supplying information, answering inquiries, and resolving problems. Maximized new desk clerks' effectiveness by providing training, motivation, and support.

- Contributed to sales team's gains, making cold calls and signing contracts.
- Identified root source of high turnover on the front desk: lack of training and information. Took the initiative to create a comprehensive, user-friendly reference guide that provided clerks with readily available answers to frequently asked questions.

Results: Lowered front-desk turnover 50% through improved training and increased support.

NONPROFIT EXPERIENCE

BAY AREA CONCIERGE ASSOCIATION, San Diego, CA   2000–2012

Board Member / **President** (3 years) / **Vice President** (2 years) / **Secretary** (3 years) / **Treasurer** (2 years)

As President, led all-volunteer organization and directed 10-member board. Instated practice of holding supplementary functions in addition to monthly meetings. Coordinated certification testing for all active concierges in the San Diego area.

- Improved outreach and internal communication by creating website and newsletter.
- Brought in new associate members from restaurants and tourist sites to build reciprocal relationships.
- Launched a scholarship fund for the hospitality program at San Diego College.

Results: Doubled membership from 50 to nearly 100.

WOMEN IN TOURISM, San Diego, CA   2010–2012

Board Member / **Director of Membership**

Elected to leadership roles with association uniting professional women for educational and networking activities for promotion and sale of tourism.

- Coordinated and hosted 2008 Silent Auction to benefit Habitat for Humanity.
- Spearheaded efforts to support CASA (Community Action Stops Abuse), a spousal abuse center, through member donations.

SAN DIEGO CHAMBER OF COMMERCE, San Diego, CA   2003–2012

Member / **Hospitality Marketing Committee**

Facilitated partnership with Los Angeles Concierge Association, supporting co-marketing strategies to promote each area's tourism business.

EDUCATION / TRAINING / MEMBERSHIP & CERTIFICATION

A.A. Degree, San Diego College—San Diego, CA (1998)
TIPS Trained (current) • CPR & AED Certified (current) • Basic First Aid Certified (current)

Member Les Clef d'Or—One of 5 Gold Keys concierges in the San Diego area
Certified Hospitality Supervisor—American Hotel & Motel Association (1999)
Certified Concierge—American Hotel & Lodging Association (2009)

KEY POINTS: Includes pertinent experience from both hotel and nonprofit • Shaded "results" boxes draw attention

Yvette R. Brousseau
CORPORATE FLIGHT ATTENDANT
PROFESSIONALISM WITH A HEART

517.555.5555 ➤ 822 Morris Avenue, Lansing, MI 48917 ➤ YBrousseau@yahoo.com ➤ **Linked**in YvetteBrousseau

Energetic and expressive communicator with 7 years of experience providing outstanding customer service to clients of all ages and backgrounds. Respected negotiator with a reputation for quick thinking and composure during crises. Conscientious team player, master of resolving difficult social situations. Bilingual in English and French, conversational Mandarin. U.S. passport holder.

YVETTE HAS BUILT A GREAT REPUTATION BY GIVING CLIENTS MORE THAN THEY EXPECT. —SB, Jet Professionals

CORE SKILLS SUMMARY

Command of Safety and Emergency Procedures (SEP)	Meticulous attention to delivery of food service
Currency in CPR/AED/Advanced First Aid	Sensitivity to passengers with special needs
Knowledge of Federal Aviation Regulations (FARs)	Superb interpersonal skills

EXPERIENCE and ACHIEVEMENTS

JET PROFESSIONALS, LLC, Teterboro, NJ *A leader in global business-aviation staffing*	**Contract Flight Attendant** 2003–Present

Deliver front-line service to up to 19 executives and their guests on international flights, ensuring passenger comfort and safety. Provide leadership in emergencies while consistently demonstrating poise and calm demeanor. Manage passengers and ground staff during pre-departure procedures to meet departure schedules.

➤ Work with medical professionals and handle emergencies. Interpreted for American physician assisting French passenger who delivered her child in flight.

➤ Promptly respond to passengers' needs and offer compassionate and attentive care.

➤ Prepare and provision cabins in Gulfstream IV and V/G550, Challenger 600, and Falcon 50 and 900-series.

PROFESSIONAL TRAINING

➤ **Recurrent Cabin Attendant Training,** *FlightSafety International, Toledo, OH, 2011*

➤ **CPR/AED/Advanced First Aid Recertification,** *Advantage First Aid Training and Safety, West Bloomfield, MI, 2009*

➤ **Professional Cabin Attendant Training, Initial; Corporate Cabin Service; General Emergency; MedAire; CPR/AED/Advanced First Aid Certification,** *FlightSafety International, Toledo, OH, 2003*

➤ **Food Handler Certification, ServSafe Food Safety Training,** *The National Restaurant Association Educational Foundation, Chicago, IL, 2002*

EDUCATION

Bachelor of Arts in International Studies *Michigan State University, East Lansing, MI 2002*	➤ Studied third year abroad in Tianjin, PR of China ➤ Graduated summa cum laude

KEY POINTS: Distinctive, colored design and graphic • Useful table format • LinkedIn profile in contact information

Submitted by John Leggatt & Jitka Vesela

Dana T. Singer

dtsinger@austin.rr.com

7551 Texas Trail
Austin, TX 78728
Home: 512-555-8345
Cell: 512-555-0904

Senior Management Executive

Driving Strategic, Profitable Growth for Start-up to Fortune 500 Organizations

Creative business strategist with a strong record of career achievements that include:

- Leading fast-growth start-ups
- Revitalizing flagging operations
- Delivering strong and sustained revenue growth
- Consolidating and cost-cutting to improve profit performance
- Repositioning sales strategies for long-term growth

Multimillion-dollar P&L responsibility for Fortune 500 and early-stage companies with U.S. and international operations. Extensive M&A experience, from assessment through integration. Unquestionable integrity and total commitment to providing outstanding customer service and creating value for shareholders.

Experience and Accomplishments

Safety Software (Subsidiary of Software Central, Inc.), Austin, TX   2007–Present

World's largest provider of public-safety software and consulting services — $500M revenue, 12 global locations

PRESIDENT

Brought on board to spearhead rapid, profitable growth — to create and execute growth strategies, develop a strong management team, acquire and integrate complementary businesses, negotiate strategic alliances, and drive sales/business development. Manage P&L, operations, and sales. Directly manage 4 VPs who oversee 400 employees in the U.S., Europe, and Asia.

- Grew revenues from $120M to $500M through acquisition and organic growth.

- Increased EBITDA from 10% to 17% through consolidation strategies.

- Spearheaded active acquisition drive and managed due diligence, negotiations, and integration for 5 acquisitions in 2 years.

- Retained experienced, entrepreneurial managers in each location, successfully renewing management contracts of more than 80% of original business owners into second year of Safety Software ownership.

- Vigorously pursued strategic partnerships to build visibility, support the development of complementary products and services, and firmly position Safety as the industry leader. Partners include:

  ○ Manufacturers of handheld and in-vehicle data terminals
  ○ Professional associations within the law-enforcement and fire-prevention fields
  ○ Leading online training companies specializing in public-safety training
  ○ Major web portals with high visibility and credibility in the public-safety industry

CORPORATE VICE PRESIDENT, SOFTWARE CENTRAL, INC. (concurrent role)

Participate in strategy and business planning as a member of the executive team of Software Central, a fast-growing $200M conglomerate of niche software providers.

- Instrumental in acquisition of P-Plus, the market-share leader in PDA peripherals.

- Leveraged Safety Software's law enforcement expertise to position Software Central for growth opportunity in public-safety database enhancement.

Continued

Submitted by Louise Kursmark

Tempco, Inc., Austin, TX   2004–2006

Regional staffing organization with $360M revenue and 24 branches throughout South/Southwestern U.S.

VICE PRESIDENT / GENERAL MANAGER

Invigorated and refocused a stagnant organization, providing turnaround leadership to build revenues, cut expenses, and dramatically boost profitability.

Held total P&L responsibility for $360M organization with $140M operating budget and 2800 employees. Directed all facets of strategy, operations, and sales.

- Grew pre-tax profits by 30%.
- Spurred revenue growth of 22% after several years averaging 3%.
- Built high-performance sales staff by transitioning order-takers to partnership managers; improved commission compensation and provided opportunities for advancement.
- Slashed employee turnover 40%.
- Transformed the sales strategy, focusing on major corporate partnerships and national accounts. Identified and capitalized on strategic opportunities to create win-win solutions for client/partner organizations — e.g., teamed with small, growing companies and delivered cost-effective hiring solutions that led to major national contracts as companies grew.

United Telecom, Houston, TX   1990–2004

A global leader in integrated telecommunications solutions

VICE PRESIDENT SALES: SPECIAL MARKETS DIVISION, 2001–2004

Led sales, marketing, distribution, and project management for Fortune 100 accounts with domestic and international installations. Directed the activities of 5 senior managers overseeing 320 sales employees. Product technology included two-way radio, paging, mobile data, and fixed data.

- Grew area operations from $40M to $100+M in revenue with a 21% pretax profit.
- Redirected sales teams toward key account management. Created telemarketing program to support lower-tier accounts and challenged direct-sales staff to deliver revenue growth through account penetration and consultative sales. Individual sales production increased from $900K to $1.7M annually.

REGIONAL MANAGER / DISTRICT SALES MANAGER / ACCOUNT EXECUTIVE, 1990–2001

Consistent top performer with an unbroken record of meeting goals — every quarter — in progressively responsible sales and sales management roles.

Education

Graduate School of the University of Texas   Austin, TX

Graduate-level certification programs in Marketing, Management, and Acquisitions

Rice University   Houston, TX

BS Business Administration, 1989

KEY POINTS: All content written in small "bites" and organized in bullets and sub-bullets • Flush with numbers/results

MAGDA YOUNG, MBA, FACHE

9457 Heath Lane • Eagle, ID 83616
(H) 208-362-9638 • (C) 208-215-8826 • myoung@gmail.com

CHIEF EXECUTIVE OFFICER

Transformational healthcare business leader with 20+ years of experience boosting profitability, streamlining operations, and building highly engaged teams. C-level executive for 5 hospitals and senior care home. Influential change agent who defines strategies, establishes productive relationships, and inspires people to action.

Areas of Proven Strength

Strategic Planning	Change Management	Turnarounds
Restructuring	Operations Management	Workforce Planning
Process Improvements	Strategic Partnerships	Cost Control
Project Management	Margin Growth	Negotiations

Professional Experience

MATHER HOSPITAL & HEALTH SCIENCES CENTER   Boise, ID • 2008–Present
257-bed level II trauma center; $220M rev., 266 physicians, 1,400 employees; part of Cassatt Health & Services.
CHIEF OPERATING OFFICER

Led major initiatives, generated new revenue, and established beneficial strategic partnerships. Direct operations of 12 departments with 600 FTEs.

- Generated $13.5M in net operating income with positive operating margins year-over-year.

2009	2010	2011
1.3%	5.2%	5.9%

- Spearheaded multiple initiatives, including new physician services division (153 physicians) and $15M construction/renovation of Emergency Department.
- Facilitated seamless continuum of care by establishing partnerships with other healthcare providers such as hospice, home health agencies, nursing homes, and other hospitals.
- Improved communications and patient care by implementing a standardized, consensus-based communication process.
- Launched new technologies, e.g., single IT platform (EPIC) for inpatient and ambulatory care.
- Developed provisioning strategy for independent physicians and Critical Access Hospitals.

GERMAN HEALTH RESOURCES   Idaho Falls and Caldwell, ID • 1997–2008
Subsidiary of Loblaw Health Systems, serving 1,000 hospitals.
CHIEF EXECUTIVE OFFICER — North Valley Hospital (Idaho Falls, ID • 2000–2008)

Achieved strategic goals including hospital's critical access status, construction of replacement hospital, and fundraising targets. Held full P&L responsibility for nonprofit 25-bed hospital with $30M in net revenue, 100 physicians, and 300 staff. Reported to 15-member board of directors.

- Delivered positive operating margins:

2002	2003	2004	2005	2006	2007
2.0%	2.7%	0.4%	4.4%	7.3%	5.2%

- Led construction of $30M replacement hospital, medical office complex, and medical office building in adjacent Gem County.
- Raised 100% of $6.3M capital campaign goal.
- Introduced new services: full-time MRI, full-time hospitalist program, full-time sleep lab, and Picture Archive Communication System (PACS).
- Succeeded in recruiting 3 surgeons and 9 specialist physicians. Led 2001 union decertification.
- Received 5-Star patient satisfaction awards from Avatar International in 2002, 2003, 2004, 2005.

Page 1 of 2

Submitted by Mary Schumacher

MAGDA YOUNG, MBA, FACHE   208-215-8826 • myoung@gmail.com

GERMAN HEALTH RESOURCES (continued)
CHIEF EXECUTIVE OFFICER — Justine Memorial Hospital (Caldwell, ID • 1997–2000)
Delivered dramatic improvements in financial position and employee relations. Set strategic direction for county-owned 18-bed acute care hospital plus attached 36-bed skilled nursing facility. Reported to 9-member board of directors.

- Implemented financial controls and procedures that increased bottom line by $167K, reduced accounts receivable by $352K, and accelerated average payment from 120 days to 30 days.
- Attained high levels of performance through new human resource program, reducing employee turnover and increasing employee satisfaction scores.

SUN DANCE RETIREMENT COMMUNITY   Meridian, ID • 1994–1996
Nonprofit joint venture 125-bed continuum of care retirement community.
ADMINISTRATOR

Guided strategic planning process designed to achieve local market leadership. Directed day-to-day operations of 125-bed nonprofit facility providing skilled nursing, transitional care, and assisted living apartments. Reported to 5-member board.

- Reduced employee turnover 122% through numerous workforce development projects, including employee handbook, clear policies and procedures, benefits package, job descriptions, performance appraisals, and defined salary program.

BINGTON HEALTH SYSTEMS   ID, WY, and MT • 1984–1993
Leading nonprofit healthcare system in the country, with 20,000 employees.
CHIEF OPERATING OFFICER — Ada County Memorial Hospital (Nampa, ID • 1993–1994)
Transformed hospital through multiple initiatives that improved internal operations and delivered new offerings. Steered administration of nonprofit 119-bed acute care county hospital with 12-bed psychiatric department and 300 FTEs.

- Achieved market objectives through development of Physician Hospital Organization and acquisition of private home health agency.
- Implemented Continuous Quality Improvement Plan to control costs and streamline functions.
- Introduced new programs, including community health club and work hardening program.

CHIEF EXECUTIVE OFFICER — Ada County Hospital (Nampa, ID • 1987–1993)
Achieved JCAHO accreditation for 29-bed nonprofit hospital and $1.1M for capital campaign.

Held earlier positions with Bington Health Systems as Administrative Fellow and Facility Administrator at hospitals in Wyoming and Montana.

EDUCATION
MBA, 1999   Boise State University — Boise, ID
BA in Business & Healthcare Administration, 1984   University of Wyoming — Laramie, WY

PROFESSIONAL AFFILIATIONS
Fellow (FACHE), American College of Healthcare Executives   Idaho Regent, ACHE
Idaho Hospital Association, Board of Directors 2007–2008   American Hospital Association

LICENSES
Licensed Idaho Nursing Home Administration

KEY POINTS: Tables illustrate impressive results • Bold first sentence of every job highlights big-picture achievement

KENDALL A. RICHMOND

7269 Woodview Way
Columbus, OH 43210

linkedin.com/in/kendallrichmond

740-815-1290
krichmond@gmail.com

CAREER TARGET: GAS COMPANY MANAGEMENT TRAINEE

✓ Unique blend of broad exposure to start-up operations in natural gas industry, a business management education, and multiple customer service work experiences in team-oriented environments.
✓ Strong leadership talents, interpersonal communication skills, and proven ability to work collaboratively with others to contribute to business goals and profitability.
✓ Record of outstanding performance in all academic, internship, and employment endeavors.

EDUCATION

PENN STATE UNIVERSITY, University Park, PA
B.A.—Business Administration with Management concentration, May 2012
GPA: 3.75/4.0—Dean's List all semesters, Sigma Beta Delta International Business Honor Society

Study Abroad
Estudio Sampere, Madrid, Salamanca, and Alicante, Spain, Spring 2011
Four-month immersion program with emphasis on study of language, history, and culture of Spain.

Leadership & Co-curricular
Professional Management Association, President
Campus Recreation Board, Secretary

Habitat for Humanity, Team Leader
Women's Cross Country Team, Member

EMPLOYMENT EXPERIENCE

CHAMBER OF BUSINESS AND INDUSTRY, State College, PA   August 2011–May 2012
Intern / Assistant to Executive Vice President
Researched and learned about great impact of Marcellus Shale natural gas exploration in Pennsylvania. Attended weekly staff meetings and recorded and compiled minutes for future organizational reference.

✓ Selected to meet with top-level gas company officials to discuss office space lease options, employment opportunities, and employee long-term housing and recreational needs.
✓ Partnered with Marketing Director to compile extensive directory of company contacts and design informational flyer promoting environmental and economic benefits of natural gas.

MULLIGAN'S PUB & BREWERY, Ocean City, MD   Summers 2009–2011
Server
Provided friendly, expedient service and wait-staff support in one of area's largest high-volume dining establishments. Maintained positive, upbeat attitude and patience in all interactions.

✓ Sold add-ons and extras to consistently achieve highest per-night sales average.
✓ Named **Employee of the Month** among 50+ employees during first summer of employment.

BROWN'S PHARMACY, Columbus, OH   June 2006–August 2008
Customer Service Representative / Night Manager
Demonstrated excellent communication, interpersonal relations, and cash management skills.
✓ Promoted to night supervisor position after only 10 months; trained and supervised 4 staff.

LANGUAGES & TECHNOLOGY

Cross-cultural communicator with fluency in Spanish and conversational ability in French.
Proficient in Microsoft Office Suite: Word, Excel, PowerPoint, Access, Publisher, and Outlook.

KEY POINTS: Summary captures unique value • Internship and seasonal work experience are both featured

Submitted by Anne Landon

Rocky Christopher
Rocky@hotmail.com
(817) 492-8740
4411 Freedom Creek, Ft. Worth, TX 76118

ENTRY-LEVEL FINANCIAL ANALYST

*Highly Motivated * Hardworking * Strategic Thinker * Strong Analytical Skills*

Recent graduate with **Bachelor of Science Degree in Economics** seeking Financial Analyst position where a passion for investments, strong analytical skills, and client relationship-building talents may be used to contribute to operational objectives and advance company growth. Extensive background in conducting research and financial analysis on domestic and international companies. **Academic preparation includes:**

☑ Financial Planning & Analysis	☑ International Finance	☑ Money & Banking
☑ International Trade	☑ Data Collection/Research/Analysis	☑ Negotiations
☑ Economic Policies	☑ Game Theory/Strategy	☑ Client Services
☑ Management Accounting	☑ Investments	☑ Presentations

Computer savvy with experience in Microsoft Word, Works, Excel, Access, PowerPoint, and Outlook; DCI Teller; I core Deposit System; Safari; Peachtree Accounting; Gary Jonas Software; Adobe Acrobat; Mozilla Firefox; Netscape Navigator; and Internet.

Education

University of Texas
Austin, TX
Bachelor of Science in Economics; Minor in Business
Spring 2012

Internship

Smith Barney Investments Firm
Fort Worth, TX
Financial Analyst
July 2012 to December 2012
- Reviewed and analyzed client company portfolios to determine financial status, profitability on investments, and debt ratios.
- Researched and retrieved SEC filings for individual companies, analyzed data, and developed presentations for upper-level management on profitability and financial stability of company.

Work History

- Bank Teller, Douglas County Bank, Ft. Worth, Texas, 2012–Present
- Marketing Intern, Herndon Sports Marketing, Inc., Austin, Texas, 2011
- Remote CSR III, Intrust Bank, N.A., Ft. Worth, Texas, 2008–2011
- Bank Teller, Bank of America, Ft. Worth, Texas, 2007–2008
- Customer Service Retail Sales, Circuit City, Ft. Worth, Texas, 2005–2007

Activities / Honors

- Philanthropy Chair, Sigma Phi Epsilon Fraternity, Austin, Texas, 2010–2012
- Outstanding New Member, Sigma Phi Epsilon Fraternity, Austin, Texas, 2009
- Listed in the Who's Who Among American High School Students, 2008
- Ambassador, Youth Entrepreneurs of Texas, 2008
- Winner, Outstanding Business Plan Award, Youth Entrepreneurs of Texas, 2008.

KEY POINTS: Expansive summary that "paints the picture" of an ideal candidate • Jobs listed without detail

Submitted by Roxie Herrman

JAMES PRITCHARD GONZALES

145 Lake Ave., Los Angeles, CA 90095
jpgonzales@gmail.com • (310) 341-4463

INTERNATIONAL SALES AND MARKETING
SALES LEADERSHIP–CLIENT ENGAGEMENT–MARKET DEVELOPMENT
RESIDENTIAL EXPERIENCE IN SPAIN
FLUENT SPANISH AND ENGLISH—CONVERSATIONAL FRENCH AND ITALIAN

Determined, enthusiastic, results-delivering college graduate prepared to contribute to the bottom line of a multinational company. International experience gained by living, working, and studying in European countries. Track record of meeting or exceeding sales and marketing goals.

EDUCATION
COMBINED COURSEWORK AND STUDY ABROAD TO PREPARE FOR INTERNATIONAL BUSINESS CAREER

Bachelor of Arts Degree, University of California, Los Angeles, CA   2012

Major:	European Studies
Minors:	Political Science and Spanish
Semester Abroad:	Universidad de Granada, Granada, Spain
Awards/Honors:	Outstanding Honors: Political Science, Anthropology, Physical Science Dean's List (2009, 2010, 2011, 2012)

INTERNATIONAL EXPERIENCE
FACILITATED FOREIGN SCHOLAR ACCULTURATION AND PARTICIPATED IN INTERNATIONAL PROJECTS

UNIVERSITY OF CALIFORNIA, Los Angeles, CA   2009–2010
Member of the Global Community Institute
- Mentored and lived with newly arrived international scholars.
- Provided support and structure for integration into campus and American culture.

EL AYUNTAMIENTO DE SANTA FE (CITY COUNCIL), Santa Fe, Spain   2009
Assistant to City Councilman Amador Rodriguez Silvar
- International consultant on sustainability and land conservation.
- Implemented sustainable transport program utilized daily by 300+ people.
- Planned and coordinated local concerts and festivals.

WORK HISTORY
DELIVERED OUTSTANDING CONTRIBUTIONS TO BUSINESS MARKETING AND SALES SUCCESSES

THE GRADUATE, Los Angeles, CA   2010–2012
Bartender/Server
- Delivered average weekly gross receipts in excess of $4000: management's "go-to" guy.
- Collaborated with executive chef to develop customer-securing strategies and promotions.

OFFICE MAX, Pasadena, CA   2004–2008
Resident Technician
- Up-sold $3000+ in service plans per month.
- Diagnosed and repaired 20+ computers per week.
- Promoted to Sales Team Leader; supervised sales floor operations and trained new staff.

PROFESSIONAL DEVELOPMENT
COMPLETED FIRST STEPS IN BUILDING STRONG PROFESSIONAL NETWORK

Bruins Toastmasters Club—Toastmasters International—Los Angeles, CA

KEY POINTS: Striking design • Short, easy-to-skim paragraphs and bullets • Emphasis on international experience

Submitted by Lorraine Beaman

Jessica Levitz

215 New Street, Apartment D | Columbus, GA 31801
229.341.7704 | jmlevitz@hotmail.com

ENTRY-LEVEL FINANCIAL SERVICES REPRESENTATIVE

✓ **Outstanding analytical abilities** honed through finance degree and additional coursework in marketing, management, and actuarial science.
✓ **Strong work ethic** developed through extensive experience in diverse environments that include retail, telemarketing, food service, and administration.
✓ **Excellent communication, multitasking, adaptability, and time management skills** sharpened through multiple customer service positions.

SKILLS & QUALIFICATIONS

Financial Management: Crystal Ball Software | Excel | Financial Statements | DuPont Analysis Governmental Accounting Regulations (SEC, GAAP) | IFRS Guidelines | Hoover's | MSN Money.com Balance Sheets | Income Statements | Microeconomics | Macroeconomics

Customer Service: Cash-Handling Procedures | Customer Complaint Resolution | Phone Etiquette Shift Closing Procedures | Active Listening | Communication with Managers and Team Members Patron Safety during Emergencies | Special Assistance for Customers with Specific Needs

EDUCATION

Columbus State University, Columbus, GA   May 2012
Bachelor of Science, Finance and Economics
GPA 3.25/4.0 | University Scholarship (2007–2008) | Honors College (2008–2009)

EXPERIENCE

FITTERS, Columbus, GA   August 2009–Present
Waitress
Perform full scale of customer service functions in a fast-paced bar/restaurant. Take orders, respond to customer requests and complaints, serve food, and stock and clean kitchen.

✓ Work 20–25 hours per week during school year, including most Friday and Saturday nights.
✓ Informally given the title of head waitress; play significant role in training new staff.

PREFERRED FAMILY HEALTHCARE, Albany, GA   May–August 2010
Secretary
Completed numerous office administration tasks, including sorting and filing confidential client information, faxing client information to other facilities, and preparing handouts and instructional materials for weekend classes for DUI and MIP offenders.

✓ Worked 40 hours per week.
✓ Received a raise within three months of employment.

PANHELLENIC HALL, Columbus, GA   December 2008–May 2010
Office Assistant
Monitored and assisted 500 building residents by providing directions, giving advice, and sorting and filing mail. Implemented security measures such as securing doors and notifying authorities in case of fire, tornado, or intruder. Received emergency training.

✓ Worked four days per week 3:00 a.m.–7:00 a.m.
✓ Frequently worked immediately prior and after breaks, allowing other workers to spend more time at home with their families.

Page One

Submitted by Lesa Kerlin

Jessica Levitz   jmlevitz@hotmail.com   **Page Two**

BREAK TIME, Albany, GA   May 2009–May 2010
Cashier
Provided friendly and competent service to customers at a high-volume gas station/convenience store. Operated cash register for customers purchasing gasoline, groceries, and retail merchandise. Balanced daily receipts and prepared for deposit.

  ✓ Managed an average daily drawer take of $2K.
  ✓ Worked alone 1:00 p.m.–10:00 p.m., five days each week.
  ✓ Secured facility for closing at end of shift.
  ✓ Reconciled funds at end of each shift; secured money and receipts in safe for manager.

UNIVERSITY BOOKSTORE, Columbus, GA   August–October 2008
Cashier
Assisted students, faculty, staff, and community members utilizing the University's only bookstore. Assisted students in locating and purchasing required textbooks as well as supplementary materials. Operated cash register, frequently handling large purchases. Worked the first week of fall semester, the bookstore's busiest time. Completed weekly inventory process and received shipments of books.

MARITZ RESEARCH CENTER, Albany, GA   May–August 2008
Research Telemarketer
Conducted five-minute telephone research surveys with customers who had received a company's farm equipment parts, assessing satisfaction with services, price, time to delivery, online service, and distribution process. Entered survey results into company's database.

ACTIVITIES

ALPHA BETA CHI SORORITY   Fall 2008–Present
Fundraising Chair (Fall 2009–Spring 2010)

  ✓ Raised $1K by selling tickets on campus for a raffle drawing from local businesses.

THE STUDENT FINANCE ASSOCIATION   Fall 2010–Present
Member

  ✓ Traveled to financial companies to learn about their operations and potential careers within their organizations, participated in investment simulation games, attended professional conferences, and attended seminars with various professionals in the finance field.

KEY POINTS: Extensive skills list • Emphasis on both paid work experience and college activities

CAROL HUNTER

4861 Golf Trail
Sarasota, FL 34232

941.463.7979
carol.hunter@gmail.com

ADMINISTRATIVE ASSISTANT
Non-Profit / Health Care

RECENT GRADUATE with a long-standing interest and desire to succeed in a non-profit organization. Proven ability to manage multiple responsibilities in a fast-paced environment with critical deadlines. Worked throughout college to partially self-finance education. Solid understanding of business priorities and great attention to detail.

"I can always count on Carol—she gets the job done. I get lots of compliments on her work. … Carol puts her heart into everything she does. She handles our diverse population exceedingly well, and the children love being with her."
—Jay Sibel, Manager, Jerry Blend Early Learning Center

EDUCATION

Bachelor of Arts, English
University of Florida, Gainesville, FL
Received Presidential Honor Scholarship

2012
GPA: 3.4

SKILLS / COMPETENCIES

- **Organizational Management** – Recognized for ability to manage multiple priorities in busy environments. Maintained flexibility in changing work assignments and demands. Recommended procedural changes.

- **Interpersonal/Communication** – Strong interaction and relationship-building skills acquired through dealing with individuals of all ages in a variety of settings. Well-developed verbal and written skills.
  - Hand-picked to train new servers.
  - Achieved #1 ranking for selling merchandise.

- **Computer** – Proficient in Microsoft Office Suite, email, social networking, and Internet.

WORK EXPERIENCE

Jerry Blend Early Learning Center, Sarasota, FL
A multi-cultural learning center for developmentally challenged children. Supported in part by United Way.
Assistant Teacher

2011–Present

Mario's Italian Café, Naples, FL
Server

2009–2010

LeConte Lodge, Great Smoky Mountains National Park, TN
Unique mountain accommodations designed for day hikers and adventurers.
Crew Member

2009

KEY POINTS: Endorsement from her manager • Skills section that pulls together details from all of her experiences

Submitted by Jane Falter

ROGER M. SIMONTON

The Art of the Plate, Delivered with Timely Excellence

SOUS CHEF

Valedictorian ▪ The Culinary Institute of America ▪ Class of 2012

Impassioned "foodie" with 4 years of hospitality achievement, including *Summa cum Laude* performance at The Culinary Institute of America. Promoted twice in 4 years with Marriott for food service and cost-cutting excellence. ServSafe-certified.

First Place ▪ The Marguerite Stein Culinary Contest ▪ 2011 & 2012

EDUCATION

THE CULINARY INSTITUTE OF AMERICA ▪ **Bachelor of Arts in Culinary Arts Management** [2012]
- Gained diverse menu development, food and beverage pairing, sustainable agriculture, and produce distribution experience through a 21-day Food, Wine, and Agriculture Trip to Italy. Toured 8 of 20 gastronomic regions.

CULINARY KNOWLEDGE & SKILLS

Hospitality & Service Management	Formal Restaurant Cooking	Accounting & Budget Management
Advanced Cooking & Nutrition	Advanced Wine Studies	Food Purchasing & Cost Control
Cookies, Tarts & Mignardises	Hearth Breads & Rolls	Menu Development
Chocolates & Confections	Classical Banquet Cuisine	Marketing & Food Promotion

CULINARY EXPERIENCE

NORTH FORK MARRIOTT [2007 –Present]
Four-star conference center and hotel with 300 rooms, banquet offerings for 1,000, and meeting facilities seating 2,000 patrons.
Prep Cook [2009–Present]
- Ensure stellar food service, crafting soups, sauces, vegetables, and pastries from ingredient preparation to completion, in accordance with corporate recipe and brand guidelines. Carve and plate meats and fish while complying with standard portion sizing, kitchen, and quality standards.

Soup Maker | Pantry Cook [2007–2008]
Promoted to Soup Maker within 6 months for prompt, accurate order preparation as Pantry Cook. Created salads, dressings, appetizers, sandwiches, and desserts for restaurant / banquet operations serving up to 200 people per hour.
- Cooked 8 varieties of house soups in 40-gallon batches and soups du jour in 5-gallon batches.
- Selected to complete Garde Manger cross-training in salad / salad dressing preparation and plate painting.

CERTIFICATIONS & AFFILIATIONS

ServSafe Certification ▪ American Culinary Federation ▪ Treasurer, Upstate New York Chefs' Association

1234 Pebble Lane ▪ Buffalo, NY 14201 ▪ 716.238.3329 ▪ rmsimonton@mail.com

KEY POINTS: Exciting visual design • Brief yet meaningful and relevant descriptions of skills, jobs, and accomplishments

Submitted by Cheryl Simpson

JEREMY WALTON

247 Columbus Avenue
Kendall, FL 33156

305-555-1543
jerwalton@isp.com

PROFESSIONAL PROFILE

- ❏ Innovative, lifelong Mac user possessing a thorough understanding of the Macintosh operating system and effectively communicating technical information to computer users of all skill levels.
- ❏ Proficiency with cutting-edge technology maintained through ongoing research and self-teaching.
- ❏ Innate curiosity to learn, master, and maximize system capabilities.
- ❏ Passion for technology balanced with approachable, friendly personality.
- ❏ Experience working in educational setting and regularly interfacing with administrators, IT specialists, instructors, and students.

TECHNICAL INVENTORY

Expertise in Macintosh operating system. In-depth knowledge of dual- and triple-booting operating systems. Experience working from command line. Understanding of network protocols.

Platforms
- Mac OS X (including Apple Remote Desktop)
- Linux (Ubuntu, Debian, Fedora)
- Windows (familiarity)

Servers
- Apple Xserve
- Linux

Hardware
- Apple iMac
- Apple MacBook Pro
- Apple Mac Pro
- Apple Airport Express/Extreme
- HP Printers/Scanners
- M-Audio Audio Interfaces
- Behringer Audio Interfaces
- M-Audio MIDI Controllers
- RME Fireface 400 Firewire Audio Interface
- Mackie Onyx Series Audio Interface/Mixer
- OWC External Hard Drive

Software

General
- Moodle (learning management system)
- Microsoft Office
- QuickTime Pro
- Adobe Creative Suite

Media
- Logic Pro
- Pro Tools
- Final Cut Pro

Music-specific
- Sibelius
- Finale
- Ableton Live
- Plogue Bidule

PROFESSIONAL EXPERIENCE

UNIVERSITY OF MIAMI • Coral Gables, Florida (2010–Present)
Studio Manager/Instructor
Manage the Frost School of Music Electronic Music Studio comprising state-of-the-art Macintosh audio/video workstations and related equipment. Carry out administrative and instructional responsibilities.

Technology
- Perform hardware and software installation, configuration, maintenance, troubleshooting, and problem solving. Provide on-site technical support for hardware and software issues.
- Interact with university IT department to maintain servers and address other technology issues.
- Set up Pro Tools sessions and interface with engineering staff at Criteria Recording Studios to facilitate the recording of graduate students' thesis scores.
- Create scripts to automate routine procedures.
- Serve as School of Music webmaster.

Page 1 of 2

Submitted by Janet Beckstrom

UNIVERSITY OF MIAMI
Studio Manager/Instructor (continued)
Administration
- Interview, hire, train, and supervise graduate student lab assistants.
- Act as liaison with and advocate for the program's technology-intensive needs with college administration, purchasing, and related departments.
- Conducted and documented the program's first comprehensive inventory of software, hardware, and related equipment.

Instruction
- Teach 2 lab classes per week training students to use hardware and software and to facilitate completion of assignments. Co-teach weekly Pro Tools & Music Editing class alternating semesters.
- Understandably communicate technical concepts to students with abilities ranging from novice to technically savvy. Developed 60+ online tutorials to support students' learning.
- Refined and enhanced curricula to better meet students' needs.

Highlights of Projects
- Awarded internal $3,000 grant for Technology Upgrade Project. Collaborated with instructor to develop technical infrastructure to offer online placement exam for incoming undergraduate students. Acted as liaison with IT department during execution.
- Collaborated with IT department to maximize network efficiency to facilitate professor's biweekly remote instruction.
- Initiated effort to facilitate offsite access to lab resources by relocating the lab's server. Played key role in 6-month process to obtain administrative approval and oversee logistics of move.
- Created dedicated site for studio classes as clearinghouse for information relating to assignments, syllabi, schedules, tutorials, links, and breaking information (http://ems.student.fsm.com).

EDUCATION

MANHATTAN SCHOOL OF MUSIC • New York, New York
Master of Fine Arts in Music Composition (2009)
- Completed 5-week internship

UNIVERSITY OF NORTH TEXAS • Denton, Texas
Bachelor of Arts Cum Laude in Music and **Spanish** [double major] (2007)
- Awarded 4-year School of Music and Saxophone Studio scholarships
- Completed 2-month study abroad experience in Morelia, Mexico

PERSONAL PROFILE

Extensive experience as performing musician, composer, and arranger.
Fluent Spanish speaker.

KEY POINTS: Rich technology section for musician seeking technical career • Tech-related job activities shown first

Elizabeth A. Gulickson

1875 Massachusetts Ave.
Fort Collins, CO 80525

lizgulickson@isp.com

(H) 970.555.1849
(C) 970.555.9624

PROFILE

Consummate professional with 20+ years of experience supporting people, projects, and processes. Scope of background demonstrates ability to manage multiple priorities and adhere to deadlines. Hands-on experience performing general office/clerical duties enhanced by innate leadership qualities. Reputation for developing rapport with others while earning trust and respect.

CORE QUALIFICATIONS

FUNCTIONAL AREAS OF EXPERTISE		PERSONAL ASSETS
Office Administration	Event Planning	Vision
Management	Basic Bookkeeping	Self-Motivation
Customer Relationship Building	Contracts	Integrity & Commitment
Project Management	Sales & Marketing	Presentation & Communication Skills

CAREER HISTORY

FORT COLLINS REALTY & MANAGEMENT, INC. • Fort Collins, Colorado   1992–Present

Associate Broker/Co-owner/Property Manager
Co-lead commercial real estate agency recognized for its professionalism, integrity, and focus on long-term client relationships. Manage office administration and staffing. Provide comprehensive real estate services including sales, leasing, and property management for individuals and corporations. Draft and negotiate sale, lease, and management agreements.

Administration & Staffing — Provide financial management of company and client accounts including vendor contracts, AR/AP, and purchasing. Hire, train, and supervise office staff. Maintain online property databases. Generate monthly marketing reports for property owners.

Property Management — Manage as much as 450,000 sq. ft. of retail, industrial, office, and residential property (at peak). Oversee maintenance, renovation, and capital improvements; select, monitor, negotiate, and act as liaison with contractors.

Sales & Leasing — Communicate with individuals and corporations to assess their needs. Make sales presentations. Manage all aspects of sale, purchase, and lease from initial showing through closing. Conduct property searches. Design marketing campaigns to promote properties.

Notable Projects —
☑ Presented concept of converting commercial space formerly occupied by big-box retailers to educational institutions. Subsequent sale of properties benefited the community by filling empty buildings (which had the potential to become eyesores) and affordably meeting the schools' needs.

☑ Assisted local electronics manufacturer throughout multiple-year process to locate and lease facility for expansion. Vied with competing states, municipalities, and Realtors to identify suitable location. Teamed with Larimer County Chamber of Commerce to ensure manufacturer's presence in the county.

☑ Contracted by local charter school to identify property for the school's relocation effort. Surveyed the community for available land and buildings that matched specifications. Documented pros and cons, calculated anticipated costs, and devised fact sheets to facilitate comparison of properties.

Submitted by Janet Beckstrom

Elizabeth A. Gulickson	lizgulickson@isp.com 970.555.9624	Page 2

LARIMER COUNTY FAIR AND RODEO • Loveland, Colorado   1983–1992

Assistant Director (1990–1992 year-round)
Assisted director in developing and planning annual county fair hosting 200,000 guests on 250-acre site over 7 days. Supervised office, maintenance, and volunteer staff. Managed daily activities during event.

> *Administration* — Maintained accounting records, processed premium [prize] payments, and prepared mandatory reports for the state. Coordinated compilation and printing of exhibitor book.

> *Promotion/Event Management* — Marketed the fair through the media and other tools. Ensured compliance with local and state regulations. Managed facility rental during off season.

Seasonal Staff (1983–1990)
Participated in virtually every aspect of operations immediately before, during, and after the fair each summer.

MOUNTAIN REALTY, INC. • Fort Collins, Colorado   1987–1990

Office Manager/Residential Property Manager
Supervised office staff. Developed and implemented office procedures. Monitored accounting. Created marketing packages to showcase properties. Managed rental property.

LAKESIDE AMUSEMENT PARK • Denver, Colorado   1984–1986

Maintenance/Operation Supervisor/Festival Show Supervisor (1985–1986)
Coordinated entertainment for the facility. Hired performers and oversaw their technical requirements. Developed and published daily entertainment schedule. Continued to perform earlier assignments.

Maintenance/Operation Supervisor/Front Gate & Guest Relations Supervisor (1984–1985)
Hired prior to facility's opening to establish front gate system and guest relations department. Responded to and resolved issues with guests. Trained, scheduled, motivated, and supervised staff. Completed training in and launched new computer system; subsequently trained local employees as well as staff from other locations.

COMMUNITY SERVICE

RIDGEVILLE CLASSICAL SCHOOL • Fort Collins, Colorado   Ongoing

Loyalty Sales Program Coordinator (2004–Present)
Administer all facets of fundraising program that has generated more than $1.5 million in orders to date.

Athletic Association Golf Outing Co-chair (2008 & 2009)
Participated in planning and hosting annual fundraiser that generated $45,000+ in 2 years.

Athletics Boosters President & Vice President (2002–2006)
Led organization in wide range of activities supporting the school's athletic program.

COLORADO CANCER COALITION/NORTH CENTRAL CHAPTER • Fort Collins, Colorado   1990–2006

Memory Walk Chairperson (2001 & 2002) and **Member**
Planned and orchestrated the chapter's major fundraiser, raising more than $85,000 over 2 years.

PERSONAL SUMMARY

Technology:	Microsoft Office (Word, Excel, PowerPoint); ACT contact manager/database; QuickBooks accounting software; and Novell networking systems
Professional Development:	QuickBooks (presented by Ernst & Young) Employer-focused seminars (Fort Collins Chamber of Commerce)
Licensure:	State of Colorado Notary Public State of Colorado Real Estate Broker (since 1996) and Salesperson (since 1987)

KEY POINTS: Functional groupings within jobs position Realtor for admin roles • Distinctive "Personal Assets" section

Dawna Campise   4581 Alhambra Way • Martinez, CA 94553
(925) 228-2983   dawn@hotmail.com

HUMAN RESOURCE GENERALIST

Human Resource Professional with **20 years** of success driving efficient HR operations in domestic and international environments. Creative leader with a track record of developing and implementing cost-effective initiatives to achieve organizational goals and objectives. Detailed worker who effectively performs challenging tasks with precision and accuracy. Strategic planner, coordinator, and leader with strong technical and project management skills.

~ Areas of Expertise ~

☑ HR Program Administration	☑ File Management	☑ Data Management
☑ Policies & Procedures	☑ Employee Relations	☑ Regulatory Compliance
☑ Benefit Administration	☑ Training & Supervision	☑ Systems & Processes
☑ Reports Management	☑ Office Support	☑ Problem Resolution

Professional Experience

United States Air Force   1992 to 2012

Human Resources Supervisor, Travis AFB, Fairfield, California — 2003 to 2012

Supervised staff in performing a wide range of HR activities: maintenance of more than 6,000 personnel records; management of personnel benefits, personnel files, government documentation and reports, and regulatory compliance; and administration of policies and procedures. Interviewed and advised personnel on benefit programs, promotions, separations, retirement, retention, bonuses, training, and career progression.

* Developed and implemented technical tracking processes and procedures that improved HR data reporting accuracy by 93%.
* Completed a comprehensive audit on 2,000+ personnel records that enhanced accuracy and efficiency in program processes.
* Led the HR division in achieving an "Excellent" rating during a compliance inspection.
* Saved government $100K through the effective resolution of HR recordkeeping discrepancies.
* Awarded the Air Force Commendation Medal (Third Oak Leaf Cluster) for meritorious service and outstanding achievements in HR operations.

Human Resources Personnel Technician, Pope AFB, North Carolina — 1995 to 2003

Performed HR administrative functions for as many as 1,000 military personnel.

* Achieved an "Excellent" rating during Operational Readiness Inspection for significant improvements made to the chemical environment operational safety procedures program.
* Improved productivity 60% by creating an awards / decorations database for 4,700 personnel.
* Earned the "Outstanding Personnel Manager of the Year" award for dedication and superior performance managing HR programs.

Page 1 of 2

Submitted by Roxie Herrman

Customer Service / Records Specialist, Rhein-Main AFB, Frankfurt, Germany — 1992 to 1995

Performed human resource functions for 3,000+ personnel.

- Counseled military personnel on programs, policies and procedures, and benefits.
- Flawlessly managed the Individualized Newcomer Orientation Program, ensuring a smooth and informative transition for newcomers.
- Managed the Enlisted Performance Report program at a 98% accuracy rate.

Education & Training

Southwestern College
Bachelor of Science in Human Resources

Wichita, Kansas
2010

United States Air Force
- Executive Leadership Academy
- Business and Administration
- Performance Management
- Microsoft Office

KEY POINTS: Keyword-rich expertise list • Accomplishment-rich job descriptions • Clear transition to civilian HR

JOHN HAMMOND

10 Arbor Lane
Louisville, KY 40204

jhammond@gmail.com

Cell: 502-600-5555
Home: 502-991-5555

OPERATIONS LEADER

Intensely focused, goal-driven leader who consistently lifts organizations to new levels of operational performance. Proven experience managing complex and changing operations, with full accountability for people, equipment, and processes. Strategic and creative problem solver. Calm under pressure.

Fifteen+ years of experience leading large teams and collaborating with cross-functional leaders and groups. Valued mentor and trainer. Recognized with repeated promotions and numerous awards for service and achievement.

KEY AREAS OF EXPERTISE

- Strategic Planning
- Organizational Development
- Logistics & Scheduling

- Systems & Process Improvement
- Compliance & Safety
- Measurement & Reporting

- People Leadership
- Training
- Project Management

LEADERSHIP EXPERIENCE

United States Army
OPERATIONS SERGEANT/COMPANY FIRST SERGEANT, Fort Knox, KY   2009–Present
Direct operations for 79-person, 24-vehicle company that provides tactical support to 750-person organization. Oversee maintenance of all vehicles and 300+ pieces of equipment, valued at ~$20 million. Lead training and manage company's work and workflow; track and report extensive information and statistics on people and equipment. Report/present directly to Company Commander and operations officers. Participate in brigade leadership group.

- **Tapped to lead newly formed company**; directed training, created and continuously refined operations and policies, and achieved highest rankings within 3,500-person brigade in efficiency, timeliness, training, and equipment quality.
- **Crafted new tools and tracking systems from scratch** to manage people, equipment, and training data.
- **Managed move of 3,500 people** (plus families and $800 million in equipment) from Fort Hood, TX, to Fort Knox; facilitated interagency coordination and agreements to ensure smooth, efficient transition and full functioning on new base within 3 months.
- **Wrote and implemented all functions and procedures for brigade operations** after relocation.
- **Co-developed 13-month training plan** (normally done by higher-ranked officers) to prepare entire brigade for next combat deployment, balancing requirements of 6 battalions and ensuring best sequence and timing.

INSTRUCTOR/OPERATIONS NCO, Kentucky University Army ROTC, Louisville, KY   2006–2009
Planned all logistical operations, including acquisition of weapons and equipment, for unit of 90 cadets each year. Also taught leadership and management courses to university students. Reported directly to Commander.

- Taught 8 classroom courses in leadership and management to 200+ sophomores and juniors over 3 years; integrated prepared material and personal experience to ready students for leadership roles.
- Contributed directly to program's **MacArthur Award recognition for 3 consecutive years**; named best small-sized ROTC out of 300 programs in nation, based on factors such as cadet performance and training.
- **Co-planned 16 major offsite leadership development events** (including timing, resources, food/lodging, weapons, and equipment) and served as instructor and evaluator in programs for 12,000 future officers.
- Planned, organized, rehearsed, and flawlessly executed 30+ ceremonial events.

Continued

Submitted by Cathy Alfandre

JOHN HAMMOND—PAGE 2

Cell: 502-600-5555   jhammond@gmail.com   **Home:** 502-991-5555

BATTALION MASTER GUNNER, Fort Stewart, GA   2005–2006
Assisted Operations Officer in planning all gunnery and training exercises for 30 Bradley Fighting Vehicle (BFV) crews (90 people). Also led forecasting of all ammunition requirements for 750-person organization.
- **Developed comprehensive, 15-month training plan** for 750 soldiers following Iraq deployment, identifying and shaping all training requirements to ensure successful re-deployment.
- **Created tool to accurately forecast** 1 year's ammunition supply for entire battalion (200,000+ rounds for multiple weapons systems); tool was later adopted by every other battalion in brigade (7,000 soldiers).
- Crafted and executed technical training plan for new BFV crew members, producing 30 fully trained crews within 4 months.

INFANTRY PLATOON SERGEANT, Fort Stewart, GA   2003–2005
Led 38 people and managed fleet and equipment valued at ~$20 million. Developed junior leaders and led diverse training to ensure full readiness. Spearheaded equipment maintenance plan for home station and Iraq deployment.
- Led 125+ combat operations in Iraq including anti-IED efforts that cut strikes on U.S. forces in sector by 90%.
- **Developed 24-hour planning matrix** to balance maintenance requirements and mission requirements, ensuring continuously effective operations even with ongoing disruptions and personnel changes.
- **Proposed major infrastructure improvement projects, and then provided logistical, manpower, and security support to execute;** refurbished schools, repaired 2 sewage pumping stations, and arranged garbage removal for neighborhood of 250,000.
- **Masterminded retraining** for period between deployments through full assessment of capabilities and development of individual/group programs; earned lead role for platoon in subsequent operations.

BRADLEY SECTION LEADER/COMPANY MASTER GUNNER, Schweinfurt, Germany   2000–2003
Directly assisted Company Commander in training crews and maintaining systems. Ran Tactical Operations Center during deployment to Kosovo (2002). Held full accountability for equipment worth ~$6 million.
- Crafted and delivered comprehensive training program for all new BFV crew members (42 people) and produced 14 fully trained crews within 9 months.
- **Graduated top 20%** in Master Gunner class, ensuring full ability to assist Company Commander in planning, resourcing, and executing all multi-echelon training, both at home station and during Kosovo deployment.
- **Established and ran 24-hour Tactical Operations Center** in Kosovo to synchronize and track all operations; continuously improved analysis and tracking of intelligence and streamlined operational efficiency.
- **Managed daily inventory** for remote base camp, anticipated needs, and established rigorous inventory control procedures; ensured critical supply of food and other supplies for 100 soldiers for 6 months.

INFANTRY SQUAD LEADER/ BRADLEY SECTION LEADER, Fort Stewart, GA   1998–2000
Led groups of 4–8 soldiers and held full accountability for equipment worth up to $6 million. Reported to Platoon Sergeant and assumed all responsibilities in his absence.
- **Led 15-person group** through intense Expert Infantry Badge (EIB) training and testing; earned both EIB and recognition for top achievement in division (12,000+ soldiers): 80% earned badge (compared to 7% average).
- **Supervised all levels of maintenance** on BFVs, achieving 100% operational rate.
- **Turned around underperforming squad** through assessment and rigorous retraining.

EDUCATION

BACHELOR OF ARTS IN ORGANIZATIONAL MANAGEMENT, All American University, Louisville, KY   2008
- Graduated "with distinction," 3.74 GPA

SELECT AWARDS

Bronze Star Medal, Achievement Medal (6 times), Meritorious Service Medal (2 times), Certificate of Achievement (10 times), Commendation Medal (7 times), Presidential Unit Citation, Good Conduct Medal (6 times)

KEY POINTS: Emphasis on operational roles, large scope of responsibility, and measurable results

How to Contact the Professional Resume Writers Who Contributed to This Book

The following professional resume writers contributed resumes to this book. They are all graduates of the Resume Writing Academy who, having completed a very rigorous training program, have earned the Academy Certified Resume Writer (ACRW) credential. I appreciate their well-written examples, and I know you will, too!

Cathy Alfandre, MBA, MRW, ACRW, CCMC
Catherine A. Alfandre, LLC
Easton, CT
203-445-7906
www.cathyalfandre.com
cathy@cathyalfandre.com

Mark Bartz, ACRW
Medical Sales Mentors
Lakeland, FL
863-248-6105
MedicalSalesMentors.com
mark@hiringleaders.com

Lorraine Beaman, ACRW, Social Networking
JLB Career Consulting
Davis, CA
530-219-9651
http://jlbcareers.com
jlbcareers@sbcglobal.net

Janet Beckstrom, MRW, ACRW, CPRW
Word Crafter
Flint, MI
810-232-9257
www.wordcrafter.com
janet@wordcrafter.com

Jane Falter, ACRW, SPHR, CPC
Jane Falter Career Resources
Flat Rock, NC
828-692-4988
www.janefalter.com
jane@janefalter.com

Reneé Green, ACRW
Passionate Coaching and Career Services, LLC
763-807-1850
www.greenpassionatecoaching.com
renee@greenpassionatecoaching.com

Roxie Herrman, ACRW
Advantage Resumes
Wichita, KS
316-992-0074
www.wichitaresumes.com
advantageresumes@cox.net

Lesa Kerlin, MPA, CPRW
LEK Consultants
Kirksville, MO
660-626-4748
lekconsultants.com
lesa@lekconsultants.com

Anne Kern, ACRW
ReachHire Resume Service
Atco, NJ
856-261-1097
http://reachhire.org
reachhire@yahoo.com

Wanda Kiser, MBA, ACRW,
CPRW, CEIP, CPCC
Advantage Career Services, Inc.
Atlanta, GA
877-314-8872
www.advantagecareerservices.net
resumeinfo@
    advantagecareerservices.net

Anne Landon, ACRW, CPRW
Distinctive Resume Designs
Williamsport, PA
570-974-4398
distinctiveresumedesigns.com
annelandon@comcast.net

John Leggatt, MBA, M.Ed.,
ACRW, CPRW, & Jitka Vesela,
M.Ed., ACRW
Careers Upstairs
Sequim, WA
818-888-3626
http://CareersUpstairs.com
Experts@CareersUpstairs.com

Barbara Safani, MA, ACRW,
CMRW, NCRW, CPRW, CCM,
ROIS
Career Solvers
New York, NY
866-333-1800
www.careersolvers.com
info@careersolvers.com

Mary Schumacher, ACRW,
CPRW, CEIP
CareerFrames LLC
Madison, WI
608-242-1879
www.careerframes.com
mary@careerframes.com

Cheryl Lynch Simpson, ACRW,
COPNS
ExecutiveResumeRescue.com
Westerville, OH
614-891-9043
www.executiveresumerescue.com
info@executiveresumerescue.com

Index

A

accomplishments
  in chronological resumes, 24
  quantifying, 85, 101
accounting sample resumes, 147–152
ACRW (Academy Certified Resume Writer), 84
action words
  list of, 23
  in resumes, 8
administrative assistant sample resume, 168
administrative management sample resume, 156–157
administrative sample resumes. *See* clerical, administration, and human resources sample resumes
appearance
  of cover letters, 50
  of resumes, 7, 102–104
art teacher sample resume, 120
awards in resumes, 25

B

blogs, 78
breaking rules in resumes, 8
business cards, JIST Cards as, 60
business development and sales professional sample resume, 131
business manager sample resume, 44–45

C

career changer sample resumes, 170–173
career counselors, evaluating, 84–85
career portfolios, 79
CARW (Certified Resume Writer), 84
CDI (Career Directors International), 84
Certified Resume Writer (CARW, CERW, CMRW), 84
chief executive officer sample resume, 161–162
chronological resumes, 9–10
  comparison of samples, 14–15
  education and training in, 22
  email address in, 18–19
  final draft, 26–27
  job objective in, 19–22
  mailing address in, 18
  name in, 15
  personal information in, 25
  phone number in, 18
  professional organizations in, 25
  recognition and awards in, 25
  references in, 25–26
  samples of, 16–17
  who should use, 14
  work and volunteer history in, 23–24
clerical, administration, and human resources sample resumes, 123–129
CMRW (Certified Resume Writer), 84
computer programmer sample resume, 42–43
contact information, 18–19
contacts, developing network of, 4
converting existing resume to electronic resume, 74
corporate flight attendant sample resume, 158
cover letters, writing, 49–59
  to people you don't know, 57–59
  to people you know, 51–56
  samples of, 53–56, 58–59
  tips for, 50–51
CPRW (Certified Professional Resume Writer), 84
creative resumes, 10–11
credentials of professional resume writers, 84
curriculum vitae (CV), 11, 110–111
customer service sample resume, 156–157

D

dates of employment in resumes, 24
dental hygienist sample resume, 107
Department of Labor website, 23
design. *See* appearance
director of operations sample resume, 145–146
district sales manager sample resume, 136
draft resumes, 101
duties in resumes, 24

E

economic analyst sample resume,
147–148
editing
for appearance, 104
importance of, 102
editor sample resume, 155
education sample resumes, 119–122
education section
in chronological resumes, 22
improving, 85
electronic resumes, 15, 70–74
converting existing resume to, 74
keywords in, 75–76
samples of, 72–74
email address in resumes, 18–19
employment dates in resumes, 24
enclosures, including with resume, 86
engineering sample resumes. *See* science,
engineering, and technology sample
resumes
envelopes, quality of, 104
environmental scientist sample resume,
112
errors, avoiding in resumes, 6–7
executive sample resumes, 159–162
executive secretary sample resume,
124–125
experience. *See* volunteer history; work
history

F–G

Farr, Mike, 60
final draft
of chronological resume, 26–27
of skills resume, 41
finance sample resumes, 147–152
financial analyst sample resume, 164
financial planning and analysis manager
sample resume, 149–150
financial services representative sample
resume, 166–167
flight attendant sample resume, 158
fonts, 103
functional resumes. *See* skills resumes
gas company management sample resume,
163
Google, 76–77
graphics in resumes, 103
graphs in resumes, samples of, 136,
145–146

H

handwritten thank-you notes, 67
health care sample resumes, 107–111
honesty in resumes, 6, 99–100
hospitality sample resumes, 156–158
human resource generalist sample resume,
174–175
human resources director sample resume,
128–129
human resources sample resumes. *See*
clerical, administration, and human
resources sample resumes
humility in resumes, 100
hybrid resumes, 9–10. *See also*
chronological resumes

I

international sales and marketing sample
resume, 165
Internet, job searches on, 69–70, 79–80.
See also electronic resumes; online
identity management
internship sample resume, 153–154
interviews
cover letters prior to, 52–56
defined, 13
thank-you notes after, 65
thank-you notes prior to, 64
IT help desk supervisor sample resume,
115–116

J

JIST Cards
sending with thank-you notes, 65
writing, 60–63
job aggregators, 70
job-content skills, 39
job duties in resumes, 24
Job-Hunt website, 80
job interviews. *See* interviews
job objective
in chronological resumes, 19–22
in skills resumes, 37
job search counselors, evaluating, 84–85
job searches
on Internet, 69–70, 79–80. See also
electronic resumes
thank-you notes for helping on, 66
tips for, 12
job titles in resumes, 23

K–L

key skills list, 38–39
keywords in resumes, 75–76
length of resumes, 6, 103
LinkedIn, 77–78
logistics and operations sample resumes, 144–146
logistics manager sample resume, 144

M

mailing address in resumes, 18
manufacturing engineer sample resume, 113–114
marketing director sample resume, 140–141
marketing leader sample resume, 142–143
marketing sample resumes, 130–143
mechanical supervisor sample resume, 113–114
media sample resumes, 153–155
microbiology group leadership sample resume, 110–111
middle school art teacher sample resume, 120
military-to-civilian career changer sample resumes, 174–177
MRW (Master Resume Writer), 84
music teacher sample resume, 121–122

N

name in resumes, 15
NCRW (Nationally Certified Resume Writer), 84
negatives in resumes, 100
network of contacts, developing, 4
new graduate sample resumes. *See* recent graduate sample resumes
NRWA (National Resume Writers' Association), 84
nurse practitioner sample resume, 108–109

O

Occupational Outlook Handbook (OOH), 23
office manager sample resume, 123, 126
online career portfolios, 79
online identity management, 76–79
 blogs and tweets, 78
 career portfolios and personal websites, 79

 Google, 76–77
 LinkedIn, 77–78
online job searches, 69–70, 79–80. *See also* electronic resumes
online profile sites, 77–78
online reputation services, 77
operations leader sample resume, 176–177
operations sample resumes, 144–146

P

paper
 for JIST Cards, 61
 quality of, 104
 for resumes, 7–8
 for thank-you notes, 68
paralegal sample resume, 127
PARW/CC (Professional Association of Resume Writers and Career Coaches), 84
personal information in resumes, 25
personal references, 25–26
personal websites, 79
personalizing
 cover letters, 50
 thank-you notes, 68
phone numbers in resumes, 18
photocopying resumes, 7
plain text format sample resume, 73–74
portfolios
 including with resume, 86
 online career portfolios, 79
previous employers in resumes, 24
printing resumes, 7
product marketing professional sample resume, 139
professional organizations in resumes, 25
professional resume writers
 evaluating, 81–84
 list of, 178–179
project management sample resume, 117–118
proof stories for key skills, 40–41
proofreading
 cover letters, 50
 importance of, 102
 resumes, 6–7
public relations internship sample resume, 153–154

Q–R

quantifying accomplishments, 85, 101
recent graduate sample resumes, 47–48
   dental hygienist, 107
   economic analyst, 147–148
   environmental scientist, 112
   gas company management, 163–169
   public relations internship, 153–154
recognition and awards in resumes, 25
references, 25–26
responses to want ads, 58
resume samples
   administrative assistant, 168
   *business development and sales profes-
      sional, 131*
   business manager, 44–45
   career changers, 170–173
   chief executive officer, 161–162
   chronological resumes, 16–17
   computer programmer, 42–43
   corporate flight attendant, 158
   *customer service and administrative
      management, 156–157*
   dental hygienist, 107
   director of operations, 145–146
   district sales manager, 136
   economic analyst, 147–148
   editor, 155
   environmental scientist, 112
   executive secretary, 124–125
   financial analyst, 164
   *financial planning and analysis manager,
      149–150*
   financial services representative, 166–167
   gas company management, 163
   human resource generalist, 174–175
   human resources director, 128–129
   international sales and marketing, 165
   *IT help desk supervisor/technical man-
      ager, 115–116*
   logistics manager, 144
   *manufacturing engineer/mechanical
      supervisor, 113–114*
   marketing director, 140–141
   marketing leader, 142–143
   microbiology group leadership, 110–111
   middle school art teacher, 120
   *military-to-civilian career changers,
      174–177*
   music teacher, 121–122
   office manager, 123, 126
   operations leader, 176–177
   paralegal, 127
   plain text format, 73–74
   product marketing professional, 139
   project management, 117–118
   public relations internship, 153–154
   *recent graduates, 47–48, 107, 112,
      147–148, 153–154, 163–169*
   sales professional, 130
   senior account executive, 132–133
   senior finance executive, 151–152
   senior management executive, 159–160
   skills resumes, 36, 42–48
   sous chef, 169
   substitute teacher, 119
   *technology sales and business development
      leader, 134–135*
   technology sales leader, 137–138
   truck driver, 45–47
   *women's health nurse practitioner,
      108–109*
   Word format, 72
Resume Writing Academy, 84
resumes
   action words in, 8
   appearance of, 7, 102–104
   breaking rules in, 8
   *chronological resumes. See chronological
      resumes*
   creative resumes, 10–11
   defined, 3
   electronic resumes, 15, 70–74
   honesty in, 6, 99–100
   *hybrid resumes, 9–10. See also chrono-
      logical resumes*
   importance of using right away, 9
   JIST Cards as, 60–63, 65
   length of, 6, 103
   other names for, 4
   paper for, 7–8, 104
   photocopying, 7
   printing, 7
   proofreading, 6–7
   reasons against having, 3–4
   reasons for having, 5
   sending out indiscriminately, 11–12
   skills resumes, 10, 34–48
   special formats, 11
   unsolicited resumes, cover letters for, 59
   word-processing software for, 7
   *writing. See chronological resumes; skills
      resumes; writing resumes*
ResuMiniMe, 61
rules, breaking in resumes, 8

S

sales professional sample resume, 130
sales sample resumes, 130–143
science, engineering, and technology
  sample resumes, 112–118
"search me" button, creating, 77
searches. *See* job searches
senior account executive sample resume,
  132–133
senior executive sample resumes, 159–162
senior finance executive sample resume,
  151–152
senior management executive sample
  resume, 159–160
signatures on thank-you notes, 68
skills, emphasizing, 101
skills resumes, 10
  final draft, 41
  job objective in, 37
  samples of, 36, 42–48
  skills section in, 38–41
  who should use, 34–35
skills section in skills resumes, 38–41
social media. *See* online identity
  management
sous chef sample resume, 169
special resume formats, 11
special sections, including in resume,
  85–86
stories for key skills, 40–41
substitute teacher sample resume, 119
summary sections
  in chronological resumes, 19
  improving, 85

T

tables in resumes, samples of, 137–138
teacher sample resumes, 119–122
technical manager sample resume, 115–116
technology sales and business development
  leader sample resume, 134–135
technology sales leader sample resume,
  137–138
technology sample resumes. *See* science,
  engineering, and technology sample
  resumes
thank-you notes, writing, 8, 64–68
  paper for, 68
  samples of, 64, 66–67
  tips for, 67–68
  when to use, 64–67

training section
  in chronological resumes, 22
  improving, 85
transition services, evaluating, 84–85
truck driver sample resume, 45–47
tweets, 78
type styles, 103

U–V

unsolicited resumes, cover letters for, 59
verbs. *See* action words
VistaPrint, 61
VisualCV website, 79
Vizibility website, 77
voicemail messages, 18
volunteer history in resumes, 23–24

W–Z

want ads, responses to, 58
Web portfolios, 79
women's health nurse practitioner sample
  resume, 108–109
Word format sample resume, 72
word-processing software for resumes, 7
work history in resumes, 23–24
worksheets
  Comprehensive Resume Worksheet,
    87–98
  Identify Your Key Transferable Skills, 39
  Instant Resume Worksheet, 27–33
  The Job Objective Worksheet, 20–21
writing
  blogs, 78
  cover letters, 49–59
  JIST Cards, 60–63
  thank-you notes, 8, 64–68
writing resumes. *See also* chronological
  resumes; skills resumes
  career counselors and transition services,
    84–85
  Comprehensive Resume Worksheet,
    87–98
  design tips for, 102–104
  improvement on basic resume, 85–86
  Instant Resume Worksheet, 27–33
  professional resume writers, 81–84
  tips for, 99–102

guardrails

avoiding regrets in your life

Andy Stanley

ZONDERVAN®

NORTH POINT
RESOURCES

ZONDERVAN.com/
AUTHORTRACKER
follow your favorite authors

CONTENTS

Introduction: Design Your System 5

Session 1: Direct and Protect 9

Session 2: Why Can't We Be Friends? 19

Session 3: Flee Baby Flee! 31

Session 4: Me and the Mrs 43

Session 5: The Consumption Assumption. 55

Session 6: Once and for All 67

Leader's Guide 75

INTRODUCTION

Design Your System

by Andy Stanley

Everybody knows what guardrails are. But you probably don't know the official definition.

Guardrails are actually "a system designed to keep vehicles from straying into dangerous or off-limit areas."

So they keep us *out* of danger . . . and *inside* the proper limits.

A Little Hurt Is Better than a Lot

The theory behind a guardrail is that you'll experience less injury to yourself, and maybe even less damage to your vehicle, if you strike a guardrail rather than crashing into something on the other side of it. The whole idea is that it's okay to cause a small amount of harm in order to keep from experiencing something worse.

And think about this. Many guardrails exclude us from areas where, theoretically at least, we *actually could drive*. But driving there could be bad news.

We don't pay much attention to guardrails until the moment comes when we need one. As we drive along, they're an invisible part of our traveling experience.

We're glad they're there—on bridges, in medians, and around curves—but for the most part, we pay no attention to them.

Bypassing Regrets

Guardrails. It's a concept that relates keenly to other areas of our lives.

Because chances are, if we'd had some form of guardrails established in a certain area, we could have avoided our greatest regrets in life. It might be something that hurt us financially, relationally, morally, or professionally. Whatever it was, and however much it hurt, it *might never have happened* if only we'd established some protective barriers.

The Tragic Results Nobody Wants

In our dangerous culture, we're all aware of certain destructive consequences, the kind we don't want in our lives.

If we could set up some guardrails that would always keep those tragic consequences on the other side of them—wouldn't that be worth it? Then whenever we bumped against them, they would keep us from destroying our lives.

We never *plan* to mess up, but it happens so easily when we fail to establish guardrails.

We shouldn't ignore this whole concept because we think, *Well, I just hope God will protect me.* Because God's protection for us actually comes through the guardrails he's given us throughout the Bible. Yes, he intends to protect us, and that's how.

To the Edge

What's sad is how we flirt with disaster in so many significant arenas of life. Many of us naturally assume we can play as close to the edge of the abyss as we want without experiencing harm. We like the thrill of just being there. And though we know about the danger (after all, that's why it's so thrilling), we don't *really* think we're personally at risk of falling.

We're so self-confident. But believe me, so were those who went over the cliff, right up until the moment they plunged uncontrollably into tragedy.

For the Future's Sake

Think about your future a moment. Can you imagine what it might be like if, from now on, you had adequate guardrails in place in all the significant areas of your life? We need them because our culture is baiting us to the edge of disaster, only to scold or punish us if we ever step across the line.

So let's stop flirting with disaster and take time now to set up the protections we need.

No one has ever regretted establishing a guardrail—but there are plenty of us who look back and regret not having them.

SESSION 1

Direct and Protect

Good fathers want to keep their children out of harm's way. So they set protective barriers, and they talk to their children about them. They establish rules and boundaries to keep their behavior from getting them too close to damaging consequences.

Isn't that exactly what a good father *should* do?

This fatherly approach is a big part of both the Old and New Testaments—just as we might expect, knowing how much God, our heavenly Father, loves us. He wants to keep his children away from life's danger zones. And in his goodness, he's done what it takes to help us do exactly that.

He knows the kinds of boundaries we need to set for ourselves. Are you willing to look at this with him, to hear the kind of help he wants to give you?

DISCUSSION STARTER

Have you ever been in a traffic accident (or seen one) where a vehicle hit a guardrail? If so, what function did the guardrail serve? What did it prevent?

How would you define a guardrail's purpose, in your own words?

VIDEO OVERVIEW

For Session 1 of the DVD

We can think of a guardrail as a *personal standard of behavior* that becomes a matter of conscience. Whenever we bump against these guardrails, we receive an internal warning.

In our culture there are behaviors that almost everyone agrees are bad—serious mistakes and dangerous actions to avoid—whether relationally, financially, morally, ethically, or professionally. Nevertheless, our culture's warning system can be very weak.

In fact, our culture doesn't like the kinds of guardrails we're talking about here. They're seen as stupid, silly rules—too confining and restrictive.

In the book of Ephesians, as he addressed people living in a culture even more immoral than ours, the apostle Paul lists several things people needed to be on their guard about. And to help them do this, he also uses the concept of guardrails.

He urged them to "be very careful" how they lived, reminding them that "the days are evil" (5:15–16). They were living in dangerous times, as we are today.

Paul adds, "Therefore do not be foolish, but understand what the Lord's will is" (5:17). He wants them to face up to God's will for their lives in every area.

The first illustration Paul gives of a guardrail concerns alcohol. He tells his readers not to get drunk, because it leads to debauchery—the kind of extreme indulgence that results in loss of control. Paul sets up the avoidance of drunkenness as a guardrail against something worse.

Throughout the Scriptures, we discover warnings to avoid whatever leads to this kind of loss of control in our lives—whether it's lust, drunkenness, greed, anger, gluttony, or whatever.

To emphasize his point, Paul presents a contrast. He says that instead of getting drunk, they should "be filled with the Spirit" (5:18).

Paul knows that our heavenly Father wants to be the preeminent influencer in our lives. And the Bible teaches that when we put our faith in Christ, the Spirit of God comes to live in us in a unique way, to prompt us, guide us, and direct us.

Paul is saying, *When you sense that still, small voice warning you on the inside, then pay attention. Be careful! Because your life's too important and time's too short and the world's too dangerous not to.*

VIDEO NOTES

_____

_____

_____

_____

_____

_____

_____

_____

_____

_____

_____

_____

_____

_____

_____

_____

_____

_____

_____

DISCUSSION QUESTIONS

1. Andy defines a guardrail as "a personal standard of behavior that becomes a matter of conscience." Why is it important that we think of these guardrails *personally*—as something individually for us and not necessarily for everyone?

2. In establishing guardrails, why is it important that they be linked to our consciences?

3. What are the kinds of disasters and danger zones that you especially want to guard against—in your marriage and family, as well as financially, professionally, morally, ethically, relationally, and in other areas?

4. How can establishing guardrails help open us to the protective love of God?

5. What kind of protection from God should we be able to count on? What kind of protection from him should we not count on?

6. In various areas of your life, how strong is your desire to live by God's will and God's plan? How well do you know his will and his plan in each of these areas?

MILEPOSTS

- We all need to establish guardrails in significant areas of our lives. They protect us from the "danger zones," where the consequences are most destructive.

- Guardrails are valuable because they help us avoid the great regrets of life. All of us have areas of regret that could have been avoided if we'd established guardrails in those areas.

- A guardrail is a personal standard of behavior that becomes a matter of conscience. It's personal—meant just for us (and not as a rule that applies to everyone). And it involves the conscience, so that it triggers our sense of danger and brings a sense of guilt when we bump against it.

MOVING FORWARD

At this point, what is your attitude and response concerning the whole idea of establishing guardrails in your life? Is this something you see a need for? Why or why not?

CHANGING YOUR MIND

Allow this passage to help you focus on our highest aim when we establish guardrails:

Therefore do not be foolish,
but understand what the Lord's will is.
Ephesians 5:17

PREPARATION FOR SESSION 2

To help you prepare for Session 2, use these suggested devotions during the week leading up to your small group meeting.

Day One

Look at Proverbs 13:20. In your own words, how would you restate both the *promise* and the *warning* found in that verse?

Day Two

How does 1 Corinthians 15:33 relate to the truths you saw in Proverbs 13:20?

Day Three

Look at what we're told to do with others in Hebrews 10:24–25. To what extent does this happen when you are with your friends?

Day Four

Look also at what we're told to do with others in 1 Thessalonians 5:11. To what extent does this happen when you are with your friends?

Day Five

Look also at what we're told to do with others in Hebrews 3:13. To
what extent does this happen when you are with your friends?

Last Session

A guardrail is a personal standard of behavior that becomes a matter of conscience. We need guardrails in every significant area of our lives, because they protect us from the "danger zones," where we're likely to be deeply hurt. These guardrails help us avoid the big regrets of life.

SESSION 2

Why Can't We Be Friends?

What makes friendship so great is the same thing that makes it so dangerous. With friends, we drop our guards. We're most open to influence from others when we're with people who accept us the way real friends do.

Acceptance leads to influence. And it can work for us—or against us. Some of the most addictive behaviors imaginable are those that people began as pastimes with friends.

Our friends greatly influence the direction and the quality of our lives. In fact, they can actually *determine* the direction and the quality of our lives. Think about it: how much have your friends impacted who you are?

Friendships are valuable. But because friendships can also be dangerous, we need guardrails.

DISCUSSION STARTER

Who are some of the most influential friends you've known, and how did they influence you? What did you appreciate most about them and their friendship? What did the relationships teach you about friendship?

In general, how would you describe the value of friendship?

VIDEO OVERVIEW

For Session 2 of the DVD

In the Bible, we see an important principle about friendship stated in an unmistakable way by Solomon. It's in Proverbs 13:20, which offers both a promise and a warning: "Walk with the wise and become wise, for a companion of fools suffers harm."

Solomon says that wisdom is contagious. If we surround ourselves with wise people, we too will become wise.

According to Scripture, a wise person is someone who understands that all of life is connected. He or she knows that what we do today—our decisions, thoughts, and actions—will influence who we are tomorrow. There are no isolated events or thought patterns or relationships or habits. They are all connected.

So, the wise person makes decisions based not simply on today, but on tomorrow and the day after.

The warning in Proverbs 13:20 is not that a companion of fools will become a fool himself. Rather, the companion of fools will eventually be hurt in some way by the fool's behavior. We might spend our entire lives with fools and never see the world in the same way they do or behave as they do. But eventually the shrapnel from the devastation in their lives will impact us, no matter how strong and disciplined we think we are.

Some of us have defended unhealthy relationships by thinking, *I'll never go along with the wrong things they participate in or the wrong things they believe; therefore, I'm safe.* Solomon would answer that by saying, *You're dead wrong, because the companion of fools will eventually be harmed by the outcome of the fool's behavior.*

The Bible describes a fool as someone who knows the difference between right and wrong but doesn't care. Fools live as if today has no bearing on tomorrow. If we have friends who don't care about their own lives, they won't be concerned about ours either.

If we ignore this principle, we will ultimately suffer the consequences. But if we leverage it to our benefit, we'll be rewarded.

In light of this principle, here are four suggested guardrails for friendships. These are things that should cause us concern, things that should bother us when we recognize them:

- When our core group of friends isn't moving in the direction we want our lives to go

- When we catch ourselves pretending to be someone other than who we know we are

- When we hear ourselves saying, *I'll go, but I won't participate*

- When we hope the people we care about most won't discover where we've been or who we've been with

These things should concern us to the point that we do something about them, rather than wait until there's a serious problem.

VIDEO NOTES

_____

_____

_____

_____

_____

_____

_____

_____

_____

_____

_____

_____

_____

_____

_____

_____

_____

_____

DISCUSSION QUESTIONS

1. How fully do you agree with this statement: "Our friends ultimately influence the direction and quality of our lives"?

2. As you see it, how strong is the connection between being *accepted* by others and being open to their influence?

3. If it's true that "friendships can be dangerous," how would you describe the danger?

4. How would you define "wisdom"? And what are the most important ways it can be learned from our friends?

5. If a fool can be biblically defined as "someone who knows the difference between right and wrong, but doesn't care," how can we discover whether this is actually true of someone we know?

6. What kind of pressure do you experience in your circle of friends? Is it mostly positive or negative?

MILEPOSTS

- We need guardrails in our friendships because our friends greatly impact the direction and quality of our lives. In many ways, they actually *determine* the direction and quality of our lives.

- Friendships are valuable. If we surround ourselves with friends who understand life's connectedness, we'll grow in our own understanding of this important truth.

- Friendships can also be dangerous. If we surround ourselves with friends who are fools—who *do not* understand life's connectedness—we'll be negatively impacted by the destructive consequences in their lives.

MOVING FORWARD

Take time to evaluate your circle of friends. Are they moving in the direction you want your life to go? When you're around them, do you find yourself pretending to be someone you really aren't? Do you feel pressure to compromise?

CHANGING YOUR MIND

Reflect on this session's key Scripture passage, and use it to deepen

your understanding of the dynamics of friendship.

Walk with the wise and become wise,
for a companion of fools suffers harm.
Proverbs 13:20

PREPARATION FOR SESSION 3

To help you prepare for Session 3, use these suggested devotions during the week leading up to your small group meeting.

Day One

Read 1 Corinthians 6:18–20. What are we commanded to do in the opening words of this passage? And what do you see as the significance of that command?

Day Two

Read 1 Corinthians 6:18–20. After the brief opening command in verse 18, one reason for that command is given in the rest of verse 18. How would you explain that reason in your own words?

Day Three

Read 1 Corinthians 6:18–20. What reason for fleeing sexual immorality is given in the first part of verse 19? How would you explain this in your own words?

Day Four

Read 1 Corinthians 6:18–20. What additional reasons for fleeing sexual immorality are given in the last part of verse 19 and in the first part of verse 20? How would you restate these in your own words?

Day Five

Read 1 Corinthians 6:18–20. Notice the command that is given in the last line in verse 20. What does this mean?

Last Session

Friendships are valuable, but they can also be dangerous. The right friends wisely understand life's connectedness, and they enable us to do the same. The wrong friends are fools who don't understand life's connectedness, and when their lives are shattered, the impact brings harm to us as well.

SESSION 3

Flee Baby Flee!

When it comes to establishing guardrails, there's one area more than any other where they are needed. Yet, it's the area where we find the most resistance to them. For some reason, we have a hard time facing up to this issue until we finally begin seeing it realistically.

Guardrails are needed in every area of our lives where we experience desire, but when it comes to sexual intimacy, we need the strongest and toughest guardrails.

In other areas of life—financially, educationally, professionally—we can fully recover from just about any kind of disaster, given enough time. We can eventually recover from our mistakes and failures; we learn from them and eventually even laugh about them.

But sexual disaster is almost impossible to fully recover from.

That's because we know intuitively that sex isn't just physical; it's much deeper than that. When people cross certain lines in their desire for physical intimacy, there are things they'll carry with them—the damage, the guilt, the ghosts—for the rest of their lives.

It goes on and on and on.

This is where all of us emphatically need guardrails.

DISCUSSION STARTER

How would you evaluate our culture's general approach to sexual intimacy? How do you see it influencing the people you know best? How has it influenced you?

VIDEO OVERVIEW

For Session 3 of the DVD

We would all be better off if we took this simple verse more seriously: "Flee from sexual immorality" (1 Corinthians 6:18). *Flee*—not "be careful" or "watch out." *Flee.* When it comes to sexual immorality, what could be any clearer?

Flee. This is exactly what we want our friends and family to do when it comes to sexual immorality. But when it comes to us, we often flirt rather than flee, don't we?

In all the areas where we need guardrails, our culture baits us to the edge of disaster, and then mocks us when we step over. This is especially true in the area of sexual immorality. Our culture isn't going to improve in this regard, so we need guardrails.

The Bible gives us great incentives for creating guardrails in this area. Paul asks, "Do you not know that your bodies are temples of the Holy Spirit, who is in you, whom you have received from God?" (1 Corinthians 6:19). He goes on: "You are not your own. You were bought at a price" (6:19–20). When Christ died for our sins, he purchased us from sin. We're no longer slaves to sin and to our desires and appetites. So Paul concludes with this application: "Therefore honor God with your bodies" (6:20).

Here are some specific guardrails to consider as we honor God with our bodies.

First, a list for married people:

1. Don't travel alone with someone of the opposite sex.

2. Don't eat alone or have coffee alone with someone of the opposite sex.

3. Don't hire "cute" members of the opposite sex because you want to help them.

4. Don't confide in or counsel someone of the opposite sex.

5. When you feel an attraction toward a specific person, tell someone immediately (not necessarily your spouse).

6. Make sure your spouse knows where your guardrails are so he or she can be comfortable with them and hold you accountable to them.

And for singles:

1. In any relationship with a married person of the opposite sex, don't travel alone or have meals alone with that person, and don't confide in or counsel that person.

2. No sleepovers.

3. In your social environment, if a date has become equivalent to having sex, then decide on a one-year break from relationships with the opposite sex. Use that time to allow God to renew your mind and heart.

VIDEO NOTES

_____

_____

_____

_____

_____

_____

_____

_____

_____

_____

_____

_____

_____

_____

_____

_____

_____

DISCUSSION QUESTIONS

1. In your own understanding, why do we especially need guardrails to protect us from sexual immorality? Why is this a strategic area for strengthening our own protections?

2. Without reavealing names, what examples can you give of people whose lives have been permanently altered by sexual immorality?

3. Why do you think our culture—and all of us, in general—is often so resistant to the idea of establishing protective barriers in this area?

4. Why exactly can we *not* expect our culture to become a healthier environment for promoting higher standards of sexual morality?

5. With a biblical perspective in mind, why is it so important to "flee from sexual immorality" (1 Corinthians 6:18)? Why is this kind of avoidance and escape so strategic and valuable?

6. What exactly does it mean to you to "honor God" with your body (as we're told to do in 1 Corinthians 6:20)?

MILEPOSTS

- We need stronger guardrails in the area of sexual intimacy than anywhere else in life, because sexual disaster has permanent consequences.

- The Bible is clear about sexual immorality: *Flee!* (1 Corinthians 6:18). We're to actively shun temptations to sexual immorality.

- There are a number of proven guardrails we can establish to help us in this area to honor God with our bodies.

MOVING FORWARD

Think carefully through the specific guardrails suggested by Andy in this session. Which ones do you need to immediately establish in your life? If you find yourself resisting some of them—why exactly is that? What other similar guidelines come to mind as being appropriate for you?

CHANGING YOUR MIND

Allow this biblical instruction to be a powerful motivation for you to

"flee from sexual immorality" (1 Corinthians 6:18).

Do you not know that your bodies are temples of the Holy Spirit,
who is in you, whom you have received from God?
You are not your own; you were bought at a price.
Therefore honor God with your bodies.
1 Corinthians 6:19–20

PREPARATION FOR SESSION 4

To help you prepare for Session 4, use these suggested devotions during the week leading up to your small group meeting.

Day One

Proverbs 27:12 is a "guardrail" verse. Look it up, and think about its meaning. How could you apply it in prayer, asking for God's help? And how could it apply in helping you establish guardrails in your life?

Day Two

A potential "guardrail" verse is Proverbs 4:23. For this verse, answer the same questions as you did in Day One for Proverbs 27:12.

Day Three

Another guardrail passage to consider is Psalm 119:9–11. For this passage, answer the questions for Day One.

Day Four

A passage to conisder is 1 Corinthians 6:12. Again, apply to this verse the questions for Day One.

Day Five

Another passage to consider is 1 Corinthians 10:31. Again, apply to this verse the questions given in Day One.

Last Session

Flee sexual immorality—that's a clear biblical principle that should govern our behavior in responding to sexual temptation.

SESSION 4

Me and the Mrs.

Maybe setting up guardrails in your life sounds like a wise thing to do, but you're thinking it's easier said than done. Especially if you're a husband or a wife, and you're thinking through how the two of you can approach this whole concept together.

DISCUSSION STARTER

Among the couples you know, what good examples have you seen of deciding on protective strategies together to ensure the health and vitality of their marriages?

VIDEO OVERVIEW

For Session 4 of the DVD

Guardrails not only protect; they also direct. They guide us in discerning the will of God.

Establishing and living by guardrails earns respect from others who appreciate personal standards.

Proverbs 27:12 is a guardrail verse: "The prudent see danger and take refuge, but the simple keep going and suffer for it." From it comes this prayer:

"Lord, help us see danger coming before it gets here; and as we see it, give us the wisdom to know what to do and the courage to do it."

Inappropriate relationships at work can have undesirable effects on our homes and families. So, another guardrail is for managers and executives to solicit their spouses' feedback and buy-in on their hiring decisions. There's normally a high wall dividing work and home, but what happens emotionally and relationally at work crosses over in its impact on the home. So why not bring down that wall by inviting that kind of involvement from spouses?

"Small groups" at church offer another relational guardrail. The relationships built there—through sharing life together, praying together, and exploring God's Word together—will quickly offer deep support, accountability, and friendship.

Wise financial guardrails in marriage include recording all expenses, deciding up-front what percentage of our income to live on (allowing for margin, avoiding debt, and being generous), and deciding to make *giving* a priority. Giving first is a guardrail against the assumption that all our income is for our own consumption—thus breaking the power of greed.

In the ongoing tension between work and home, another guardrail is choosing to let it be our professions that suffer, not our families—since there isn't really enough time to fully satisfy both. An example would be choosing to return home each day at a set time agreed to by both husband and wife.

Another guardrail is to diligently guard our schedules in order to focus on the primary task God has called us to—the kind of focus Nehemiah displayed when others tried to sidetrack him and he responded, "I am doing a great work and I cannot come down" (Nehemiah 6:3 NASB).

Another is for a couple to maintain a marriage-centered family, not a kids-centered family, with adequate time for just the two of them to continue nurturing their relationship.

VIDEO NOTES

_____

_____

_____

_____

_____

_____

_____

_____

_____

_____

_____

_____

_____

_____

_____

_____

_____

_____

DISCUSSION QUESTIONS

1. "Guardrails not only protect; they also direct." Explain how you see that working. How can guardrails function practically to help us discover God's guidance?

2. Do you respect people who establish and live by the kinds of guardrails we've discussed in this series? Why or why not?

3. What are some ways we can more clearly recognize approaching danger as it confronts our marriages or families or other relationships? Or as it threatens our personal or professional lives?

4. What accountability, support, encouragement, and friend-ship can you count on from those outside your family?

5. What do you see as the most important factors for couples to consider as they guard their finances?

6. What do you see as the most important factors for couples to consider as they guard the use of their time?

MILEPOSTS

- Guardrails have proven value. Guardrails not only protect; they also *direct*. By establishing strong guardrails, we allow ourselves to more easily receive guidance and direction from God.

- As a key guardrail verse, Proverbs 27:12 helps us understand the need to protect ourselves from approaching danger, rather than casually continuing forward and encountering negative consequences.

- The right guardrails help us make the best use of our finances and our time, as well as strengthening our families and other relationships.

MOVING FORWARD

What do you find most encouraging from the things that Sandra and Andy have learned and applied in their marriage and family? If you're married, in what ways do you identify with them? In what way is your marriage different (not better or worse; just different) from theirs? What can you learn from them? What do you think they might be able to learn from you?

CHANGING YOUR MIND

Adopt this verse into protective thinking and strategies for yourself

and your family:

> *The prudent see danger and take refuge,*
> *but the simple keep going and pay the penalty.*
> *Proverbs 27:12*

PREPARATION FOR SESSION 5

To help you prepare for Session 5, use these suggested devotions during the week leading up to your small group meeting.

Day One

Read the words of Jesus in Matthew 6:24. What truths does this passage uncover about our loyalty, devotion, and service?

Day Two

Continue reading Jesus' words in Matthew 6:25–30. What important truth is Jesus trying to teach us about God?

Day Three

Continue in this passage, this time reading Matthew 6:31–32, where Jesus sums up what he has been saying in the previous verses. How would you summarize it in your own words?

Day Four

Read Matthew 6:33. What is Jesus asking us to do here? And what promise does he make?

Day Five

Finally, read Matthew 6:34. What further emphasis does this passage give to the whole point of what you've been reading in Matthew 6:24–33?

Last Session

Guardrails have proven their protective value repeatedly. And they help *direct* us as well as protect us—they open us up to a clearer discernment of God's will. In our finances, our use of time, our family relationships, and many other areas, guardrails bring an order and security to life that we otherwise would miss.

SESSION 5

The Consumption Assumption

Most of our worst crises in life and most of our greatest regrets have to do with either sex or money. Yet, our culture usually dismisses anything Scripture has to say about these topics.

We looked earlier at one of those tough issues; now let's tackle the other. What do you need to be on your guard about when it comes to finances?

The Bible has a great deal to say on this topic. And it all comes back to one simple thing.

The reason God says so much about it actually has nothing to do with money; it has everything to do with *devotion*. God knows that his chief competition for our hearts and our devotion—for our loyalty, our fellowship, and our service—is not the devil, but rather our wealth and consumption.

God knows that if he can control your money, he has your heart—because (as Jesus taught), where your treasure is, that's where your heart is also.

When it comes to your finances, what needs guarding is not your cash, but your heart.

DISCUSSION STARTER

In your approach to finances, do you think of yourself as more of a saver or a spender? If you're married, how would you categorize your spouse?

VIDEO OVERVIEW

For Session 5 of the DVD

Jesus says, "No one can serve two masters. Either you will hate the one and love the other, or you will be devoted to the one and despise the other. *You cannot serve both God and Money"* (Matthew 6:24).

We're in tension about whether to place our trust in God or in money and the pursuit of wealth (and whatever money can buy).

As we think about our need for guardrails in this area, there are ditches on both sides of our paths when it comes to finances: consumption and hoarding. Most of us don't want to be hoarders; we're fine with being consumers. But consuming, strictly speaking, means the consumption of everything that comes our way. Meanwhile, hoarding happens because we're anxiously asking, *What if I get sick and can't work? What if the economy gets worse? What if, what if, what if?*

Both the consumer and the hoarder are self-centered; both live as if there is no God; and both are fueled by greed. Greed is simply the assumption that anything coming to us is for our own consumption—either now or later.

We can believe in God yet still be fueled by greed if finances are our chief concern and the object of our ultimate dependence. And when we face financial difficulties, we're quick to ask God for help. God is like our backup financial plan. He's on the periphery.

But the Bible tells us that God wants to be the master and ruler of our lives, not our backup plan.

The key to breaking the power of greed is simple. It's a habit we develop through our decision to allow our heavenly Father to rule our lives. That habit is described in just three words: give, save, live.

That's the order of priority. When we are paid, the first thing we do is give a percentage away. This is saying, *God, I will not be ruled by my stuff. I will not be owned by the things I own. My hands are open. The first percentage goes to you.*

Jesus later tells us not to worry about the things we truly need that money can buy. When we worry like that, we're living as if God isn't aware and doesn't care.

One of the biggest decisions we can make is to affirm for all time that God knows and God cares. Then we will begin changing our orientations from stuff-centered to God-centered, as we continually seek his help in managing our lives and finances.

Then we're free to carry out the pursuit Jesus calls us to: "Seek first his kingdom [that is, God's purpose and will] and his righteousness [God's values, God's understanding of right and wrong], and all these things [those needs that we worry about] will be given to you as well" (Matthew 6:33).

VIDEO NOTES

_____

_____

_____

_____

_____

_____

_____

_____

_____

_____

_____

_____

_____

_____

_____

_____

_____

_____

_____

DISCUSSION QUESTIONS

1. In your own life, in what ways do you see money and the pursuit of wealth (or whatever wealth promises to buy, such as security or pleasure) as competitors to your devotion to God?

2. Do you sense a tension between your approach to finances and your love of God? If so, how would you describe it?

3. In practical terms, what's your understanding of greed? What's at the root of it?

4. In what ways (if any) are finances a major, ongoing concern in your life?

5. How would you say your approach to finances affects your desire to know God's purpose and will?

6. How would you say your approach to finances affects your openness to understanding God's values and standards?

MILEPOSTS

- Our urgent need for guardrails in the area of our finances is reflected in the fact that God has so much to say in the Bible about the role of money in our lives.

- Money is the leading competitor in our hearts to our devotion to God. Jesus makes it clear that none of us can be devoted to both God and money. Our tendency to be greedy is deep-rooted.

- To counter our tendency toward greed, the most practical guardrail in the area of our finances is to develop the habit of *give, save, live* as our system of financial priorities.

MOVING FORWARD

How conscious are you of the fact that God fully *knows* all your needs (including your financial needs), and that he completely *cares* for you and is entirely committed to meeting all your true needs? Is this something you have already affirmed to him in prayer? Is that something you need to do now?

CHANGING YOUR MIND

The words of Jesus in this passage are well known for their liberating power and perspective. Take them to heart as they relate to your own financial needs.

> *But seek first his kingdom and his righteousness,*
> *and all these things will be given to you as well.*
> *Matthew 6:33*

PREPARATION FOR SESSION 6

To help you prepare for Session 6, use these suggested devotions during the week leading up to your small group meeting.

Day One

Open your Bible to the book of Daniel. What important background information to Daniel's story is given in the first seven verses of chapter 1?

Day Two

What important decision does Daniel make in verse 8 of chapter 1? How would you explain the significance of this?

Day Three

Read Daniel 1:9–14. What "test" does Daniel propose, and how is it put into place? How do these verses demonstrate Daniel's trust in God?

Day Four

What was the outcome of the test that Daniel proposed, according to verses 15–16 in chapter 1?

Day Five

What were the further consequences of Daniel's action, according to

Daniel 1:17–21?

Last Session

God's leading competitor to our heart's devotion is our devotion to money, which is deeply rooted in our tendency toward greed. But we can counter that tendency by establishing a practical guardrail—by practicing the habit of *give, save, live* as our system of financial priorities.

SESSION 6

Once and for All

Here's our big pushback to establishing guardrails: "They'll keep me from something I want. They'll be in my way."

But guardrails or no guardrails, the tension we feel isn't going away. The temptations will be there. Eliminating guardrails will only erode our resolve and bring us to a place of temptation where the consequences are much worse. Not having guardrails just moves the battle line closer to disaster.

Our desires and appetites are never fully and finally satisfied. They always come back for more. We shouldn't deceive ourselves into thinking that by saying yes, yes, yes, yes, yes, we'll never have to say no.

There's someone in Scripture who knew all this and demonstrated what it can mean in one of the most dramatic life stories in all of history.

DISCUSSION STARTER

If you're familiar with the story of Daniel in the Bible, what do you re-
call most from his life? What impresses you most about him?

VIDEO OVERVIEW

For Session 6 of the DVD

In 605 BC, Daniel and his three friends Hananiah, Mishael, and Aza-
riah (also known as Shadrach, Meshach, and Abednego) were among
the Jewish nobles taken captive to Babylon by King Nebuchadnez-
zar. There they were to undergo a three-year process of being indoc-
trinated and reoriented to Babylonian culture before they entered
the king's service. As Daniel realized, this would mean being slowly
stripped of their beliefs and values.

So, Daniel "resolved not to defile himself with the royal food and
wine, and he asked the chief official [whose name was Asphenaz] for
permission not to defile himself this way" (Daniel 1:8).

Then we read, "*Now God* had caused the official to show favor
and compassion to Daniel" (Daniel 1:9). Daniel knew that God uses
our guardrails not only to protect us, but also to direct us.

Because of Daniel's resolve, what happens from this point on in
his story is amazing. Daniel's decision to draw a line in the sand was
the thing God used to direct his entire life. If he hadn't made this de-

cision, we wouldn't have a book in the Bible called Daniel.

More than he could possibly imagine, everything hinged on his decision whether to eat the royal meat and drink the royal wine. Daniel said no—and God essentially responded, "This is your defining moment. I'm going to direct your entire future by this decision."

That experience is similar for many people. God becomes most real to them—and they discover the clearest direction in their lives—not when they're praying for his direction, but in moments of temptation and trials, moments of tension when they decide, *This is where I draw the line; this is as far as I'll go.* They later look back and realize, *That's the decision God used to completely redirect my life.* They were just trying to make the right ethical or moral decision, and God used it not only to protect them, but also to direct them.

Daniel had no idea what hung in the balance with his decision. We also have no idea what hangs in the balance of our decisions to establish guardrails for our lives. But later we'll be able to look back and say, "That was a defining moment. God redirected my entire life because I made up my mind."

In Daniel's story, God honored his decision. It was the beginning of a journey for his friends and him that would profoundly impact the nation of Israel. And it all started with a simple decision to say, "That's as far as I'll go."

VIDEO NOTES

_____

_____

_____

_____

_____

_____

_____

_____

_____

_____

_____

_____

_____

_____

_____

_____

_____

_____

_____

_____

DISCUSSION QUESTIONS

1. Are you experiencing any kind of continuing resistance to the idea of guardrails in your life? If so, how would you describe this resistance? And how would you explain the reason for it?

2. We all know the pressure and tension we feel when we encounter temptation. Can yielding to the temptation eliminate that feeling? Explain your understanding of this.

3. How have you personally seen the truth of this statement: "Our appetites are never fully and finally satisfied; they always come back wanting more"?

4. Do you think of establishing guardrails as a "defining mo-
    ment" in your life? If so, in what way?

5. What further help do you want or feel you need in establish-
    ing strong guardrails?

6. What have you learned most in this series about the impor-
    tance and value of guardrails?

MILEPOSTS

- We might resist the idea of guardrails, but there's no escaping the tension we'll continue to feel as we encounter temptations in every area of life. Yielding to temptation only increases the effects of the consequences later on.

- The levels of temptations will increase because in this life we never reach a point of having our desires and appetites fully satisfied.

- The story of Daniel dramatically illustrates the amazing destiny that unfolds for those who learn to draw the line, who in the face of temptation learn to say: *I refuse to go further.*

MOVING FORWARD

Have you made up your mind to keep and maintain guardrails in all the significant areas of your life? Have you resolved to draw the line in these areas and say, "That's as far as I'll go"? If so, what is your motivation for doing so, in light of your heavenly Father's loving care and control over your life?

CHANGING YOUR MIND

Reflect on these words, and ask God to allow you to experience the kind of integrity, uprightness, and guidance that the first line speaks of:

*The integrity of the upright guides them,
but the unfaithful are destroyed by their duplicity.
Proverbs 11:3*

Leader's Guide

So, You're the Leader...

Is that intimidating? Perhaps exciting? No doubt you have some mental pictures of what it will look like, what you will say, and how it will go. Before you get too far into the planning process, there are some things you should know about leading a small group discussion. We've compiled some tried and true techniques here to help you.

Basics About Leading

1. Cultivate discussion — It's easy to think that the meeting lives or dies by your ideas. In reality, the ideas of everyone in the group are what make a small group meeting successful. The most valuable thing you can do is to get people to share their thoughts. That's how the relationships in your group will grow and thrive. Here's a rule: The impact of your study material will typically never exceed the impact of the relationships through which it was studied. The more meaningful the relationships, the more meaningful the study. In a sterile environment, even the best material is suppressed.

2. Point to the material — A good host or hostess gets the party going by offering delectable hors d'oeuvres and beverages. You too should be ready to serve up "delicacies" from the material. Sometimes you will simply read the discussion questions and invite everyone to respond. At other times, you will encourage others to share their ideas. Remember, some of the best treats are the ones your guests will bring to the party. Go with the flow of the meeting, and be ready to pop out of the kitchen as needed.

3. Depart from the material — A talented ministry team has carefully designed this study for your small group. But that doesn't mean you should follow every part word for word. Knowing how and when to depart from the material is a valuable art. Nobody knows more about your people than you do. The narratives, questions, and exercises are here to provide a framework for discovery. However, every group is motivated differently. Sometimes the best way to start a small group discussion is simply to ask, "Does anyone have a personal insight or revelation they'd like to share from this week's material?" Then sit back and listen.

4. Stay on track — Conversation is the currency of a small group discussion. The more interchange, the healthier the "economy." However, you need to keep your objectives in mind. If your goal is to have a meaningful experience with this material, then you should make sure the discussion is contributing to that end. It's easy to get off on a tangent. Be prepared to interject politely and refocus the group. You might need to say something like, "Excuse me, we're obviously all interested in this subject; however, I just want to make sure we cover all the material for this week."

5. Above all, pray — The best communicators are the ones that manage to get out of God's way enough to let him communicate *through* them. That's important to keep in mind. Books don't teach God's Word; neither do sermons nor group discussions. God himself speaks into the hearts of men and women, and prayer is our vital channel to communicate directly with him. Cover your efforts in prayer. You don't just want God present at your meeting; you want him to direct it.

We hope you find these suggestions helpful. And we hope you enjoy leading this study. You will find additional guidelines and suggestions for each session in the Leader's Guide notes that follow.

Leader's Guide
Session Notes

Session 1 — Direct and Protect

Bottom Line

To help us avoid major regrets in the future, we need to set up protective guardrails in every significant area of our lives. These guardrails are personal standards of behavior that become a matter of conscience. They'll protect us from the "danger zones" of behavior that can so easily lead to disastrous consequences.

Discussion Starter

Use the "Discussion Starter" printed in Session 1 of the Participant's Guide to "break the ice"—and to help everyone recognize the obvious benefits of guardrails.

Notes for Discussion Questions

1. **Andy defines a guardrail as "a personal standard of behavior that becomes a matter of conscience." Why is it important that we think of these guardrails *personally*—as something individually for us and not necessarily for everyone?**

Guide the discussion toward greater recognition and under-standing that these standards represent our personal under-standing and convictions, *not* universal rules.

2. **In establishing guardrails, why is it important that they be linked to our consciences?**

    In this discussion, help foster awareness that our consciences can be informed and energized by these guardrails.

3. **What kinds of disasters and danger zones do you especially want to guard against—in your marriage and family, as well as financially, professionally, morally, ethically, relationally, and in other areas?**

    We probably prefer not to think how disastrous the conse-quences can be for wrong behavior, so use this question to help everyone face those facts honestly.

4. **How can establishing guardrails help open us to the protec-tive love of God?**

    Guardrails that are rooted in our convictions based on biblical principles are indeed a blessing made possible only by God's grace. Help guide the discussion toward recognizing this truth.

5.   **What kind of protection from God should we be able to count on? What kind of protection from him should we not count on?**

Use the discussion to help counter the thought that we don't need guardrails if we simply decide: *I'll rely on God to protect me.*

6.   **In various areas of your life, how strong is your desire to live by God's will and God's plan? How well do you know his will and his plan in each of these areas?**

You might want to use this question as a springboard into deeper discussion of Ephesians 5:15–18.

Moving Forward

The goal here is to help the group become familiar with the concept and value of guardrails as they apply to the way we live our lives.

Preparation for Session 2

Remember to point out the brief daily devotions that the group members can complete and which will help greatly in stimulating discussion in your next session. These devotions will enable everyone to dig into the Bible and start wrestling with the topics that will come up next time.

Session 2 — Why Can't We Be Friends?
Bottom Line

Despite the great value of friendships, they can be dangerous, be-cause our friends have so much influence over us—for bad as well as for good. That's why we need guardrails in our friendships to help us recognize when their influence is not as healthy as it should be.

Discussion Starter

Use the "Discussion Starter" listed for Session 2 of the Participant's Guide. This one should help everyone in your group focus on the value of friendship. It's definitely something that's worth protecting, and experiencing in the right way!

Notes for Discussion Questions

1. **How fully do you agree with this statement: "Our friends ul-timately influence the direction and the quality of our lives"?** Some who view themselves as more independently minded might not agree with this statement. And, indeed, some of us are more impressionable than others. But the influence of friends is still far more powerful than we often realize.

2.   **As you see it, how strong is the connection between being**

      accepted **by others and being open to their influence?**

      The discussion here can help everyone realize that the group

      of friends we've grown comfortable with might not be the best

      people for us to be around. There are many more things to

      seek in friendships than just our own comfort and sense of

      acceptance.

3.   **If it's true that "friendships can be dangerous," how would**

      you describe the danger?

      Some in the group might be able to testify to the destructive

      influence of some of their friends in the past.

4.   **How would you define "wisdom"? And what are the most im-**

      portant ways that it can be learned from our friends?

      You might want to bring in the definition mentioned in the

      teaching session—that a wise person is one who sees the con-

      nectedness of life (our todays have been shaped by our choic-

      es yesterday, and our tomorrows will be determined by our

      choices today)—and who makes decisions based on that truth.

5.   **If a fool can be biblically defined as "someone who knows**
     the difference between right and wrong, but doesn't care,"
     how can we discover whether this is actually true of some-
     one we know?

     This should prompt some interesting discussion as everyone
     thinks about friends whose actions have proven to be unwise.

6.   **What kind of pressure do you experience in your circle of**
     friends? Is it mostly positive or negative?

     Some in your group might be surprised once they honestly
     recognize and evaluate this pressure.

Moving Forward

All of us have a sense of loyalty to our friends, even when they dis-
appoint us. The goal here is to help the group see beyond that and
to move toward an honest evaluation of how healthy our friendships
really are.

Preparation for Session 3

Again, encourage your group members to complete the brief daily
devotions. These will help stimulate discussion in your next session.
They'll enable everyone to dig into the Bible and start wrestling with
the topics coming up next time.

Session 3 — Flee Baby Flee!

Bottom Line

We need stronger guardrails in the area of sexual temptation than anywhere else in life. And all our guardrails in this area should reflect the Bible's core teaching: "Flee from sexual immorality" (1 Corinthians 6:18). We need all the help we can get to escape sexual temptation.

Discussion Starter

Again, use the "Discussion Starter" listed for Session 3 of the Participant's Guide. This should help the group focus on the dangers and deceptions in our culture's approach to sexuality.

Notes for Discussion Questions

1. **In your own understanding, why do we especially need guardrails to protect us from sexual immorality? Why is this a strategic area for strengthening our own protections?**

    A number of factors mentioned in the teaching session touch on the uniqueness of this area. You might want to review these things with the group.

2. **Without revealing names, what examples can you give of people whose lives have been permanently altered by sexual immorality?**

The goal here is to help everyone honestly recognize the severe and lasting impact of sexual immorality.

3. **Why do you think our culture—and all of us, in general—is often so resistant to the idea of establishing protective barriers in this area?**

Encourage a wide-open discussion and evaluation about this. There might be a number of ideas mentioned.

4. **Why exactly can we not expect our culture to become a healthier environment for promoting higher standards of sexual morality?**

Help them recognize and face up to our culture's corruption.

5. **With a biblical perspective in mind, why is it so important to "flee from sexual immorality" (1 Corinthians 6:18)? Why is this kind of avoidance and escape so strategic and valuable?**

Encourage the group toward a stronger trust in God's wisdom

in this area. He knows what's best for us to do in response to
sexual temptation.

6.   **What exactly does it mean to you to "honor God" with your
      body (as we're told to do in 1 Corinthians 6:20)?**
      This might lead naturally to a deeper discussion of 1 Corinthi-
      ans 6:18–20.

Moving Forward

The goal here is to make positive, deliberate progress toward establishing strong guardrails in this crucial area.

Preparation for Session 4

Again, encourage your group members to complete the daily devotions. This will help them be better prepared for the topics coming
up next time.

Session 4 — Me and The Mrs.

Bottom Line

Guardrails have proven value, as Andy and Sandra Stanley can positively testify. Their encouraging example in the use of guardrails offers us insight in several dimensions.

Discussion Starter

Use the "Discussion Starter" listed for Session 4 of the Participant's
Guide. This should help everyone focus on looking to couples with
healthy marriages for good examples of guardrails

Notes for Discussion Questions

1. **"Guardrails not only protect; they also direct." Explain how
    you see that working. How can guardrails function practically
    to help us discover God's guidance?**
    Encourage a wider appreciation of the many benefits of guard-
    rails.

2. **Do you respect people who establish and live by the kinds of
    guardrails we've discussed in this series? Why or why not?**
    While we're generally not attracted to people who seem le-
    galistic, there's often a strong attraction to people with wise

convictions and standards. Help everyone see the difference.

3.   **What are some ways we can more clearly recognize approaching danger as it confronts our marriages or families or other relationships? Or as it threatens our personal or professional lives?**

Bring in Proverbs 27:12 for discussion here.

4.   **What accountability, support, encouragement, and friendship can you count on from those outside your family?**

Hopefully, this group will be growing in providing these very things for one another.

5.   **What do you see as the most important factors for couples to consider as they guard their finances?**

The guidelines from Andy and Sandra should be especially helpful here.

6.   **What do you see as the most important factors for couples to consider as they guard the use of their time?**

Again, the guidelines mentioned in the teaching session by Andy and Sandra should lead to good discussion here.

Moving Forward

The goal here is simply to encourage lingering reflection and re-
membrance concerning the things shared by Andy and Sandra in
the teaching session.

Preparation for Session 5

Again, encourage your group members to complete the daily devotions in preparation for the next session.

Session 5 — The Consumption Assumption

Bottom Line

There are no greater threats to our devotion to God—our loyalty, fellowship, and service toward him—than money and the pursuit of wealth. That's why we need strong guardrails in this area. One of the strongest is the simple priority pattern of *give, save, live* as a habit in determining how we allocate our money.

Discussion Starter

Use the "Discussion Starter" listed for Session 5 of the Participant's Guide. This should help the group focus on the different perspectives from which we view finances.

Notes for Discussion Questions

1. **In your own life, in what ways do you see money and the pursuit of wealth (or whatever wealth promises to buy, such as security or pleasure) as competitors to your devotion to God?**

    Many in your group might be resistant to recognizing this truth in their lives. It would be helpful to approach it from various angles.

2.   **Do you sense a tension between your approach to finances
      and your love of God? If so, how would you describe it?**

      Many will experience this, and the tension manifests itself in
      various ways. Explore this thoroughly.

3.   **In practical terms, what's your understanding of greed?
      What's at the root of it?**

      Refer back to the definition supplied in the teaching session:
      greed is simply our assumption that anything coming to us is
      for our own consumption—either now or later.

4.   **In what ways (if any) are finances a major, ongoing concern
      in your life?**

      For some, finances will represent a constant source of anxiety.
      Yet there will likely be a reluctance to admit this. Answering this
      very candidly yourself will help others to do the same.

5.   **How would you say your approach to finances affects your
      desire to know God's purpose and will?**

      This is a good time to bring in the command of Jesus in Mat-
      thew 6:33 about seeking first the kingdom of God.

6.   **How would you say your approach to finances affects your openness to understand God's values and standards?**

The words of Jesus in Matthew 6:33 are relevant, especially concerning our need to seek God's righteousness.

Moving Forward

Encourage your group to positively affirm for themselves the stunning reality of God's goodness and greatness in how he actively cares for us in all our needs.

Preparation for Session 6

Encourage your group members to complete the daily devotions in preparation for the next session.

Session 6 — Once and for All

Bottom Line

Our need for guardrails is accentuated by the fact that our various desires and appetites will never reach a point of being fully satisfied. Daniel's example in the Bible shows us the urgent need to draw a line and say, "I refuse to go further" in certain areas of our lives. The result will be a destiny that opens us up to God's amazing guidance and provision.

Discussion Starter

Once more, use the "Discussion Starter" listed for Session 6 of the Participant's Guide. This should help everyone in the group to focus on the exemplary value of Daniel's story in the Bible as it relates to guardrails.

Notes for Discussion Questions

1. **Are you experiencing any kind of continuing resistance to the idea of guardrails in your life? If so, how would you describe this resistance? And how would you explain the reason for it?** Allow plenty of time to discuss this. Encourage honest answers, and demonstrate positive acceptance toward anyone who's struggling with applying guardrails.

2.   **We all know the pressure and tension we feel when we en-**

      counter temptation. Can yielding to the temptation eliminate

      that feeling? Explain your understanding of this.

      Refer back to the points made about this in the teaching ses-

      sions. The answer is definitely no, but it will help us greatly if we

      understand why.

3.   **How have you personally seen the truth of this statement:**

      "Our appetites are never fully and finally satisfied; they al-

      ways come back wanting more"?

      Most, if not all, of us have come to recognize this unattractive

      truth. It might seem discouraging—but the Bible is full of encour-

      agement and truth in our fight against temptation.

4.   **Do you think of establishing guardrails as a "defining mo-**

      ment" in your life? If so, in what way?

      Obviously, this will become fully clear only in the future; nev-

      ertheless, it's encouraging to have a strong vision of what can

      happen later if we faithfully set up guardrails now.

5.   **What further help do you want or feel you need in establish-**

      ing strong guardrails in your life?

      Spend plenty of time here. Obviously, these teaching sessions

      do not deal with all the issues associated with our need for

      guardrails. There's much more we can learn and apply. Encour-

      age one another in a lifelong pursuit of these discoveries.

6.   **What have you learned most in this series about the impor-**

      tance and value of guardrails?

      Again, allow plenty of time for all group members to review the

      series highlights and to articulate a big picture view of what this

      series has meant for them.

Moving Forward

The goal here is to encourage a strong sense of vision of the good

things that can happen in the future when we're faithful now to es-

tablish strong guardrails.

Taking Responsibility for Your Life DVD

Because Nobody Else Will

Andy Stanley

RESPONSIBILITIES.

We all have them. But we don't all take them as seriously as we ought to. Wouldn't it be great, though, if we all took responsibility for the things we are responsible for? Wouldn't it be great if you took responsibility for everything you're responsible for? It's time to stop the finger-pointing and excuse-making and to remove the "ir" in irresponsible.

In this 4-part study, Andy Stanley tells us it's time to ask ourselves, "Am I REALLY taking responsibility for my life?"

Session titles:
1. Let the Blames Begin
2. The Disproportionate Life
3. This Is No Time to Pray
4. Embracing Your Response Ability

Designed for use with the *Taking Responsibility for Your Life Participant's Guide.*

Your Move

Four Questions to Ask When You Don't Know What to Do

Andy Stanley

We are all faced with decisions that we never anticipated having to make. And, we usually have to make them quickly. In this four session video group study, author and pastor Andy Stanley discusses four questions that will help participants make sound decisions with God's help. Follow Andy as he teaches how every decision and its outcomes become a permanent part of your story, what to do when you feel the need to pause before taking action, and how to make more of this life by making sound decisions.

The DVD-ROM and separate participant's guide contain everything you need to create your group experience:

Staying in Love

Falling in Love Is Easy, Staying in Love Requires a Plan

Andy Stanley

We all know what's required to fall in love...a pulse. Falling in love is easy. But staying there—that's something else entirely. With more than a thousand matchmaking services available today and new ones springing up all the time, finding a romantic match can be easier than ever. But staying together with the one you've found seems to be the real challenge.

So, is it possible for two people to fall in love and actually stay there? Absolutely! Let pastor and author Andy Stanley show you how in this four-session, video-based study that also features a separate participant's guide.

Session titles include:
1. The Juno Dilemma
2. Re-Modeling
3. Feelin' It
4. Multiple Choice Marriage

Available in stores and online!

Faith, Hope, and Luck

Discover What You Can Expect from God

Andy Stanley

Our faith in God often hinges on his activity— or inactivity—in our daily experiences. When our prayers are answered, our faith soars. When God is silent, it becomes harder to trust him. When God shows up in an unmistakable way, our confidence in him reaches new heights. But when he doesn't come through, our confidence often wanes.

But it doesn't have to be that way—it's not supposed to be that way.

This five-session study is guaranteed to transform your thinking about faith. As you listen or watch, you will discover the difference between faith and hope. You will be presented with a definition of faith that will shed new light on both the Old and New Testaments. Andy Stanley explains what we can expect of God every time we come to him with a request. In addition, he exposes the flaws in what some have labeled The Faith Movement.

With both a DVD and separate participant's guide, *Faith, Hope, and Luck* is not just another group study. This content is foundational for everyone who desires to be an informed, active follower of Christ.

Five sessions include:
1. Better Odds
2. Betting on Hope
3. Beating the Odds
4. No Dice
5. All In

Available in stores and online!

Five Things God Uses to Grow Your Faith

Andy Stanley

Imagine how different your outlook on life would be if you had absolute confidence that God was with you. Imagine how differently you would respond to difficulties, temptations, and even good things if you knew with certainty that God was in all of it and was planning to leverage it for good. In other words, imagine what it would be like to have PERFECT faith. In this DVD study, Andy Stanley builds a biblical case for five things God uses to grow BIG faith.

In six video sessions, Andy covers the following topics:

• Big Faith
• Practical Teaching
• Providential Relationships
• Private Disciplines
• Personal Ministry
• Pivotal Circumstances

Along with the separate participant's guide, this resource will equip groups to become more mature followers of Jesus Christ.

Available in stores and online!

ZONDERVAN®
.com

Twisting the Truth

Learning to Discern in a Culture of Deception

Andy Stanley

In six insight-packed sessions, Andy Stanley exposes four destructive and all-too-prevalent lies about authority, pain, sex, and sin. They're deceptions powerful enough to ruin our relationships, our lives, even our eternities—but only if we let them. Including both a small group DVD and participant's guide that work together, *Twisting the Truth* untwists the lies that can drag us down. With his gift for straight, to-the-heart communication, Andy Stanley helps us exchange falsehoods for truths that can turn our lives completely around.

Available in stores and online!

Starting Point Starter Kit

Find Your Place in the Story

Andy Stanley and the Starting Point Team

Starting Point is an exploration of God's grand story and where you fit into the narrative. This proven, small group experience is carefully designed to meet the needs of

- Seekers that are curious about Christianity
- Starters that are new to a relationship with Jesus
- Returners that have been away from church for a while

Starting Point is an accepting, conversational environment where people learn about God's story and their places in it. Starting Point helps participants explore the Bible and begin to understand key truths of the Christian faith.

Carefully refined to enhance community, the ten interactive sessions in Starting Point encourage honest exploration. The *Conversation Guide*, which includes a five-disk audio series featuring Andy Stanley, helps each participant enjoy and engage fully with the small group experience.

About This Starter Kit

The *Starting Point Starter Kit* is geared for ministry leaders. It consists of the following:

- Four-color *Starting Point Conversation Guide* containing five audio disks, with over five hours of teaching by Andy Stanley
- *Starter Guide* providing step-by-step instructions on how to successfully launch and sustain the Starting Point ministry
- A Starting Point TNIV Bible
- One-hour leader training DVD
- Interactive CD containing promotional videos, pre-service marketing graphics, leader training tools, and administrative resources

Share Your Thoughts

With the Author: Your comments will be forwarded to the author when you send them to zauthor@zondervan.com.

With Zondervan: Submit your review of this book by writing to zreview@zondervan.com.

Free Online Resources at

www.zondervan.com

Zondervan AuthorTracker: Be notified whenever your favorite authors publish new books, go on tour, or post an update about what's happening in their lives at www.zondervan.com/authortracker.

Daily Bible Verses and Devotions: Enrich your life with daily Bible verses or devotions that help you start every morning focused on God. Visit www.zondervan.com/newsletters.

Free Email Publications: Sign up for newsletters on Christian living, academic resources, church ministry, fiction, children's resources, and more. Visit www.zondervan.com/newsletters.

Zondervan Bible Search: Find and compare Bible passages in a variety of translations at www.zondervanbiblesearch.com.

Other Benefits: Register yourself to receive online benefits like coupons and special offers, or to participate in research.

ZONDERVAN®

ZONDERVAN.com/
AUTHORTRACKER
follow your favorite authors